Feature Store for Machine Learning

Curate, discover, share and serve ML features at scale

Jayanth Kumar M J

BIRMINGHAM—MUMBAI

Feature Store for Machine Learning

Publishing Product Manager: Dhruv Jagdish Kataria
Content Development Editor: Manikandan Kurup
Technical Editor: Rahul Limbachiya
Copy Editor: Safis Editing
Project Coordinator: Farheen Fathima
Proofreader: Safis Editing
Indexer: Rekha Nair
Production Designer: Roshan Kawale
Marketing Coordinators: Shifa Ansari and Abeer Riyaz Dawe

First published: June 2022

Production reference: 1270522

Published by Packt Publishing Ltd.
Livery Place
35 Livery Street
Birmingham
B3 2PB, UK.

ISBN 978-1-80323-006-1

`www.packt.com`

ನಮಗೆ ಒಳ್ಳೆ ಶಿಕ್ಷಣ ಕೊಡಿಸಲೇ ಬೇಕೆಂಬ ನನ್ನ ತಾಯಿ ಗಾಯತ್ರಿ ಅವರ

ದೃಢತನ ಹಾಗು ಸಮರ್ಪಣೆಗೆ, ನನ್ನ ಅಣ್ಣ ಸಂತೋಷ್ ಮತ್ತು

ಕುಟುಂಬದ ಬೆಂಬಲಕ್ಕೆ ಹಾಗು ನನ್ನ ಪತ್ನಿ ದೀಪಾಳ ಬೆಂಬಲಕ್ಕೆ,

ನಾನು ಈ ಪುಸ್ತಕವನ್ನು ಸಮರ್ಪಿಸುತೇನೆ.

To my mother Gayatri, for her dedication and determination in educating us, to my brother Santhosh and his family for being supportive, last but not the least to my wife Deepa for being kind and supportive during no fun weekends for the last six months.

– Jayanth Kumar M J

Contributors

About the author

Jayanth Kumar M J is a lead data engineer at Cimpress USA. He specializes in building platform components for data scientists and data engineers to make MLOps smooth and self-service. He is also a Feast feature store contributor.

I want to thank, the whole team who made this possible, all my colleagues, mentors throughout my career from Sapient to Cimpress and to my friends and family who made life easy and fun when they are around.

About the reviewer

Nilan Saha is pursuing a master's degree in data science with a specialization in computational linguistics at the University of British Columbia, Canada. He has worked as an NLP contractor for multiple start-ups in the past and also has brief experience in research, which has resulted in a few publications. He is also a Kaggle kernels and discussion expert.

Table of Contents

Section 2 – A Feature Store in Action

3
Feature Store Fundamentals, Terminology, and Usage

4
Adding Feature Store to ML Models

5

Model Training and Inference

6

Model to Production and Beyond

Section 3 – Alternatives, Best Practices, and a Use Case

7

Feast Alternatives and ML Best Practices

8

Use Case – Customer Churn Prediction

Preface

Data-driven decision-making has been the key to the success of any business, and **Machine Learning** (**ML**) plays a key role in achieving that and helping businesses stay ahead of the competition. Though ML helps in unlocking the true potential of a business, there are many obstacles along the way. According to a study, 90 percent of ML models never make it to production. The disconnect between model development and productionization as well as bad or mediocre ML practices are a few of the many reasons for this. This is why there are so many end-to-end ML platforms offering to make ML development easy. One of the primary goals of these platforms is to encourage data scientists/ML engineers to follow **Machine Learning Operations** (**MLOps**) standards that help in the faster productionization of a model. In recent years, feature management has been one of the aims of the ML platform – whether it is built in-house or offered as a **Platform as a Service** (**PaaS**). A feature store that provides the ability to create, share, and discover curated ML features has become an integral part of most of these ML platforms.

The aim of this book is to discuss the significance of a feature store in ML pipelines. Hence, we will start with an ML problem and try to develop a model without a feature store. We will then discuss what aspects of ML can benefit from a feature store and how a few capabilities of feature stores not only help in creating better ML practices but also help in the faster and more cost-effective development of the model. As we move from *why* we should use a feature store to the *what?* and *how?* aspects of it, we will go through feature engineering, model training, inference, and also productionization of batch and online models with practical examples. In the first and second sections of the book, we will use an open source feature store, Feast. In the last section, we will look for alternatives that are available on the market and also try out an end-to-end use case with a managed feature store.

Who this book is for

This book is for data/ML/platform engineers, data scientists, and also data science enthusiasts who want to learn about feature management, how to deploy Feast on the AWS cloud, how to create curated ML features, and how to use and collaborate with other data scientists in model building, using a feature store for batch and online model prediction, as well as moving a model from development to production. This book will be beneficial to ML projects that range from small university projects to enterprise-level ML applications.

What this book covers

Chapter 1, An Overview of the Machine Learning Life Cycle, starts with a small introduction to ML and then dives deep into an ML use case – a customer lifetime value model. The chapter runs through the different stages of ML development, and finally, it discusses the most time-consuming parts of ML and also what an ideal world and the real world look like in ML development.

Chapter 2, What Problems Do Feature Stores Solve?, introduces us to the main focus of the book, which is feature management and feature stores. It discusses the importance of features in production systems, different ways to bring features into production, and common issues with these approaches, followed by how a feature store can overcome these common issues.

Chapter 3, Feature Store Fundamentals, Terminology, and Usage, starts with an introduction to an open source feature store – Feast – followed by installation, different terminology used in the feature store world, and basic API usage. Finally, it briefly introduces different components that work together in Feast.

Chapter 4, Adding Feature Store to ML Models, will help readers install Feast on AWS as it goes through the different resource creations, such as S3 buckets, a Redshift cluster, and the Glue catalog, step by step with screenshots. Finally, it revisits the feature engineering aspect of the customer lifetime value model developed in *Chapter 1, An Overview of the Machine Learning Life Cycle*, and creates and ingests the curated features into Feast.

Chapter 5, Model Training and Inference, continues from where we left in *Chapter 4, Adding Feature Store to ML Models*, and discusses how a feature store can help data scientists and ML engineers collaborate in the development of an ML model. It discusses how to use Feast for batch model inference and also how to build a REST API for online model inference.

Chapter 6, Model to Production and Beyond, discusses the creation of an orchestration environment using Amazon **Managed Workflows for Apache Airflow** (**MWAA**), uses the feature engineering, model training, and inference code/notebooks built in the previous chapters, and deploys the batch and online model pipelines into production. Finally, it discusses aspects beyond production, such as feature monitoring, changes to feature definitions, and also building the next ML model.

Chapter 7, Feast Alternatives and ML Best Practices, introduces other feature stores, such as Tecton, Databricks Feature Store, Google Cloud's Vertex AI, Hopsworks Feature Store, and Amazon SageMaker Feature Store. It also introduces the basic usage of the latter so that users can get the gist of what is it like to use a managed feature store. Finally, it briefly discusses the ML best practices.

Chapter 8, Use Case – Customer Churn Prediction, uses a managed feature store offering of Amazon SageMaker and runs through an end-to-end use case to predict customer churn on a telecom dataset. It also covers examples of feature drift monitoring and model performance monitoring.

To get the most out of this book

The book uses AWS services for Feast deployment, pipeline orchestration, and a couple of SageMaker offerings. If you create a new AWS account, all the services used are under free-tier or featured products, except the Managed Workflows for Apache Airflow (MWAA) environment. However, we have listed alternatives for Airflow installation that can be used for running the examples.

All the examples are run using Python 3.7 – `feast==0.19.3`. The appropriate library versions are also mentioned in the notebooks wherever necessary. To run through the examples, all you need is a Jupyter notebook environment (local, Google Colab, SageMaker, or another of your choice) and the mentioned AWS resources and permissions for each chapter or section.

Software/hardware covered in the book	Operating system requirements
Python 3.7	Windows, macOS, or Linux
Jupyter notebook environment	

If you are using the digital version of this book, we advise you to type the code yourself or access the code from the book's GitHub repository (a link is available in the next section). Doing so will help you avoid any potential errors related to the copying and pasting of code.

To get the most out of the book, you should have Python programming experience, and a basic understanding of notebooks, Python environments, and ML and Python ML libraries, such as XGBoost and scikit-learn.

Download the example code files

You can download the example code files for this book from GitHub at `https://github.com/PacktPublishing/Feature-Store-for-Machine-Learning`. If there's an update to the code, it will be updated in the GitHub repository.

We also have other code bundles from our rich catalog of books and videos available at `https://github.com/PacktPublishing/`. Check them out!

Download the color images

We also provide a PDF file that has color images of the screenshots and diagrams used in this book. You can download it here: `https://static.packt-cdn.com/downloads/9781803230061_ColorImages.pdf`.

Conventions used

There are a number of text conventions used throughout this book.

`Code in text`: Indicates code words in text, database table names, folder names, filenames, file extensions, pathnames, dummy URLs, user input, and Twitter handles. Here is an example: "The preceding code block scales the numerical columns: `tenure`, `MonthlyCharges`, and `TotalCharges`."

A block of code is set as follows:

```
le = LabelEncoder()
for i in bin_cols:
    churn_data[i] = le.fit_transform(churn_data[i])
```

When we wish to draw your attention to a particular part of a code block, the relevant lines or items are set in bold:

```
project: customer_segmentation
registry: data/registry.db
provider: aws
online_store:
```

```
type: dynamodb
region: us-east-1
```

Any command-line input or output is written as follows:

```
$ docker build -t customer-segmentation .
```

Bold: Indicates a new term, an important word, or words that you see onscreen. For instance, words in menus or dialog boxes appear in **bold**. Here is an example: "On the cluster home page, select the **Properties** tab and scroll down to **Associated IAM roles**."

> Tips or Important Notes
> Appear like this.

Get in touch

Feedback from our readers is always welcome.

General feedback: If you have questions about any aspect of this book, email us at customercare@packtpub.com and mention the book title in the subject of your message.

Errata: Although we have taken every care to ensure the accuracy of our content, mistakes do happen. If you have found a mistake in this book, we would be grateful if you would report this to us. Please visit www.packtpub.com/support/errata and fill in the form.

Piracy: If you come across any illegal copies of our works in any form on the internet, we would be grateful if you would provide us with the location address or website name. Please contact us at copyright@packt.com with a link to the material.

If you are interested in becoming an author: If there is a topic that you have expertise in and you are interested in either writing or contributing to a book, please visit authors.packtpub.com.

Share Your Thoughts

Once you've read *Feature Store for Machine Learning*, we'd love to hear your thoughts! Scan the QR code below to go straight to the Amazon review page for this book and share your feedback.

`https://packt.link/r/1-803-23006-1`

Your review is important to us and the tech community and will help us make sure we're delivering excellent quality content.

Section 1 – Why Do We Need a Feature Store?

This section concentrates on the significance of a feature store (*why?*) in **Machine Learning** (**ML**) pipelines. We will start with an ML problem and go through the different stages of ML development, such as data exploration, feature engineering, model training, and inference. We will discuss how the availability of features in production affects model performance and start looking into ways in which features are brought to production and the common problems with them. At the end of the section, we will introduce a feature store in the ML pipeline and look at how it resolves the common problems that other alternatives struggle with.

This section comprises the following chapters:

1
An Overview of the Machine Learning Life Cycle

Machine learning (**ML**) is a subfield of computer science that involves studying and exploring computer algorithms that can learn the structure of data using statistical analysis. The dataset that's used for learning is called training data. The output of training is called a model, which can then be used to run predictions against a new dataset that the model hasn't seen before. There are two broad categories of machine learning: **supervised learning** and **unsupervised learning**. In supervised learning, the training dataset is labeled (the dataset will have a target column). The algorithm intends to learn how to predict the target column based on other columns (features) in the dataset. Predicting house prices, stock market changes, and customer churn are some supervised learning examples. In unsupervised learning, on the other hand, the data is not labeled (the dataset will not have a target column). In this, the algorithm intends to recognize the common patterns in the dataset. One of the methods of generating labels for an unlabeled dataset is using unsupervised learning algorithms. Anomaly detection is one of the use cases for unsupervised learning.

The idea of the first mathematical model for machine learning was presented in 1943 by Walter Pitts and Warren McCulloch (*The History of Machine Learning: How Did It All Start?* – `https://labelyourdata.com/articles/history-of-machine-learning-how-did-it-all-start`). Later, in the 1950s, Arthur Samuel developed a program for playing championship-level computer checkers. Since then, we have come a long way in ML. I would highly recommend reading this article if you haven't.

Today, as we try to teach real-time decision-making to systems and devices, ML engineer and data scientist positions are the hottest jobs on the market. It is predicted that the global machine learning market will grow from $8.3 billion in 2019 to $117.9 billion by 2027. As shown in the following diagram, it's a unique skill set that overlaps with multiple domains:

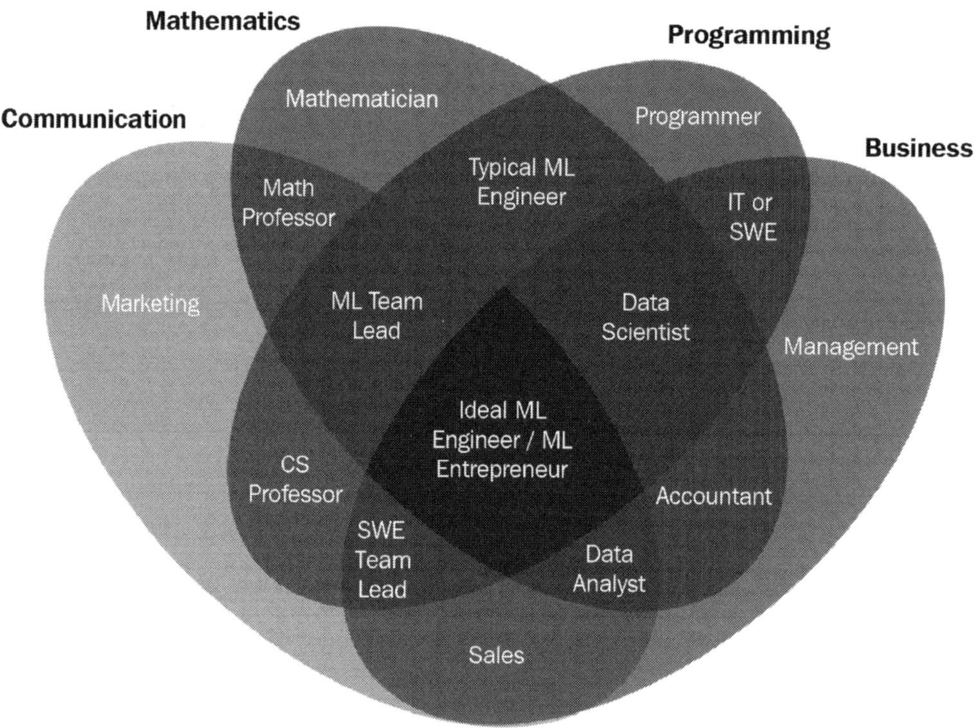

Figure 1.1 – ML/data science skill sets

In 2007 and 2008, the DevOps movement revolutionized the way software was developed and operationalized. It reduced the time to production for software:

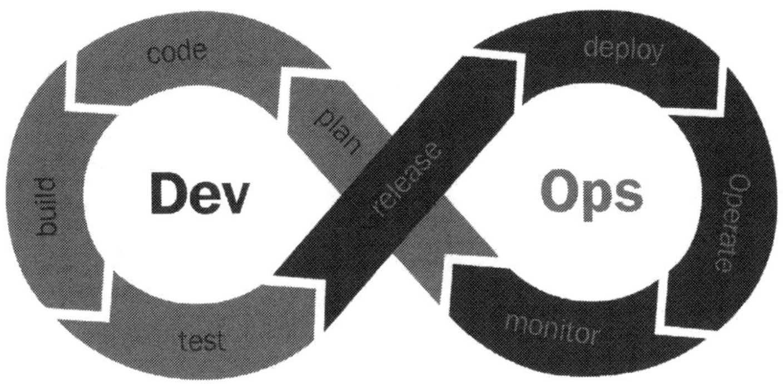

Figure 1.2 – DevOps

Similarly, to take a model from experimentation to operationalization, we need a set of standardized processes that makes this process seamless. Well, the answer to that is **machine learning operations (MLOps)**. Many experts in the industry have come across a set of patterns that would reduce the time to production of ML models. 2021 is the year of MLOps – there are a lot of new start-ups that are trying to cater to the ML needs of the firms that are still behind in the ML journey. We can assume that this will expand over time and only get better, just like any other process. As we grow with it, there will be a lot of discoveries and ways of working, best practices, and more will evolve. In this book, we will talk about one of the common tools that's used to standardize ML and its best practices: the feature store.

Before we discuss what a feature store is and how to use it, we need to understand the ML life cycle and its common oversights. I want to dedicate this chapter to learning about the different stages of the ML life cycle. As part of this chapter, we will take up an ML model-building exercise. We won't dive deep into the ML model itself, such as its algorithms or how to do feature engineering; instead, we will focus on the stages an ML model would typically go through, as well as the difficulties involved in model building versus model operationalization. We will also discuss the stages that are time-consuming and repetitive. The goal of this chapter is to understand the overall ML life cycle and the issues involved in operationalizing models. This will set the stage for later chapters, where we will discuss feature management, the role of a feature store in ML, and how the feature store solves some of the issues we will discuss in this chapter.

In this chapter, we will cover the following topics:

- The ML life cycle in practice
- An ideal world versus the real world
- The most time-consuming stages of ML

Without further ado, let's get our hands dirty with an ML model.

Technical requirements

To follow the code examples in this book, you need to be familiar with Python and any notebook environment, which could be a local setup such as Jupyter or an online notebook environment such as Google Colab or Kaggle. We will be using the Python3 interpreter and PIP3 to manage the virtual environment. You can download the code examples for this chapter from the following GitHub link: `https://github.com/PacktPublishing/Feature-Store-for-Machine-Learning/tree/main/Chapter01`.

The ML life cycle in practice

As Jeff Daniel's character in HBO's *The Newsroom* once said, the first step in solving any problem is recognizing there is one. Let's follow this knowledge and see if it works for us.

In this section, we'll pick a problem statement and execute the ML life cycle step by step. Once completed, we'll retrospect and identify any issues. The following diagram shows the different stages of ML:

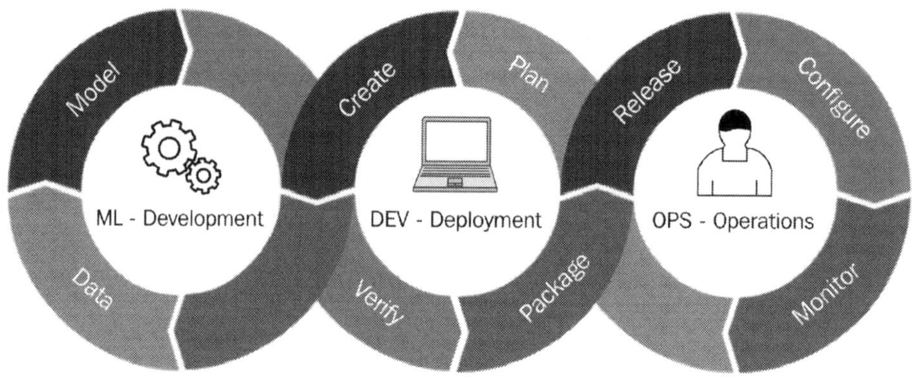

Figure 1.3 – The ML life cycle

Let's take a look at our problem statement.

Problem statement (plan and create)

For this exercise, let's assume that you own a retail business and would like to improve customer experience. First and foremost, you want to find your customer segments and customer **lifetime value (LTV)**. If you have worked in the domain, you probably know different ways to solve this problem. I will follow a medium blog series called *Know Your Metrics – Learn what and how to track with Python* by Barış Karaman (`https://towardsdatascience.com/data-driven-growth-with-python-part-1-know-your-metrics-812781e66a5b`). You can go through the article for more details. Feel free to try it out for yourself. The dataset is available here: `https://www.kaggle.com/vijayuv/onlineretail`.

Data (preparation and cleaning)

First, let's install the `pandas` package:

```
!pip install pandas
```

Let's make the dataset available to our notebook environment. To do that, download the dataset to your local system, then perform either of the following steps, depending on your setup:

- **Local Jupyter**: Copy the absolute path of the `.csv` file and give it as input to the `pd.read_csv` method.
- **Google Colab**: Upload the dataset by clicking on the folder icon and then the upload icon from the left navigation menu.

Let's preview the dataset:

```
import pandas as pd
retail_data = pd.read_csv('/content/OnlineRetail.csv',
                          encoding= 'unicode_escape')
retail_data.sample(5)
```

The output of the preceding code block is as follows:

	InvoiceNo	StockCode	Description	Quantity	InvoiceDate	UnitPrice	CustomerID	Country
137258	548150	72802B	OCEAN SCENT CANDLE IN JEWELLED BOX	2.0	3/29/2011 12:55	4.25	17315.0	United Kingdom
191407	553356	84991	60 TEATIME FAIRY CAKE CASES	24.0	5/16/2011 14:05	0.55	14038.0	United Kingdom
180983	552410	22665	RECIPE BOX BLUE SKETCHBOOK DESIGN	1.0	5/9/2011 12:40	2.95	14527.0	United Kingdom
7753	537054	85227	SET OF 6 3D KIT CARDS FOR KIDS	6.0	12/5/2010 11:40	0.85	16931.0	United Kingdom
205853	554839	22191	IVORY DINER WALL CLOCK	1.0	5/26/2011 17:15	8.50	14056.0	United Kingdom

Figure 1.4 – Dataset preview

As you can see, the dataset includes customer transaction data. The dataset consists of eight columns, apart from the index column, which is unlabeled:

- `InvoiceNo`: A unique order ID; the data is of the `integer` type
- `StockCode`: The unique ID of the product; the data is of the `string` type
- `Description`: The product's description; the data is of the `string` type
- `Quantity`: The number of units of the product that have been ordered
- `InvoiceDate`: The date when the invoice was generated
- `UnitPrice`: The cost of the product per unit
- `CustomerID`: The unique ID of the customer who ordered the product
- `Country`: The country where the product was ordered

Once you have the dataset, before jumping into feature engineering and model building, data scientists usually perform some exploratory analysis. The idea here is to check if the dataset you have is sufficient to solve the problem, identify missing gaps, check if there is any correlation in the dataset, and more.

For the exercise, we'll calculate the monthly revenue and look at its seasonality. The following code block extracts year and month (yyyymm) information from the `InvoiceDate` column, calculates the `revenue` property of each transaction by multiplying the `UnitPrice` and `Quantity` columns, and aggregates the revenue based on the extracted year-month (yyyymm) column.

Let's continue from the preceding code statement:

```
##Convert 'InvoiceDate' to of type datetime
retail_data['InvoiceDate'] = pd.to_datetime(
    retail_data['InvoiceDate'], errors = 'coerce')

##Extract year and month information from 'InvoiceDate'
```

```
retail_data['yyyymm']=retail_data['InvoiceDate'].
dt.strftime('%Y%m')

##Calculate revenue generated per order
retail_data['revenue'] = retail_data['UnitPrice'] * retail_
data['Quantity']

## Calculate monthly revenue by aggregating the revenue on year
month column
revenue_df = retail_data.groupby(['yyyymm'])['revenue'].sum().
reset_index()
revenue_df.head()
```

The preceding code will output the following DataFrame:

	yyyymm	revenue
0	201012	748957.020
1	201101	560000.260
2	201102	498062.650
3	201103	683267.080
4	201104	493207.121

Figure 1.5 – Revenue DataFrame

Let's visualize the `revenue` DataFrame. I will be using a library called `plotly`. The following command will install `plotly` in your notebook environment:

```
!pip install plotly
```

Let's plot a bar graph from the `revenue` DataFrame with the `yyyymm` column on the *x* axis and `revenue` on the *y* axis:

```
import plotly.express as px

##Sort rows on year-month column
revenue_df.sort_values( by=['yyyymm'], inplace=True)

## plot a bar graph with year-month on x-axis and revenue on
y-axis, update x-axis is of type category.
```

```
fig = px.bar(revenue_df, x="yyyymm", y="revenue",
             title="Monthly Revenue")
fig.update_xaxes(type='category')
fig.show()
```

The preceding codes sort the revenue DataFrame on the yyyymm column and plot a bar graph of revenue against the year-month (yyyymm) column, as shown in the following screenshot. As you can see, September, October, and November are high revenue months. It would have been good to validate our assumption against a few years of data, but unfortunately, we don't have that. Before we move on to model development, let's look at one more metric – the monthly active customers – and see if it's co-related to monthly revenue:

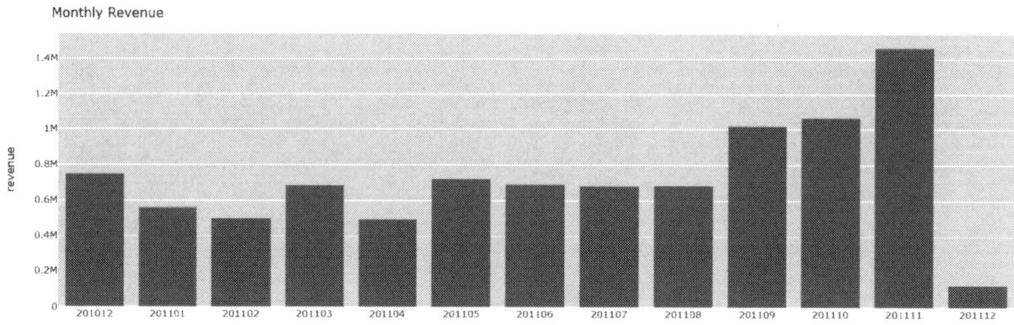

Figure 1.6 – Monthly revenue

Continuing in the same notebook, the following commands will calculate the monthly active customers by aggregating a count of unique CustomerID on the year-month (yyyymm) column:

```
active_customer_df = retail_data.groupby(['yyyymm'])
['CustomerID'].nunique().reset_index()
active_customer_df.columns = ['yyyymm',
                              'No of Active customers']
active_customer_df.head()
```

The preceding code will produce the following output:

	yyyymm	No of Active customers
0	201012	948
1	201101	783
2	201102	798
3	201103	1020
4	201104	899

Figure 1.7 – Monthly active customers DataFrame

Let's plot the preceding DataFrame in the same way that we did for monthly revenue:

```
## Plot bar graph from revenue data frame with yyyymm column on
x-axis and No. of active customers on the y-axis.
fig = px.bar(active_customer_df, x="yyyymm",
            y="No of Active customers",
            title="Monthly Active customers")
fig.update_xaxes(type='category')
fig.show()
```

The preceding command plots a bar graph of `No of Active customers` against the year-month (`yyyymm`) column. As shown in the following screenshot, `Monthly Active customers` is positively related to the monthly revenue shown in the preceding screenshot:

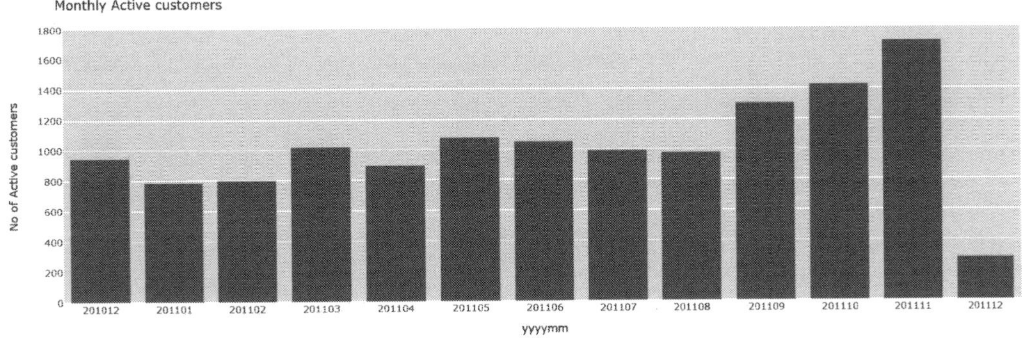

Figure 1.8 – Monthly active customers

In the next section, we'll build a customer LTV model.

Model

Now that we have finished exploring the data, let's build the LTV model. **Customer lifetime value** (**CLTV**) is defined as *the net profitability associated with a customer's life cycle with the company. Simply put, CLV/LTV is a projection for what each customer is worth to a business* (reference: `https://www.toolbox.com/marketing/customer-experience/articles/what-is-customer-lifetime-value-clv/`). There are different ways to predict lifetime value. One could be predicting the value of a customer, which is a regression problem, while another way could be predicting the customer group, which is a classification problem. In this exercise, we will use the latter approach.

For this exercise, we will segment customers into the following groups:

- **Low LTV**: Less active or low revenue customers
- **Mid-LTV**: Fairly active and moderate revenue customers
- **High LTV**: High revenue customers – the segment that we don't want to lose

We will be using 3 months worth of data to calculate the **recency** (**R**), **frequency** (**F**), and **monetary** (**M**) metrics of the customers to generate features. Once we have these features, we will use 6 months worth of data to calculate the revenue of every customer and generate LTV cluster labels (low LTV, mid-LTV, and high LTV). The generated labels and features will then be used to train an XGBoost model that can be used to predict the group of new customers.

Feature engineering

Let's continue our work in the same notebook, calculate the R, F, and M values for the customers, and group our customers based on a value that's been calculated from the individual R, F, and M scores:

- **Recency (R)**: The recency metric represents how many days have passed since the customer made their last purchase.
- **Frequency (F)**: As the term suggests, F represents how many times the customer made a purchase.
- **Monetary (M)**: How much revenue a particular customer brought in.

Since the spending and purchase patterns of customers differ based on demographic location, we will only consider the data that belongs to the United Kingdom for this exercise. Let's read the `OnlineRetails.csv` file and filter out the data that doesn't belong to the United Kingdom:

```
import pandas as pd
from datetime import datetime, timedelta, date
from sklearn.cluster import KMeans

##Read the data and filter out data that belongs to country
other than UK
retail_data = pd.read_csv('/content/OnlineRetail.csv',
                          encoding= 'unicode_escape')
retail_data['InvoiceDate'] = pd.to_datetime(
    retail_data['InvoiceDate'], errors = 'coerce')
uk_data = retail_data.query("Country=='United Kingdom'").reset_
index(drop=True)
```

In the following code block, we will create two different DataFrames. The first one (`uk_data_3m`) will be for `InvoiceDate` between `2011-03-01` and `2011-06-01`. This DataFrame will be used to generate the RFM features. The second DataFrame (`uk_data_6m`) will be for `InvoiceDate` between `2011-06-01` and `2011-12-01`. This DataFrame will be used to generate the target column for model training. In this exercise, the target column is LTV groups/clusters. Since we are calculating the customer LTV group, a larger time interval would give a better grouping. Hence, we will be using 6 months worth of data to generate the LTV group labels:

```
## Create 3months and 6 months data frames
t1 = pd.Timestamp("2011-06-01 00:00:00.054000")
t2 = pd.Timestamp("2011-03-01 00:00:00.054000")
t3 = pd.Timestamp("2011-12-01 00:00:00.054000")
uk_data_3m = uk_data[(uk_data.InvoiceDate < t1) & (uk_data.
InvoiceDate >= t2)].reset_index(drop=True)
uk_data_6m = uk_data[(uk_data.InvoiceDate >= t1) & (uk_data.
InvoiceDate < t3)].reset_index(drop=True)
```

Now that we have two different DataFrames, let's calculate the RFM values using the `uk_data_3m` DataFrame. The following code block calculates the `revenue` column by multiplying `UnitPrice` with `Quantity`. To calculate the RFM values, the code block performs three aggregations on `CustomerID`:

- To calculate **R**, `max_date` in the DataFrame must be calculated and for every customer, we must calculate `R = max_date - x.max()`, where `x.max()` calculates the latest `InvoiceDate` of a specific `CustomerID`.
- To calculate **F**, `count` the number of invoices for a specific `CustomerID`.
- To calculate **M**, find the `sum` value of `revenue` for a specific `CustomerID`.

The following code snippet performs this logic:

```
## Calculate RFM values.
uk_data_3m['revenue'] = uk_data_3m['UnitPrice'] * uk_
data_3m['Quantity']
# Calculating the max invoice date in data (Adding additional
day to avoid 0 recency value)
max_date = uk_data_3m['InvoiceDate'].max() + timedelta(days=1)
rfm_data = uk_data_3m.groupby(['CustomerID']).agg({
        'InvoiceDate': lambda x: (max_date - x.max()).days,
        'InvoiceNo': 'count',
        'revenue': 'sum'})
rfm_data.rename(columns={'InvoiceDate': 'Recency',
                         'InvoiceNo': 'Frequency',
                         'revenue': 'MonetaryValue'},
                         inplace=True)
```

Here, we have calculated the R, F, and M values for the customers. Next, we need to divide customers into the R, F, and M groups. This grouping defines where a customer stands concerning the other customers in terms of the R, F, and M metrics. To calculate the R, F, and M groups, we will divide the customers into equal-sized groups based on their R, F, and M values, respectively. These were calculated in the previous code block. To achieve this, we will use a method called `pd.qcut` (`https://pandas.pydata.org/pandas-docs/stable/reference/api/pandas.qcut.html`) on the DataFrame. Alternatively, you can use any *clustering* methods to divide customers into different groups. We will add the R, F, and M groups' values together to generate a single value called `RFMScore` that will range from 0 to 9.

In this exercise, the customers will be divided into four groups. The *elbow method* (`https://towardsdatascience.com/clustering-metrics-better-than-the-elbow-method-6926e1f723a6`) can be used to calculate the optimal number of groups for any dataset. The preceding link also contains information about alternative methods you can use to calculate the optimal number of groups, so feel free to try it out. I will leave that as an exercise for you.

The following code block calculates `RFMScore`:

```
## Calculate RFM groups of customers
r_grp = pd.qcut(rfm_data['Recency'], q=4,
                labels=range(3,-1,-1))
f_grp = pd.qcut(rfm_data['Frequency'], q=4,
                labels=range(0,4))
m_grp = pd.qcut(rfm_data['MonetaryValue'], q=4,
                labels=range(0,4))
rfm_data = rfm_data.assign(R=r_grp.values).assign(F=f_grp.
values).assign(M=m_grp.values)
rfm_data['R'] = rfm_data['R'].astype(int)
rfm_data['F'] = rfm_data['F'].astype(int)
rfm_data['M'] = rfm_data['M'].astype(int)
rfm_data['RFMScore'] = rfm_data['R'] + rfm_data['F'] + rfm_
data['M']
rfm_data.groupby('RFMScore')
['Recency','Frequency','MonetaryValue'].mean()
```

The preceding code will generate the following output:

RFMScore	Recency	Frequency	MonetaryValue
0	76.633588	5.206107	94.023359
1	58.500000	9.074074	158.990864
2	54.380208	13.968750	239.346354
3	38.091633	16.605578	271.437331
4	36.647619	24.180952	363.867000
5	34.000000	33.558252	535.423204
6	28.516432	44.920188	742.487324
7	18.431138	51.317365	974.310120
8	14.316547	80.064748	2192.578568
9	7.142012	126.763314	2335.736805

Figure 1.9 – RFM score summary

This summary data gives us a rough idea of how `RFMScore` is directly proportional to the `Recency`, `Frequency`, and `MonetaryValue` metrics. For example, the group with `RFMScore=0` has the highest mean recency (the last purchase day of this group is the farthest in past), the lowest mean frequency, and the lowest mean monetary value. On the other hand, the group with `RFMScore=9` has the lowest mean recency, highest mean frequency, and highest mean monetary value.

With that, we understand `RFMScore` is positively related to the value a customer brings to the business. So, let's segment customers as follows:

- 0-3 => Low value
- 4-6 => Mid value
- 7-9 => High value

The following code labels customers as having either a low, mid, or high value:

```
# segment customers.
rfm_data['Segment'] = 'Low-Value'
rfm_data.loc[rfm_data['RFMScore']>4,'Segment'] = 'Mid-Value'
rfm_data.loc[rfm_data['RFMScore']>6,'Segment'] = 'High-Value'
rfm_data = rfm_data.reset_index()
```

Customer LTV

Now that we have RFM features ready for the customers in the DataFrame that contains 3 months worth of data, let's use 6 months worth of data (`uk_data_6m`) to calculate the revenue of the customers, as we did previously, and merge the RFM features with the newly created revenue DataFrame:

```
# Calculate revenue using the six month dataframe.
uk_data_6m['revenue'] = uk_data_6m['UnitPrice'] * uk_
data_6m['Quantity']
revenue_6m = uk_data_6m.groupby(['CustomerID']).agg({
        'revenue': 'sum'})
revenue_6m.rename(columns={'revenue': 'Revenue_6m'},
                  inplace=True)
revenue_6m = revenue_6m.reset_index()
revenue_6m = revenue_6m.dropna()
```

```
# Merge the 6m revenue data frame with RFM data.
merged_data = pd.merge(rfm_data, revenue_6m, how="left")
merged_data.fillna(0)
```

Feel free to plot `revenue_6m` against `RFMScore`. You will see a positive correlation between the two.

In the flowing code block, we are using the `revenue_6m` columns, which is the *lifetime value of a customer*, and creating three groups called *Low LTV*, *Mid LTV*, and *High LTV* using K-means clustering. Again, you can verify the optimal number of clusters using the *elbow method* mentioned previously:

```
# Create LTV cluster groups
merged_data = merged_data[merged_data['Revenue_6m']<merged_
data['Revenue_6m'].quantile(0.99)]
kmeans = KMeans(n_clusters=3)
kmeans.fit(merged_data[['Revenue_6m']])
merged_data['LTVCluster'] = kmeans.predict(merged_
data[['Revenue_6m']])
merged_data.groupby('LTVCluster')['Revenue_6m'].describe()
```

The preceding code block produces the following output:

	count	mean	std	min	25%	50%	75%	max
LTVCluster								
0	1170.0	828.670189	621.405282	-609.40	324.4675	663.525	1245.465	2447.57
1	21.0	14123.309048	3653.311262	9313.18	11464.6700	12913.990	16756.310	20530.00
2	186.0	4137.019892	1477.396388	2503.30	2964.2275	3635.200	4987.535	8910.04

Figure 1.10 – LTV cluster summary

As you can see, the cluster with label 1 contains the group of customers whose lifetime value is very high since the mean revenue of the group is $14,123.309, whereas there are only 21 such customers. The cluster with label 0 contains the group of customers whose lifetime value is low since the mean revenue of the group is only $828.67, whereas there are 1,170 such customers. This grouping gives us an idea of which customers should always be kept happy.

The feature set and model

Let's build an XGBoost model using the features we have calculated so far so that the model can predict the LTV group of the customers, given the input features. The following is the final feature set that will be used as input for the model:

```
feature_data = pd.get_dummies(merged_data)
feature_data.head(5)
```

The preceding code block produces the following DataFrame. This includes the feature set that will be used to train the model:

	CustomerID	Recency	Frequency	MonetaryValue	R	F	M	RFMScore	Revenue_6m	LTVCluster	Segment_High-Value	Segment_Low-Value	Segment_Mid-Value
0	12747.0	7	35	1082.09	3	2	3	8	1666.11	1	1	0	0
1	12748.0	1	582	4336.73	3	3	3	9	18679.01	2	1	0	0
2	12749.0	8	54	782.10	3	3	3	9	2323.04	1	1	0	0
4	12823.0	63	1	459.00	0	0	2	2	765.00	1	0	1	0
7	12836.0	28	62	814.71	1	3	3	7	951.46	1	1	0	0

Figure 1.11 – Feature set for model training

Now, let's use this feature set to train the `Xgboost` model. The prediction label (`y`) is the `LTVCluster` column; the rest of the dataset except for the `Revenue_6m` and `CustomerID` columns are the `X` value. `Revenue_6m` will be dropped from the feature set as the `LTVCluster` column (`y`) is calculated using `Revenue_6m`. For the new customer, we can calculate other features without needing at least 6 months worth of data and also predict their `LTVCluster(y)`.

The following code will train the `Xgboost` model:

```
from sklearn.metrics import classification_report, confusion_
matrix
import xgboost as xgb
from sklearn.model_selection import KFold, cross_val_
score, train_test_split
#Splitting data into train and test data set.
X = feature_data.drop(['CustomerID', 'LTVCluster',
                       'Revenue_6m'], axis=1)
y = feature_data['LTVCluster']
X_train, X_test, y_train, y_test = train_test_split(X, y, test_
size=0.1)
xgb_classifier = xgb.XGBClassifier(max_
depth=5, objective='multi:softprob')
```

```
xgb_model = xgb_classifier.fit(X_train, y_train)
y_pred = xgb_model.predict(X_test)
print(classification_report(y_test, y_pred))
```

The preceding code block will output the following classification results:

```
              precision    recall  f1-score   support

           0       0.92      0.99      0.95       121
           1       1.00      0.50      0.67         2
           2       0.67      0.27      0.38        15

    accuracy                           0.91       138
   macro avg       0.86      0.59      0.67       138
weighted avg       0.89      0.91      0.89       138
```

Figure 1.12 – Classification report

Now, let's assume that we are happy with the model and want to take it to the next level – that is, to production.

Package, release, and monitor

So far, we have spent a lot of time looking at data analysis, exploration, cleaning, and model building since that is what a data scientist should concentrate on. But once all that work has been done, can the model be deployed without any additional work? The answer is no. We are still far away from deployment. We must do the following things before we can deploy the model:

- We must create a scheduled data pipeline that performs data cleaning and feature engineering.
- We need a way to fetch features during prediction. If it's an online/transactional model, there should be a way to fetch features at low latency. Since customers' R, F, and M values change frequently, let's say that we want to run two different campaigns for mid-value and high-value segments on the website. There will be a need to score customers in near-real time.
- Find a way to reproduce the model using the historical data.
- Perform model packaging and versioning.
- Find a way to AB test the model.
- Find a way to monitor model and data drift.

As we don't have any of these ready, let's stop here and look back at what we have done, if there is a way to do this better, and see if there are any common oversights.

In the next section, we'll look at *what we think we have built (ideal world) versus what we have built (real world).*

An ideal world versus the real world

Now that we have spent a good amount of time building this beautiful data product that can help the business treat customers differently based on the value they bring to the table, let's look at what we expect from this versus what it can do.

Reusability and sharing

Reusability is one of the common problems in the IT industry. We have this great data for a product in front of us, the graphs we built during exploration, and the features we generated for our model. These can be reused by other data scientists, analysts, and data engineers. With the state it is in currently, can it be reused? The answer is maybe. Data scientists can share the notebook itself, can create a presentation, and so on. But there is no way for somebody to discover if they are looking for, say, customer segmentation or RFM features, which could be very useful in other models. So, if another data scientist or ML engineer is building a model that needs the same features, the only option they are left with is to reinvent the same wheel. The new model may be built with the same, more accurate, or less accurate RFM features based on how the data scientist generates it. However, it could be a case where the development of the second model could have been accelerated if there was a better way to discover and reuse the work. Also, as the saying goes, *two heads are better than one*. A collaboration would have benefitted both the data scientist and the business.

Everything in a notebook

Data science is a unique skill that is different from software engineering. Though some of the data scientists might have a software engineer background, the needs of the role itself may push them away from software engineering skills. As the data scientists spend more time in the data exploration and model building phases, the **integrated development environments** (**IDEs**) may not be sufficient as the amount of data they are dealing with is huge. The data processing phase will run for days if we have to explore, do feature engineering, and do model building on our personal Mac or PC. Also, they need to have the flexibility to use different programming languages such as Python, Scala, R, SQL, and others to add commands dynamically during analysis. That is one of the reasons why there are so many notebook platform providers, including Jupyter, Databricks, and SageMaker.

Since data product/model development is different from traditional software development, it is always impossible to ship the experimental code to production without any additional work. Most data scientists start their work in a notebook and build everything in the same way as we did in the previous section. A few standard practices and tools such as feature store will not only help them break down the model building process into multiple production-ready notebooks but can also help them avoid re-processing data, debugging issues, and code reuse.

Now that we understand the reality of ML development, let's briefly go through the most time-consuming stages of ML.

The most time-consuming stages of ML

In the first section of this chapter, we went through the different stages of the ML life cycle. Let's look at some of the stages in more detail and consider their level of complexity and the time we should spend on each of them.

Figuring out the dataset

Once we have a problem statement, the next step is to figure out the dataset we need to solve the problem. In the example we followed, we knew where the dataset was and it was given. However, in the real world, it is not that simple. Since each organization has its own way of data warehousing, it may be simple or take forever to find the data you need. Most organizations run data catalog services such as Amundsen, Atlan, and Azure Data Catalog to make their dataset easily discoverable. But again, the tools are as good as the way they are used or the people using them. So, the point I'm making here is that it's always easy to find the data you are looking for. Apart from this, considering the access control for the data, even if you figure out the dataset that's needed for the problem, it is highly likely that you may not have access to it unless you have used it before. Figuring out access will be another major roadblock.

Data exploration and feature engineering

Data exploration: once you figure out the dataset, the next biggest task is to *figure out the dataset again!* You read that right – for a data scientist, the next biggest task is to make sure that the dataset they've picked is the right dataset to solve the problem. This would involve data cleaning, augmenting missing data, transforming data, plotting different graphs, finding a correlation, finding out data skew, and more. The best part is that if the data scientists find that something is not right, they will go back to the previous step, which is to look for more datasets, try them out again, and go back.

Feature engineering is not easy either; domain knowledge becomes key to building the feature set to train the model. If you are a data scientist who has been working on the pricing and promotion models for the past few years, you would know what dataset and features would result in a better model than a data scientist who has been working on customer value models for the past few years and vice versa. Let's try out an exercise and see if feature engineering is easy or not and if domain knowledge plays a key role. Have a look at the following screenshot and see if you can recognize the animals:

Figure 1.13 – A person holding a dog and a cat

I'm sure you know what these animals are, but let's take a step back and see how we correctly identified the animals. When we looked at the figure, our subconscious did feature engineering. It could have picked features such as *it has a couple of ears*, a *couple of eyes*, *a nose*, *a head*, and *a tail*. Instead, it picked much more sophisticated features, such as *the shape of its face*, *the shape of its eyes*, *the shape of its nose*, and *the color and texture of its fur*. If it had picked the first set of features, both animals would have turned out to be the same, which is an example of bad feature engineering and a bad model. Since it chose the latter, we identified it as different animals. Again, this is an example of good feature engineering and a good model.

But another question we need to answer would be, when did we develop expertise in animal identification? Well, maybe it's from our kindergarten teachers. We all remember some version of the first 100 animals that we learned about from our teachers, parents, brothers, and sisters. We didn't get all of them right at first but eventually, we did. We gained expertise over time.

Now, what if, instead of a picture of a cat and a dog, it was a picture of two snakes and our job was to identify which one of them is venomous and which is not. Though all of us could identify them as snakes, almost none of us would be able to identify which one is venomous and which is not. Unless the person has been a snake charmer before.

Hence, domain expertise becomes crucial in feature engineering. Just like the data exploration stage, if we are not happy with the features, we are back to square one, which involves looking for more data and better features.

Modeling to production and monitoring

Once we've figured out the aforementioned stage, taking the model to production is very time-consuming unless the right infrastructure is ready and waiting. For a model to run in production, it needs a processing platform that will run the data cleaning and feature engineering code. It also needs an orchestration framework to run the feature engineering pipeline in a scheduled or event-based way. We also need a way to store and retrieve features securely at low latency in some cases. If the model is transactional, the model must be packaged so that it can be accessed by the consumers securely, maybe as a REST endpoint. Also, the deployed model should be scalable to serve the incoming traffic.

Model and data monitoring are crucial aspects too. As model performance directly affects the business, you must know what metrics would determine that the model needs to be retrained in advance. Other than model monitoring, the dataset also needs to be monitored for skews. For example, in an e-commerce business, traffic patterns and purchase patterns may change frequently based on seasonality, trends, and other factors. Identifying these changes early will affect the business positively. Hence, data and feature monitoring are key in taking the model to production.

Summary

In this chapter, we discussed the different stages in the ML life cycle. We picked a problem statement, performed data exploration, plotted a few graphs, did feature engineering and customer segmentation, and built a customer lifetime value model. We looked at the oversights and discussed the most time-consuming stages of ML. I wanted to get you onto the same page as I am and set a good foundation for the rest of this book.

In the next chapter, we will set the stage for the need for a feature store and how it could improve the ML process. We will also discuss the need to bring features into production and some of the traditional ways of doing so.

2

What Problems Do Feature Stores Solve?

In the last chapter, we discussed the different stages in the **machine learning** (**ML**) life cycle, the difficult and time-consuming stages of ML, and how far we are from an ideal world. In this chapter, we'll explore one area of ML, which is ML feature management. ML feature management is the process of creating features, storing them in persistent storage, and serving them at scale for model training and inference. It is one of the most important stages of ML, although it is often overlooked. In data science/engineering teams in the early stages of ML, the absence of feature management has been a major hindrance to getting their ML models to production.

As a data scientist/ML engineer, you may have found innovative ways to store and retrieve features for your ML model. But mostly, the solutions we build are not reusable, and every solution has limitations. For example, some of us might be using S3 buckets to store features, whereas other data scientists in the team might be using transactional databases. One may be more comfortable using CSV files and the other might prefer using Avro or Parquet files. Due to personal preference and a lack of standardization, each model will probably have a different way of managing features. Good feature management, on the other hand, should do the following:

- Make features discoverable
- Lead to easy reproducibility of models
- Accelerate model development and productionization
- Fuel reuse of features within and across teams
- Make feature monitoring easy

The aim of this chapter is to explain how data scientists and engineers strive to achieve better feature management and yet fall short of expectations. We will review different approaches adopted by teams to bring features into production, common problems with these approaches, and how we can do better with a feature store. By the end of this chapter, you will understand how a feature store meets the objectives mentioned previously and provides standardization across teams.

In this chapter, we will cover the following topics:

- Importance of features in production
- Ways to bring features to production
- Common problems with the approaches used for bringing features to production
- Feature store to the rescue
- Philosophy behind feature stores

Importance of features in production

Before discussing how to bring features to production, let's understand why features are needed in production. Let's go through an example.

We often use taxi and food delivery services. One of the good things about these services is that they tell us how long it will take for our taxi or food to arrive. Also, most of the time, it is approximately correct. How does it predict this accurately? It uses ML, of course. The ML model predicts how long it will take for the taxi or food to arrive. For a model like that to be successful, not only does it need a good feature engineering and ML algorithm, but also the most recent features. Though we don't know the exact feature set that the model uses, let's look at a couple of features that change dynamically and are very important.

With food delivery services, the major components that affect the delivery time are restaurants, drivers, traffic, and customers. The model probably uses a set of slow-changing features that are updated regularly, maybe daily or weekly, and a set of dynamic features that change every few minutes. The slow-changing features might include the average number of orders a restaurant receives at different times of the day from the app and in person, the average time it takes for an order to be ready, and so on. It might seem like these features are not slow-changing, but if you think about it, the average number of orders might differ based on restaurant location, seasonality, time of the day, day of the week, and more. Dynamic features include how long the last five orders took, the number of cancelations in the past 30 minutes, and the current number of orders for the restaurant. Similarly, driver features might include average order delivery time with respect to distance, how often the driver cancels orders, and whether the driver is picking up multiple orders. Apart from these features, there will be traffic features, which change much more dynamically.

With many dynamic features in play, even if one of them is an hour old, the model's predictions will go off the charts. For example, if there is a crash on the delivery route and traffic features don't capture it and use it for inference, the model will predict that food will arrive more quickly than it actually will. Similarly, if the model cannot get the current number of orders at the restaurant, it will use the old value and predict a value that may be far from the truth. Hence the more up-to-date features a model gets, the better the predictions will be. Also, another thing to keep in mind is that the app will not give the features; the app can only give information such as the restaurant ID and the customer ID. The model will have to fetch the features and facts from a different location, ideally a feature store. Wherever the features are being fetched from, the infrastructure serving it must scale in and scale out based on traffic to efficiently use resources and also to accommodate requests at low latency with a very low percentage of errors, if any.

Just like the food delivery service, the model we built in the first chapter needs the features during inference and the more up to date the features are, the better the customer's **lifetime value** (**LTV**) prediction will be. Good predictions will lead to better actions, resulting in excellent customer experience, hence better customer affinity, and better business.

Ways to bring features to production

Now that we understand the need for features in production, let's look at some traditional ways of bringing features to production. Let's consider two types of pipelines: batch model pipelines and online/transactional model pipelines:

- **Batch models**: These are models that are run on a schedule, such as hourly, daily, weekly, and so on. Two of the common batch models are forecasting and customer segmentation. Batch inference is easier and less complex than its counterpart since it doesn't have any latency requirements; inference can run for minutes or hours. Batch models can use distributed computational frameworks such as Spark. Also, they can be run with simple infrastructure. Most ML models start as batch models and, over time, depending on the available infrastructure and requirements, they go on to become online/transactional models.

  Though batch models' infrastructure is simple to build and manage, these models have drawbacks, such as the predictions not always being up to date. Since there is a time lag on predictions, it might cost business. For example, let's say a manufacturing plant uses order forecasting models to acquire raw materials. Depending on the time lag of the batch forecast models, the business might need to bear the cost of the shortage in raw materials versus overstocking raw materials in the warehouse.

- **Online/transactional models**: Online models follow the pull paradigm; the prediction will be generated on demand. Online models take advantage of the current reality and use that for predictions. Online models are transactional, need low-latency serving, and should scale based on incoming traffic. A typical online model is a recommendation model, which could be product recommendation, design recommendation, and so on.

> Though real-time prediction sounds fancy, online models face a different set of challenges. It is easier to build applications whose latency is 8 hours than it is to build an application with a latency of 100 milliseconds. The latency of online models is usually in milliseconds. That means the model has a few milliseconds to figure out what the most up-to-date value is (which means generating or getting the latest features for the model) and predict the outcomes. For this to happen, the model needs a supporting infrastructure to serve the data required for prediction. Online models are usually hosted as REST API endpoints, which again need scaling, monitoring, and more.

Now that we understand the difference between batch and online models, let's look at how batch model pipelines work.

Batch model pipeline

As discussed, batch model pipeline latency requirements can range from minutes to hours. Batch models usually run on a schedule, hence they will be orchestrated using tools such as Airflow or AWS Step Functions. Let's look at a typical batch model pipeline and how features are brought to production.

Figure 2.1 depicts typical batch model pipelines:

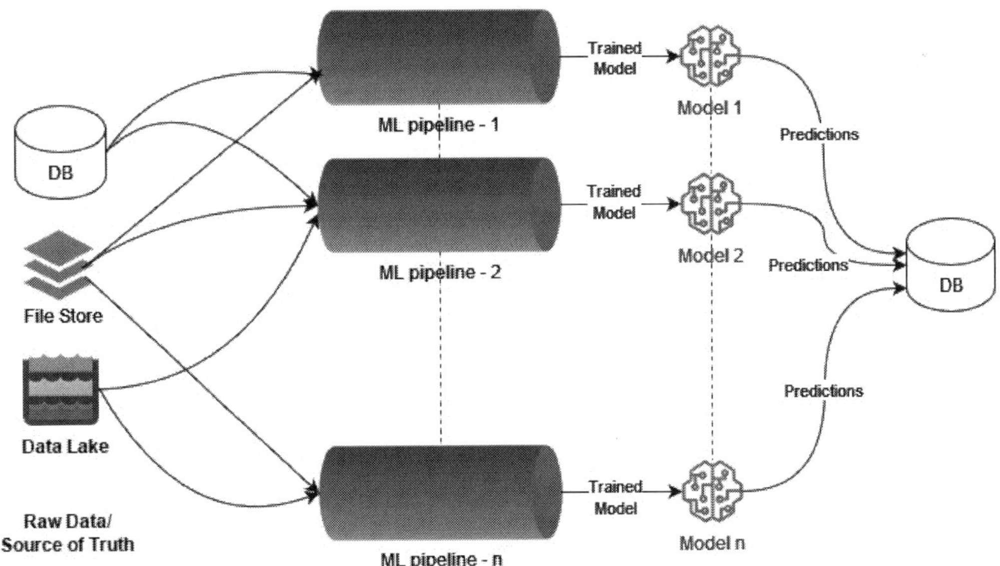

Figure 2.1 – Batch model pipelines

As discussed in *Chapter 1, An Overview of the Machine Learning Life Cycle*, once the model development is complete and it's ready for productionization, the notebook will be refactored to remove unwanted code. Some data engineers also break down a single notebook into multiple logical steps, such as feature engineering, model training, and model prediction. The refactored notebooks or refactored Python scripts generated from the notebook are scheduled using an orchestration framework such as Airflow. In a typical pipeline, the first stage will read the raw data from different data sources, perform data cleaning, and carry out feature engineering, which will be used by subsequent stages in the pipeline. Once the model prediction stage is complete, the prediction output will be written to a persistent store, maybe a database or an S3 bucket. The results will be accessed from the persistent storage as and when needed. If a stage in the pipeline fails for any reason (such as a data accessibility issue or errors in the code), the pipeline will be set up to trigger an alarm and stop further execution.

If you haven't already noticed, in the batch model pipeline, the features are generated when the pipeline runs. In some cases, it also retrains a new model with the latest data, and in others, it uses a previously trained model and predicts using the features generated from the data available at the time when the pipeline is run. As you can see in *Figure 2.1*, every new model that is built starts at the raw data source, repeats the same steps, and joins the production pipeline list. We will discuss the problems in this approach in the later section. Let's look at the different ways to bring features to production in online models next.

Online model pipeline

Online models have the special requirement of serving features in near real time, as these models are customer-facing or need to make business decisions in real time. There are different ways to bring features to production in an online model. Let's discuss them one by one in this section. One thing to keep in mind is that these approaches are not exactly how everybody does it; they are merely a representation of group approaches. Different teams use different versions of these approaches.

Packaging features along with models

To deploy an online model, it will have to be packaged first. Again, there are different standards that teams follow depending on the tools they use. Some might use packing libraries such as MLflow, joblib, or ONNX. Others might package the model directly as the REST API Docker image. As data scientists and data engineers have a different set of skills, as mentioned in *Figure 1.1* of *Chapter 1, An Overview of the Machine Learning Life Cycle*, the ideal approach is to provide data scientists with tools to package models using libraries such as MLflow, joblib, and ONNX, and save the model to a model registry. The data engineers can then use the registered model to build REST APIs and deploy it. There is also out-of-the-box support to deploy MLflow-packaged models as AWS SageMaker endpoints with a simple **command-line interface** (**CLI**) command. It also supports building REST API Docker images with a CLI command, which then can be deployed in any container environment.

While libraries such as MLflow and joblib provide a way to package Python objects, they also support adding additional dependencies if required. For example, MLflow provides a set of built-in flavors to support the packaging of models using ML libraries such as scikit-learn, PyTorch, Keras, and TensorFlow. It adds all the required dependencies for the ML library. Packaging models with built-in flavors is as simple as using the following code:

```
mlflow.<MLlib>.save_model(model_object)
## example scikit-learn
mlflow.sklearn.save_model(model_object)
```

Along with the required dependencies, you can package the `features.csv` file and load it in the `predict` method of the model. Though this might sound like an easy deployment option, the result of this is not far away from a batch model. Since features are packaged along with the model, they are static. Any change in the raw dataset will not affect the model unless a new version of the model is built with a new set of features generated from the latest data and packaged along with the model. However, this might be a good first step from batch to online models. The reason I say this is that instead of running it as a batch model, you have now made it a pull-based inference. Also, you have defined a REST endpoint input and output format for the consumer of the model. The only pending step is to get the latest features to the model instead of static features, which are packaged. Once that is implemented, the consumers of the model won't have to make any changes and consumers will be served with predictions using the latest available data.

Push-based inference

Unlike pull-based inference, where the model is scored when needed, in the push-based inference pattern, predictions are run proactively and kept ready in a transactional database or key-value store so that they can be served at low latency when the request comes. Let's look at a typical architecture of online models using push-based inference:

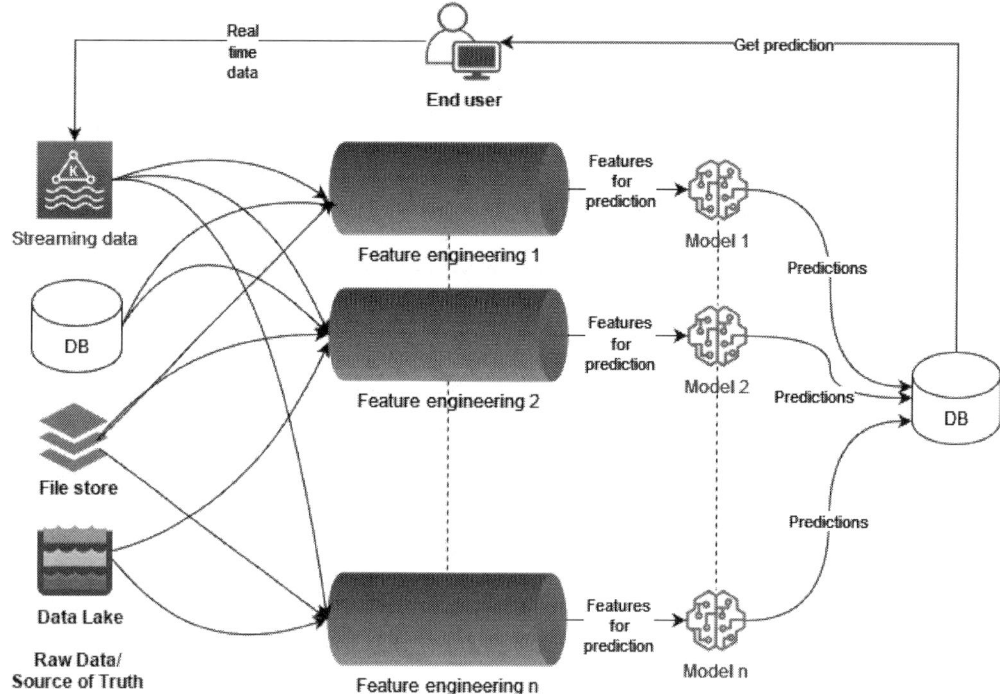

Figure 2.2 – Push-based inference

Figure 2.2 shows the architecture of push-based inference. The idea here is similar to batch model inference, but the difference is that the pipeline also considers the real-time dataset, which is changing dynamically. The operation of a push-based model works as follows:

- The real-time data (in this example, user interactions with the website) will be captured and pushed to a queue, such as Kafka, Kinesis, or Event Hubs.

- The feature engineering pipelines subscribe to a specific set of topics or a specific set of queues depending on what data is needed to generate features of the model. This also depends on the tools and the architecture. There may be a single queue or multiple queues depending on how huge/diverse the application is.
- Whenever an event of interest appears in the queue, the feature engineering pipeline will pick this event and regenerate the features of the model using other datasets.

> **Note**
>
> Not all features are dynamic. Some features may not change very much or very often. For example, a customer's geographic location might not change often.

- The newly generated features are used to run the prediction of the data point.
- The results are stored in a transactional database or a key-value store.
- Whenever required, the website or application will query the database to get new predictions for the specific ID (such as `CustomerId` when serving recommendations for a customer on a website).
- This process repeats every time a new event of interest appears on the queue.
- A new pipeline will be added for every new ML model.

This approach might seem easy and straightforward, as the only additional requirement here is real-time streaming data. However, this has limitations; the whole pipeline will have to run within milliseconds so that the recommendations are available before the application makes the next query for prediction. This is achievable but might involve a higher cost of operationalization because this is not just one pipeline: every pipeline for real-time models will have to have a similar latency requirement. Also, this will not be a copy-and-paste infrastructure because each model will have a different set of requirements when it comes to incoming traffic. For example, a model working on order features might require fewer processing instances, whereas a model working with clickstream data will require more data processing instances. Another thing to keep in mind is that although it might look like they are writing data to the same database, most of the time, it involves different databases and different technologies.

Let's look at a better solution next.

Pull-based inference

In contrast to push-based inference, in pull-based inference, predictions are run at the time of the request. Instead of storing the predictions, feature sets of a specific model are stored in a transactional database or key-value store. During prediction, the feature set can be accessed with low latency. Let's look at the typical architecture of a pull-based inference model and the components involved:

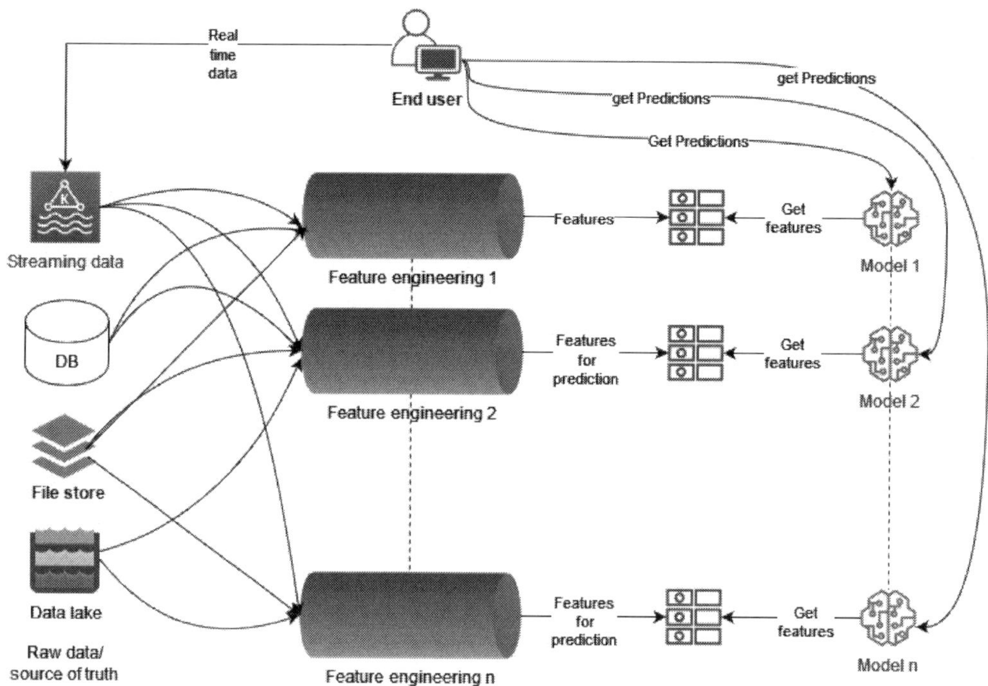

Figure 2.3 – Using transactional/key-value store for features

Figure 2.3 shows another way of bringing features to production: the pull-based mechanism. Half of the pipeline works in a similar way to the push-based inference that we just discussed. The difference here is that after feature engineering, the features are written to a transactional database or key-value store. These features will be kept up to date by the pipelines. Once the features are available, the model works as follows:

1. The model's `predict` API would have a contract similar to the one mentioned here:

```
def predict(entity_id: str) -> dict
```

2. When the application needs to query the model, it will hit the REST endpoint with `entity_id`.
3. The model will use `entity_id` to query the key-value store to get the features required to score the model.
4. The features are used to score the model and return the predictions.

This approach is ideal if you don't have the feature store infrastructure. Also, we will discuss this extensively in the next chapter. Again, there are a few concerns involved with this approach, which are the repetition of the work, deploying and scaling the feature engineering pipeline, and managing multiple key-value store infrastructures, among others.

Calculating features on demand

Let's discuss one last approach before we move on and discuss the problems with these approaches. In the approaches discussed so far, the data pipelines calculate the features proactively as and when the data arrives, or when the pipeline runs. However, it is possible to calculate the features on demand when there is a request for the inference. This means when the application queries the model for a prediction, the model will request another system for the features. The system uses raw data from different sources and calculates the features on demand. This may be the most difficult architecture to implement, but I heard on the *TWIML AI podcast with Sam Charrington, episode 326: Metaflow, A Human-Centric Framework for Data Science with Ville Tuulos*, that Netflix has a system that can generate features on demand with a latency of seconds.

The `predict` API might look similar to the one in the last approach:

```
def predict(entity_id: str) -> dict
```

It then invokes the system to get features for the given entity, runs predictions using the features, and returns the results. As you can imagine, all of this will have to happen within a few seconds. The on-demand feature engineering to be executed in real time might require a huge infrastructure with multiple caches between different storage systems. Keeping these systems in sync is not an easy architecture design. It's just a dream infrastructure for most of us. I haven't seen one so far. Hopefully, we will get there soon.

In this section, we discussed multiple ways to bring features into production for inference. There may be many other ways of achieving this, but most solutions are variations that revolve around one of these approaches. Now that we understand why and how we bring features to production, let's look at the common issues that these approaches have and what can be done to overcome them.

Common problems with the approaches used for bringing features to production

The approaches discussed in the previous section seem like good solutions. However, not only does every approach have its own technical difficulties, such as infrastructure sizing, keeping up with a service-level agreement (SLA), and interaction with different systems, but they have a few common problems as well. This is expected in a growing technical domain until it reaches a level of saturation. I want to dedicate this section to the common problems that exist in these approaches.

Re-inventing the wheel

One of the common problems in engineering is building something that already exists. The reasons for that could be many; for example, a person developing a solution may not know that it already exists, or the existing solution is inefficient, or there is a need for additional functionality. We have the same problem here.

In many organizations, data scientists work in a specific domain and with a team supporting them, which usually includes ML engineers, data engineers, and data analysts. Their goal is to get their model to production. Though the other teams working in parallel also have the goal of getting their model to production, they hardly ever collaborate with each other due to their schedules and delivery timelines. As discussed in the first chapter, every persona in the team has different skill sets, different levels of experience with the available tools, and different preferences. Also, data engineers on two different teams rarely have the same preference. This leads to each team finding a solution to productionizing their model, which involves building feature engineering pipelines, feature management, model management, and monitoring.

After coming up with a successful solution, even if the team (let's call it team-A) shares their knowledge and success with other teams, the response you would get would be *good to know, interesting, could be useful for us*. But it will never materialize into the other teams' solutions. The reason for that is not that other teams are indifferent to what team-A achieved. Apart from the knowledge, nothing that was built by team-A in many cases is reusable. The options that the other teams are left with are to copy the code and adapt it to their needs and hope it works or implement a similar-looking pipeline. Hence, most teams end up building their own solution for the model. The interesting thing is that even team-A will re-build the same pipeline for the next model they work on in most cases.

Feature re-calculation

Let's start with a question. Ask yourself this: *how much memory does your phone have?* Most probably you know the answer by heart. If you are not sure, you might check the memory in the settings and answer. Either way, if I or somebody else asks you the same question in an hour, I'm pretty sure you will not go back into the phone's settings and check again before answering, unless you have changed your phone. So why are we doing this in all our ML pipelines for features?

When you go back and look at the approaches discussed previously, all of them have this common problem. Let's say team-A just completed a customer LTV model successfully and took it to production. Now team-A has been assigned another project, which is to predict the next purchase day of the customer. There is a high chance that the features that were effective in the customer LTV model can be effective here as well. Though these features are being calculated periodically to support the production model, team-A will start again with the raw data, calculate these features from scratch, and use them for the model development. Not only that, but they replicate the whole pipeline, though there are overlaps.

As a result of this re-calculation, depending on the setup and the tools that team-A uses, they will be wasting compute, storage, and man-hours, whereas with better feature management, team-A could have gotten a head start on the new project, which is also a cost-effective solution.

Feature discoverability and sharing

As discussed, one of the problems is recalculation within the same team. The other part of this problem is even bigger. That is re-calculation across the teams and domains. Just like in the *Re-inventing the wheel* section, where teams were trying to figure out how to bring ML features to production, data scientists are re-discovering the data and features themselves here.

One of the major drivers of this is a lack of trust and discoverability. Let's talk about discoverability first. Whenever data scientists work on a model and do a great job of data mining, exploration, and feature engineering, there are very limited ways of sharing it, as we discussed in the first chapter. The data scientist can use emails and presentations to do that. However, there is no way for anybody to discover what's available and selectively build what is not and use both in the model. Even if it's possible to discover other data scientists work, it is not possible to use it without figuring out data access and re-calculating features.

The other driver for re-inventing the wheel in data discovery and feature engineering is trust. Though evidence is clear that there is a production model that uses the generated features, data scientists often find it difficult to trust programs developed by others that generate the features. Since raw data is trustworthy as it will have SLAs and schema validations, data scientists often end up re-discovering and generating the features.

Hence the solution required here is an application that can make the features generated by others discoverable, sharable, and, most importantly, trustworthy, that is, a person/team who owns and manages the features they produce.

Training vs Serving skew

One other common problem in ML is training and serving skew. This happens when the feature engineering code used to generate the features for model training is different from the code used to generate the features for model prediction/serving. This could happen for many reasons; for instance, during model training, the data scientist may have used PySpark for generating the features, where as while productionizing the pipeline, the ML/Data engineer who took over, used a different technologies that is required by the production infrastructure. There are few problems with this. One is, there are two versions of feature engineering code, and the other problem is this could cause the training versus serving skew since the data generated by two versions of the pipeline may not be same for the same raw data input.

Model reproducibility

Model reproducibility is one of the common issues to tackle in ML. I have heard the story of how after a data scientist quit his job, the model he was working on was lost and his team couldn't reproduce the model many times. One of the main reasons for this is again the lack of feature management tools. You might ask what the problem is in reproducing the same model when you have the history of raw data. Let's take a look.

Let's say there was a data scientist, Ram, working on an ML model to recommend products to customers. Ram spent a month working on it and came up with a brilliant model. With the help of data engineers on the team, the model was deployed to production. But Ram was not challenged enough in this job, so he quit and moved on to a different firm. Unfortunately, the production system went down, Ram didn't follow the MLOps standards of saving the model to a registry, so the model was lost and could not be recovered.

Now, the responsibility for rebuilding the model is given to Dee, a new data scientist on the team, who is smart and uses the same dataset that was used by Ram, and performs the same data cleansing and feature engineering as if Dee is a reincarnation of Ram. Unfortunately, Dee's model cannot get the same results as Ram's. No matter how many times Dee tries, she cannot reproduce the model.

One of the reasons for this is that the data has changed over time, which in turn affects the feature values and hence the model. There is no way to go back in time to produce the same features that were used the first time. As model reproducibility/repeatability is one of the crucial aspects of ML, we need to time travel. This means that data scientists should be able to go back in time and fetch the feature from a specific time in the past, just like in *Avengers: Endgame*, so that the models can be reproduced consistently.

Low latency

One other problem that all the approaches are trying to solve is low-latency feature serving. The ability to provide features at low latency decides whether a model can be hosted as an online model or a batch model. This has problems such as building and managing infrastructure and keeping features up to date. As it doesn't make sense to set up all models to be transactional, at the same time there is a high chance that a feature used in one batch model could be of great use in a different online model. So, the ability to switch the low-latency serving on and off would be a great benefit to data scientists.

So far in this section, we have been through some of the common problems with the approaches discussed in the previous section. The question that still remains unanswered is what can be done to make this better? Is there a single tool or set of tools that exists today that can help us solve these common problems? As it turns out, the answer is *yes*, there is one tool that can solve all the problems we have talked about so far. It is called a *feature store*. In the next section, let's see what feature stores are, how they solve these problems, and the philosophy behind them.

Feature stores to the rescue

Let's begin this section with the definition of feature stores. A **feature store** is an operational data system for managing and serving ML features to models in production. It can serve feature data to models from a low-latency online store (for real-time prediction) or from an offline store (for scale-out batch scoring or model training). As the definition points out, it's a whole package that helps you create and manage ML features, and accelerate the operationalization of models. Before we dive deeper into feature stores, let's look at how the architecture of ML pipelines changes with the introduction of a feature store:

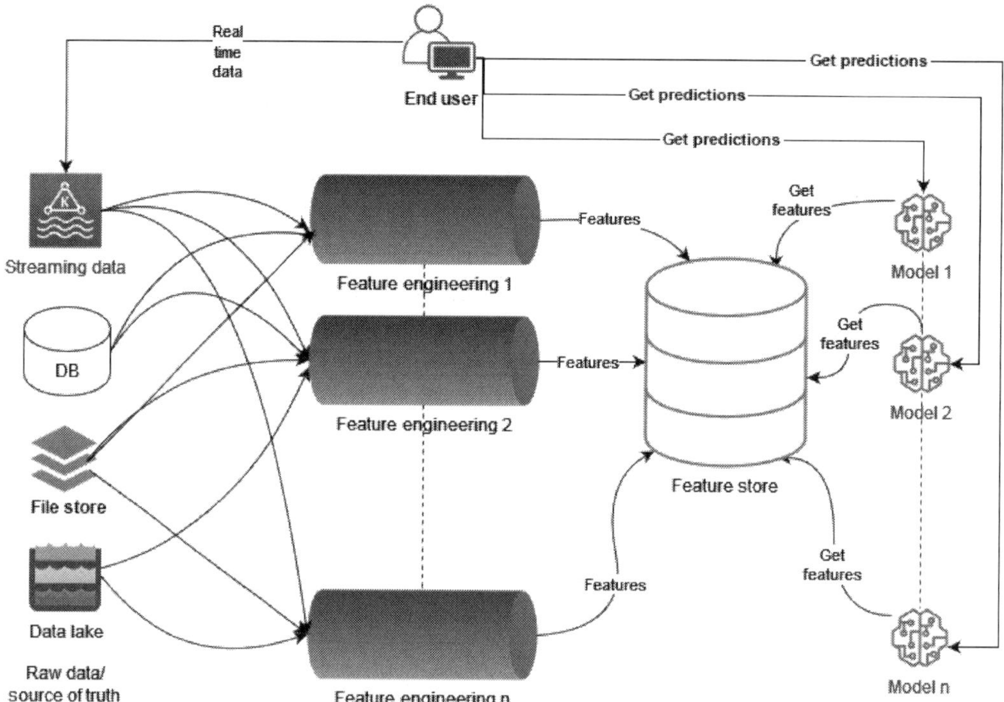

Figure 2.4 – ML pipelines with a feature store

Figure 2.4 depicts the architecture of ML pipelines when you include a feature store. You may think that *Figure 2.4* looks the same as *Figure 2.3* and I just replaced a bunch of small data stores with a bigger one and called it a feature store. Yes, it might seem that way, but there is more to it. Unlike a traditional data store, a feature store has a special set of capabilities; it is not a data store, but rather a data system (as its definition states), and it can do much more than just storage and retrieval.

With the feature store being part of the ML pipeline, this is how the entire pipeline works:

1. Once the data scientist has a problem statement, the starting point will not be raw data anymore. It will be the feature store.
2. The data scientist will connect to the feature store, browse through the repository, and use the features of interest.
3. If this is the first model, the feature store might be empty. From here, the data scientist will go into the discovery phase, figure out the dataset, build a feature engineering pipeline, and ingest the features into the feature store. The feature store decouples feature engineering pipelines from the rest of the stages in ML.
4. If the feature store is not empty but there are not enough features available in the feature store, the data scientist will discover the data of interest and another feature engineering pipeline will be added to sink a new set of features into the feature store. This approach makes the features available for the model that the data scientist is working on and for other data scientists who find these features useful in their model.
5. Once the data scientist is happy with the feature set, the model will be trained, validated, and tested. If the model performance is not good, the data scientist will go back to discover new data and features.
6. When the model is ready to be deployed, the `predict` method of the model will include code to fetch the required features for generating model predictions.
7. The ready model will be deployed as a REST endpoint if it's an online model; otherwise, it will be used to perform batch predictions.

Now that we understand how the pipeline works, let's go through the problems we discussed in the previous section and learn how the feature store solves them.

Standardizing ML with a feature store

Once the feature store is standardized at the team level, though there may be different ways of reading data and building feature engineering pipelines, but beyond feature engineering, the rest of the pipeline becomes a standard implementation. The ML engineers and data scientists don't have to come up with new ways to bring features to production. After feature engineering, the data scientists and ML engineers will ingest the features into the feature store. The feature store, by definition, can serve features at low latency. All ML engineers will have to do after that is update their `predict` method to fetch the required features from the feature store and return the predictions. This not only makes the life of the ML engineers easy, it sometimes also offloads managing feature management infrastructure.

Feature store avoids reprocessing data

As mentioned in the definition, a feature store has an offline store, and data from the offline store can be retrieved for model training or batch inference. Model training here doesn't mean training the same model. The features ingested into the feature store can be used for the training of another model.

Let's take the same example we used while discussing the problem: team-A just completed the production deployment of the customer LTV model. The next model team-A starts working on is predicting the next purchase date. When the data scientists start working on this model, they don't have to go back to raw data and re-calculate the features that were used to build the customer LTV model. The data scientist can connect to the feature store, which is being updated with the latest features of the previous model, and get the features required to train the new model. However, the data scientist will have to build a data cleaning and feature engineering pipeline for the additional features that they find useful from the raw data. Again, the newly added features can be reused in the next model. This makes model development efficient and cost-effective.

Features are discoverable and sharable with the feature store

In the previous paragraph, we discussed the reuse of features within a team. Feature stores help data scientists achieve that. The other major issue was re-calculating and re-discovering useful data and features across teams due to the lack of feature discoverability. Guess what? Feature stores solve that too. Data scientists can connect to a feature store and browse through the existing feature tables and schemas. If they find any of the existing features useful, data scientists can use them in the model without re-discovering or re-calculating them.

Another problem involved in sharing was trust. Although feature stores don't solve this completely, they address it to some extent. Since the feature tables are created and managed by a team, the data scientists can always reach out to the owners to get access and also discuss other aspects, such as SLAs and monitoring. If you haven't noticed yet, feature stores facilitate collaboration between teams. This can be beneficial for both teams, with data scientists and ML engineers from different teams working together and sharing each other's expertise.

No more training versus serving skew

With Feature Store, training versus serving skew will never occur. Once the feature engineering is complete, the features will be ingested into the feature store and feature store is the source for model training. Hence, the data scientists will use the features in feature store to train the ML model. Once the model is trained and moved to production, the production model will fetch the online store or historical store again for model prediction. As these features are used by both - training and prediction, serving is generated by the same pipeline/code and we will never have this issue with feature store.

Model reproducibility with feature stores

The other major issue with the previously discussed architecture was model reproducibility. This is an issue: the data is changing frequently, which in turn leads to features changing and hence the model changing, though the same set of features is being used to build the model. The only way to solve this problem was to go back in time and fetch the same state data that produced the old model. That may be a very complex problem to solve since it will involve multiple data stores. However, it is possible to store generated features in such a way that it allows data scientists to time travel.

Yes, that is exactly what a feature store does. A feature store has an offline store, which stores historical data and allows users to go back in time and get the value of a feature at a specific point in time. With a feature store, a data scientist can get features from a specific time in history, so reproducing the model consistently is possible. Model reproducibility is no longer an issue with feature stores.

Serving features at low latency with feature stores

Though all the solutions were able to achieve the low-latency serving in some way, the solutions were not uniform. ML engineers had to come up with a solution to solve this issue and also build and manage the infrastructure. However, having a feature store in the ML pipeline makes this simple and also offloads the infrastructure management to the other team in cases where the platform team manages the feature store. Even without that, having the ability to run a few commands and have the low-latency serving up and running is a handy tool for ML engineers.

Philosophy behind feature stores

In this chapter, we have discussed different issues with ML pipelines and how feature stores help data scientists solve them and accelerate ML development. In this section, let's try to understand the philosophy behind feature stores and try to make sense of why having a feature store in our ML pipeline may be the ideal way to accelerate ML. Let's start with a real-world example as we are trying to build real-world experience with ML. You will be given the names of two phones; your job is to figure out which one is better. The names are iPhone 13 Pro and Google Pixel 6 Pro. You have an infinite amount of time to find the answer; continue reading once you have the answer.

As Ralph Waldo Emerson said, *It's not the destination, it is the journey*. Whatever your answer may be, however long you took to arrive at it, let's look at how you might have arrived at it. Some of you might have got an answer right away, but if you haven't used either of these phones, you probably would have googled `iPhone 13 Pro vs Google Pixel 6 Pro`. You would have browsed through a few links, which would give you a comparison of the phones:

	iPhone 13 Pro	Google Pixel 6 Pro
Size	146.7 x 71.5 x 7.7 mm (5.78 x 2.81 x 0.30 inches)	163.9 x 75.9 x 8.9 mm (6.45 x 2.99 x 0.35 inches)
Weight	204 grams (7.2 ounces)	210 grams (7.41 ounces)
Screen size	6.1-inch Super Retina XDR OLED	6.71-inch LTPO AMOLED
Screen resolution	2532 x 1170 pixels (460 ppi)	3120 x 1440 pixels (512 ppi)
Operating system	iOS 15	Android 12
Storage	128 GB, 256 GB, 512 GB, 1TB	128 GB, 256 GB, 512 GB
MicroSD card slot	No	No
Processor	Apple A15 Bionic (5nm)	Google Tensor (5nm)
RAM	6 GB	12 GB
Camera	Triple lens 12-megapixel wide, 12 MP ultrawide, and 12 MP telephoto rear, 12 MP front	Triple lens 50MP wide, 12 MP ultrawide, and 48 MP telephoto rear, 11.1 MP front
Video	4K at up to 60 fps, 1080p at 120 fps	4K at up to 60 fps, 1080p at 240 fps
Bluetooth version	Bluetooth 5.1	Bluetooth 5.2
Ports	Lightning	USB-C
Fingerprint sensor	No, FaceID instead	Yes (in-display ultrasonic)
Water resistance	IP68	IP68
Battery	3,125 mAh 20 W wired charging (no charger included in the box) 15 W MagSafe charging 7.5 W wireless charging	5,003 mAh 30 W wired charging (no charger included in the box) 23 W wireless charging
App marketplace	Apple App Store	Google Play Store
Network support	All major carriers	All major carriers
Colors	Graphite, Gold, Silver, Sierra Blue	Cloudy White, Sorta Sunny, Stormy Black
Price	Starting at $999	Starting at $899
Buy from	Apple	Google
Review score	4.5 out of 5 stars	4 stars out of 5

Figure 2.5 – iPhone 13 Pro versus Google Pixel 6 Pro

This was a great way of comparing two phones. Some of you might have done a lot more to arrive at the answer, but I'm sure none of us went and bought both phones, read through the specs provided by Apple and Google, used each of them for a month, and became experts with each of them before answering the question.

In this task, we were smart enough to use the expertise and work done by others. Although there are a lot of comparisons on the internet, we chose the one that works for us. Not only in this task, but in most tasks, from buying a phone to buying a home, we try to use expert opinion to make a decision. If you look at it in a certain way, these are features in our decision-making. Along with the expert's opinion, we also include our own constraints and features, such as budget, memory if it's a phone, the number of seats if it's a car, and the number of rooms if it's a house. We use a combination of these to decide and take action. In most cases, this approach works, and in some cases, we might do a lot more research and become experts too.

The use of feature stores in ML is an attempt to achieve something similar; it is like Google for data scientists. Instead of a generic search like Google, data scientists are looking for something specific, and are also sharing their expertise with other data scientists. If what is available in the feature store doesn't work for a data scientist, they will go to raw data, explore, understand, become experts in it, and come up with distinguishing features about a particular entity, which could be products, customers, and so on. This workflow of ML with feature stores will not only help data scientists use each other's expertise but also standardize and accelerate ML development.

Summary

In this chapter, we discussed common problems in ML feature management, different architectures of productionizing ML models, and ways to bring features to production. We also explored the issues involved with these approaches and how feature stores solve these issues by standardizing practices and providing additional features that a traditional data store does not.

Now that we understand what feature stores have to offer, in the next chapter, we'll get our hands dirty with feature stores and explore the terminology, features, typical architecture of a feature store, and much more.

Further reading

- *Feast documentation*: `https://docs.feast.dev/`

Section 2 – A Feature Store in Action

This section concentrates on the *what?* and *how?* aspects of feature management in **Machine Learning** (**ML**). In this section, we will start with an introduction to an open source feature store, *Feast*, followed by different terminologies and basic API usage. We will reuse the same ML problem that we discussed in *Section 1*, *Why Do We Need a Feature Store?*, create a Feast infrastructure on AWS, and include it in our ML pipeline. This inclusion enables us to look at how a feature store decouples our ML pipeline into different stages and the changes it brings to model training and inference. Once the model development is complete, we will look at how the capabilities of a feature store make it easy to move a model into production and also help in feature monitoring.

This section comprises the following chapters:

- *Chapter 3, Feature Store Fundamentals, Terminology, and Usage*
- *Chapter 4, Adding Feature Store to ML Models*
- *Chapter 5, Model Training and Inference*
- *Chapter 6, Model to Production and Beyond*

3
Feature Store Fundamentals, Terminology, and Usage

In the last chapter, we discussed the need to bring features into production and different ways of doing so, along with a look at common issues with these approaches and how feature stores can solve them. We have built up a lot of expectations about feature stores, and it's time to understand how they work. As mentioned in the last chapter, a feature store is different from a traditional database – it is a data storage service for managing machine learning features, a hybrid system that can be used for storage and retrieval of historical features for model training. It can also serve the latest features at low latency for real-time prediction, and at sub-second latency for batch prediction.

In this chapter, we will discuss what a feature store is, how it works, and the range of terminology used in the feature store world. For this chapter, we will use one of the most widely used open source feature stores, called **Feast**. The goal of this chapter is for you to understand the basic usage of Feast feature store terms and APIs along with gaining a brief understanding of how it works internally.

In this chapter, we will discuss the following topics:

- Introduction to Feast and installation
- Feast terminology and definitions
- Feast initialization
- Feast usage
- Feast behind the scenes

Technical requirements

To follow the code examples in this chapter, all you need is familiarity with Python and any notebook environment, which could be a local setup such as Jupyter or an online notebook environment such as Google Colab or Kaggle. You can download the code examples for this chapter from the following GitHub link: `https://github.com/PacktPublishing/Feature-Store-for-Machine-Learning/tree/main/Chapter03`.

Introduction to Feast and installation

Feast is an open source feature management system for serving and managing ML features. It was a collaboration between *Google* and *Gojek*, which was then adopted by *Linux Foundation AI and Data*. Feast was initially built for **Google Cloud Platform (GCP)**, then extended to run on other cloud platforms like **Amazon Web Services (AWS)** and **Microsoft Azure**. Today, you can run Feast on **on-premise** infrastructure as well. Cloud agnosticism is the biggest advantage Feast offers over other feature stores.

However, Feast is a self-managed infrastructure. Depending on your organization structure, you need a team to create and manage the infrastructure for Feast. Another key thing to note here is Feast moved from **Service-Oriented Architecture (SOA)** to an **Software Development Kit (SDK)/Command Line Interface (CLI)** basis. This enables small teams to quickly install, run, and experiment with Feast for projects without spending a lot of time in its initial setup, only to then realize Feast isn't the right fit. However, for production environments, engineering teams might have to manage multiple infrastructures to run their set of projects. There are alternatives to Feast if you are not a fan of self-managed infrastructures. These include *Tecton*, which is one of the main contributors to Feast today, *SageMaker Feature Store* which is an AWS-managed feature store, *Databricks Feature Store*, and more.

Now that we briefly know what Feast is, let's look at the installation. Unlike other feature stores that require you to run the service on the cloud or register with a cloud provider, Feast can be installed in a notebook environment without having to set up any additional services.

The following command installs the latest version of Feast in your notebook environment:

```
!pip install feast
```

Yes, that's all you need to do to install and run Feast if you want to try it out. However, to collaborate with a team, developer, stage, and production environment, the setup involves some additional steps. We will get there in the next set of chapters. For now, this is enough to look at the APIs, terminology, and project structure.

In the next section, let's look at Feast terminology, initialization, and a few APIs.

Feast terminology and definitions

New discoveries in software applications often give birth to new terms or redefine some existing terms in the context of the new software. For example, **Directed Acyclic Graph (DAG)** in general means a type of graph; whereas in the context of Airflow (assuming you're familiar with it), it means defining a collection of tasks and their dependencies. Similarly, Feast and the wider feature store context have a set of terms that are used frequently. Let's learn what they are in this section.

Entity: *An entity is a collection of semantically related features.* Entities are domain objects to which the features can be mapped. In a ride-hailing service, *customer* and *driver* could be the entities, and features can then be grouped with their corresponding entities.

The following code block is an example of entity definition:

```
driver = Entity(name='driver', value_type=ValueType.STRING,
                join_key='driver_id')
```

Entities are part of a feature view, which acts as a primary key in the feature ingestion and retrieval process. **Point-in-time** joins and feature lookups can be done on primary keys during model training and prediction, respectively.

Feature: *A feature is individual measurable property. It is typically a property observed on a specific entity but does not have to be associated with an entity.* For instance, the average time a customer spends on the website could be a feature. A non-associated feature could be the number of new customers on the website today. The following code block is an example feature definition:

```
trips_today = Feature(name="trips_today",
                      dtype=ValueType.INT64)
```

Features represent the columns of the underlying feature data. As you can see in the preceding example, it has `name` and `dtype` properties.

Data source: The data source represents the underlying data. Feast supports a range of data sources including **FileSource** (local, S3, GCS), **BigQuery**, and **Redshift**.

The following screenshot is an example data source:

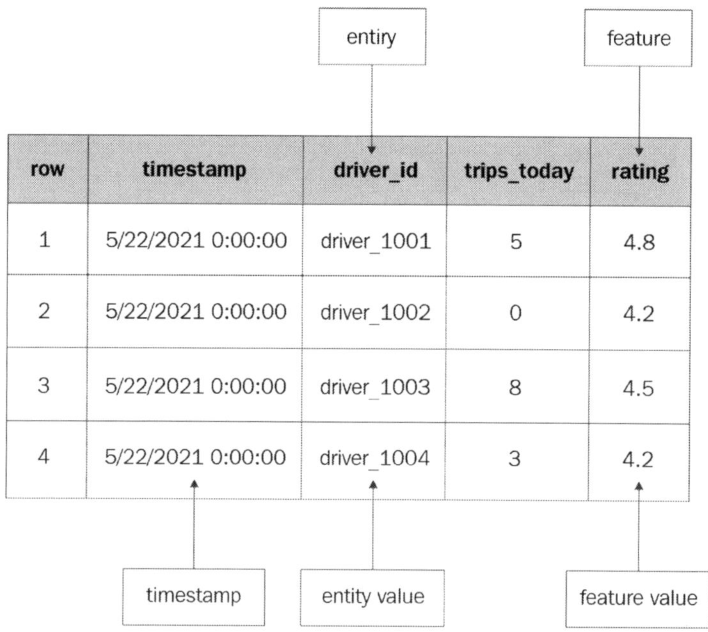

row	timestamp	driver_id	trips_today	rating
1	5/22/2021 0:00:00	driver_1001	5	4.8
2	5/22/2021 0:00:00	driver_1002	0	4.2
3	5/22/2021 0:00:00	driver_1003	8	4.5
4	5/22/2021 0:00:00	driver_1004	3	4.2

Figure 3.1 – Data source

As you can see in the preceding figure, the dataset has a `driver_id` entity, `trips_today` and `rating` features, and a `timestamp` column. The structure of the data in the table you see in *Figure 3.1* is a *Feature view*.

Feature view: A feature view is like a database table, it represents the structure of the feature data at its source. A feature view consists of entities, one or more features, and the data source. A feature view is generally modeled around a domain object similar to databases objects. There are cases where a feature view can be entity-less.

The following code block is an example `FeatureView` definition:

```
driver_stats_fv = FeatureView(
    name="driver_activity",
    entities=["driver"],
    ttl=timedelta(hours=2),
    features=[
        Feature(name="trips_today", dtype=ValueType.INT64),
        Feature(name="rating", dtype=ValueType.FLOAT),
    ],
    batch_source=BigQuerySource(
        table_ref="feast-oss.demo_data.driver_activity"
    )
)
```

As you can see in the preceding code block, `FeatureView` has a `driver` entity, `trips_today` and `rating` features, and `BigQuerySource` as the data source. Depending on the feature store, Feature view has other synonyms. For instance, in SageMaker Feature Store, it is called **Feature Group**, in Databricks Feature Store, it is called **Feature Table**, in the older version of Feast, it was called a **Feature Set** and **Feature Table**.

Point-in-time joins: In the previous chapters, we discussed the need for a data scientist in order to reproduce the state of the system for model reproducibility and for debugging any data/prediction issues. In Feast and other feature stores, the data is *modeled as time-series records*. As you can see in *Figure 3.1*, the `timestamp` column stores the information of when a particular event occurred (that is, when a particular event was produced in the system). Along with this, feature stores offer flexibility to add additional columns such as *creation time*, *ingest API invocation time*, and more. This enables data scientists and data engineers to reproduce the state of a system at any time in the past. To reproduce the state in past, the system performs **point-in-time joins**. In Feast, this capability is available out of the box as an API. In others, users might have to write code for it.

Let's look at an example of a point-in-time join in practice. The following dataset has a schema that matches the `FeatureView` defined in *Figure 3.1*.

timestamp	driver_id	trips_today	rating
2022-01-02 0:00:00	101	0	4.2
2022-01-02 1:00:00	101	2	4.9
2022-01-02 2:00:00	101	6	4.6
2022-01-02 3:00:00	101	4	4.3
2022-01-02 4:00:00	101	3	4.8
2022-01-02 5:00:00	101	0	4.7

Figure 3.2 – Point-in-time join dataset

As you will see in the later section, to fetch historical data you need an entity DataFrame like the following:

timestamp	driver_id	trip_success
2022-01-01 23:52:20	101	0
2022-01-02 1:23:20	101	1
2022-01-02 4:15:20	101	1
2022-01-02 5:42:20	101	0
2022-01-02 12:38:20	101	1

Figure 3.3 – Point-in-time join entity DataFrame

When the user invokes `store.get_historical_features()`, with the entity DataFrame in *Figure 3.3* and a feature list, Feast performs a **point-in-time join** to fetch the latest value of the features at the given timestamp. For instance, for the first row in *Figure 3.3*, the timestamp value is `2022-01-01 23:52:20`. The **point-in-time join** looks for the driver features with the latest timestamp.

The following screenshot shows the **point-in-time join** in action:

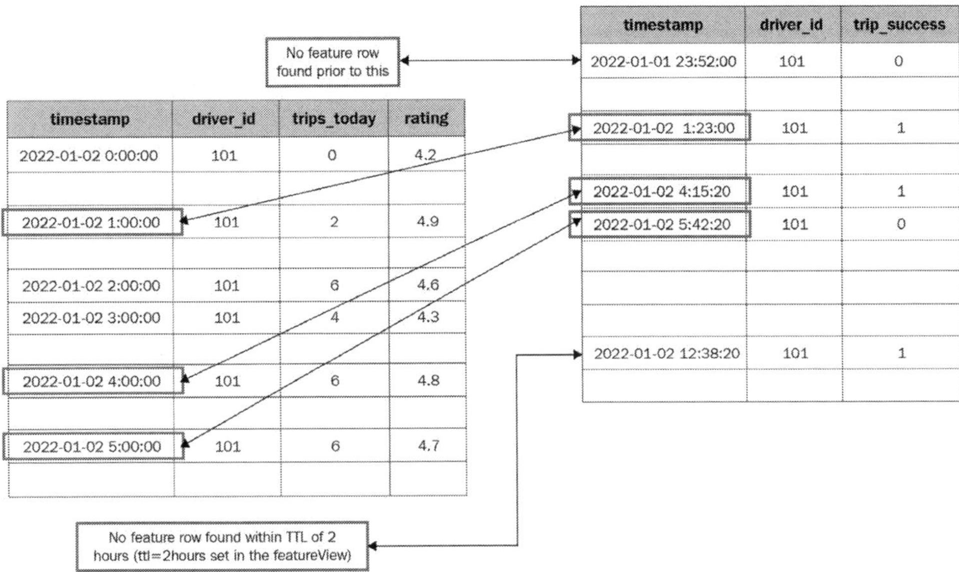

Figure 3.4 – Point-in-time join

The **time-to-live (ttl)** set in the `FeatureView` is 2 hours. This indicates that features live only for 2 hours from the time an event occurs (`event_timestamp + 2 hours` window). The logic for point-in-time joins is `timestamp_in_data >= timestamp_in_entity_dataframe` and `timestamp_in_entity_dataframe <= timestamp_in_data + ttl (2 hours)`. As you can see in *Figure 3.4*, the first row doesn't have a matching window in the data, whereas the second, third, and fourth rows of the entity DataFrame have a matching window for the events that occurred at `2022-01-02 1:00:00`, `2022-01-01 4:00:00`, and `2022-01-01 5:00:00` respectively. Following the same logic, the last row in the entity DataFrame doesn't have any matching window in the data.

The output DataFrame of the point-in-time join is as follows:

timestamp	driver_id	trip_success	trips_today	rating
2022-01-01 23:52:20	101	0	NULL	NULL
2022-01-02 1:23:20	101	1	2	4.9
2022-01-03 4:15:20	101	1	3	4.8
2022-01-04 5:42:20	101	0	0	4.7
2022-01-05 12:38:20	101	1	NULL	NULL

Figure 3.5 – Point-in-time join output

As seen in *Figure 3.5*, for the rows that don't have matching windows, the feature values are `NULL`, and for the rows with matching windows, the features are available.

In the next section, let's learn how to initialize a Feast project, what its contents are, and basic API usage.

Feast initialization

Let's open a new notebook and install a specific version of `feast` and the `Pygments` library to get a more nicely formatted view when we look at the files. The following code installs the required libraries:

```
!pip install feast==0.18.1
!pip install Pygments
```

Let's initialize the Feast project and look through the folder structure and files. The following code block initializes a Feast project called `demo`:

```
!feast init demo
```

The preceding code will output the following lines:

```
Feast is an open source project that collects anonymized error
reporting and usage statistics. To opt out or learn more see
https://docs.feast.dev/reference/usage

Creating a new Feast repository in /content/demo.
```

Let's ignore the warning message in the first line. In the second line, you can see where the Feast repo is initialized. If you are using Google Colab you will see a similar path, `/content/<repo_name>`; if not, the repo will be created in the current working directory.

To understand what the `feast init` command did in the background, we need to look through the folder that the command created. You can use the left navigation bar on Google Colab to look through the files or use the CLI:

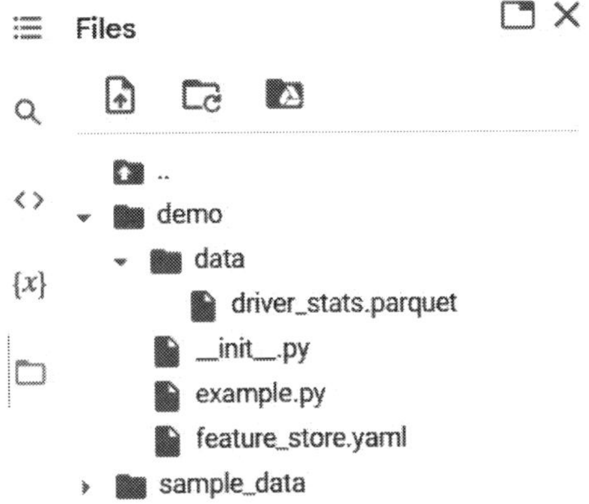

Figure 3.6 – Folder structure

Figure 3.6 is the snapshot from Google Colab. As you can see, the `feast init` command created a sample project repo for starters. There is a `driver_stats.parquet` file in the `data` folder, and a `example.py`, and `feature_store.yaml` file. Let's go through the files and see what's in them. The simplest file to understand is the `driver_stats.parquet` file in the `data` folder. As the folder says, it contains sample data for the demo project.

The following code block loads the dataset in `driver_stats.parquet` and displays the first ten rows from it:

```
import pandas as pd

df = pd.read_parquet("demo/data/driver_stats.parquet")
df.head(10)
```

The preceding code block produces the following output:

	event_timestamp	driver_id	conv_rate	acc_rate	avg_daily_trips	created
0	2022-02-02 02:00:00+00:00	1005	0.859278	0.186328	331	2022-02-17 02:52:20.886
1	2022-02-02 03:00:00+00:00	1005	0.201459	0.707427	809	2022-02-17 02:52:20.886
2	2022-02-02 04:00:00+00:00	1005	0.291222	0.177430	467	2022-02-17 02:52:20.886
3	2022-02-02 05:00:00+00:00	1005	0.845518	0.947779	140	2022-02-17 02:52:20.886
4	2022-02-02 06:00:00+00:00	1005	0.506576	0.822694	298	2022-02-17 02:52:20.886
5	2022-02-02 07:00:00+00:00	1005	0.466269	0.084688	227	2022-02-17 02:52:20.886
6	2022-02-02 08:00:00+00:00	1005	0.022204	0.956079	722	2022-02-17 02:52:20.886
7	2022-02-02 09:00:00+00:00	1005	0.404754	0.491500	788	2022-02-17 02:52:20.886
8	2022-02-02 10:00:00+00:00	1005	0.940343	0.404221	563	2022-02-17 02:52:20.886
9	2022-02-02 11:00:00+00:00	1005	0.336696	0.843453	169	2022-02-17 02:52:20.886

Figure 3.7 – Sample dataset

The `driver_stats.parquet` file is a sample feature dataset, as you can see in *Figure 3.7*. It contains driver features such as `conv_rate` and `avg_daily_trips`. It also has additional columns, such as `event_timestamp` and `created`. These are special columns used for performing point-in-time joins, as discussed in the previous section.

Let's look at the `feature_store.yaml` file next. The following command prints the file content:

```
!pygmentize demo/feature_store.yaml
```

The preceding command outputs the following:

```
project: demo
registry: data/registry.db
provider: local
online_store:
    path: data/online_store.db
```

The `feature_store.yaml` file contains the following variables:

- `project`: This is the project name. It uses the input of the `feast init` command as the project name. We ran `feast init demo`, hence the project name is `demo`.

- `registry`: This variable stores the feature registry path for the project. The registry stores all the metadata for the project including `FeatureView`, `Entity`, `DataSources`, and more. As you can see, the `registry.db` file doesn't yet exist in the `data` folder. It gets created when we run the `apply` command; we will look at it in the *Feast usage* section.
- `provider`: This variable defines where the feature store is going to run. The value is set to `local`, which indicates the infrastructure will be run on the local system. The other possible values are `aws`, `gcp`, and more. For `aws` and `gcp` providers, additional dependencies need to be installed and additional params need to be passed to the `feast init` command.
- `online_store`: As the name of the `online_store` param indicates, it is used for storing and serving features at low latency. By default, it uses SQLite, but Feast offers a variety of options for the online store, from *DynamoDB* to a *custom store*. The following page lists the supported options for online stores: `https://docs.feast.dev/roadmap`.
- `offline_store`: You don't see this variable in the `feature_store.yaml` file. However, this is another important parameter that is used to set *historical stores* from the available options. Again, Feast offers a lot of flexibility here: you can choose anything from *file store* to *Snowflake*. The link in the preceding bullet has the information on supported offline stores.

Other than the ones mentioned previously, each of the variables might include some additional setup based on what is chosen for that option. For example, if Snowflake is chosen as the offline store, it needs additional inputs like the schema name, table name, Snowflake URL, and more.

Let's look at what the `example.py` file consists of. The following command prints the contents of the file:

```
!pygmentize -f terminal16m demo/example.py
```

The output of the preceding command is very lengthy, so instead of looking at all the content at once, we'll break it down into parts. The following code block contains the first part of the file:

```
# This is an example feature definition file

from google.protobuf.duration_pb2 import Duration
```

```
from feast import Entity, Feature, FeatureView, FileSource,
ValueType

""" Read data from parquet files. Parquet is convenient for
local development mode. For production, you can use your
favorite DWH, such as BigQuery. See Feast documentation for
more info."""
Driver_hourly_stats = FileSource(
    path="/content/demo/data/driver_stats.parquet",
    event_timestamp_column="event_timestamp",
    created_timestamp_column="created",
)
```

In the preceding block, there are a couple of imports from the installed libraries, but what follows the imports is of particular interest to us. The code defines a data source of type `FileSource` and provides the path to the sample data in *Figure 3.7*. As mentioned earlier, the `event_timestamp_column` and `created_timestamp_column` columns are special columns, which indicate when a particular event (row in the data) occurred and when the row was ingested into the data source, respectively.

The following code block contains the second part of the file:

```
# Define an entity for the driver. You can think of entity as a
primary key used to fetch features.
Driver = Entity(name="driver_id",
                value_type=ValueType.INT64,
                description="driver id",)
```

In the preceding code block, a `driver_id` entity is defined along with its value type and description.

The following code block contains the last part of the file:

```
""" Our parquet files contain sample data that includes a
driver_id column, timestamps and three feature column. Here we
define a Feature View that will allow us to serve this data to
our model online."""
Driver_hourly_stats_view = FeatureView(
    name="driver_hourly_stats",
    entities=["driver_id"],
    ttl=Duration(seconds=86400 * 1),
```

```
    features=[
        Feature(name="conv_rate", dtype=ValueType.FLOAT),
        Feature(name="acc_rate", dtype=ValueType.FLOAT),
        Feature(name="avg_daily_trips",
                dtype=ValueType.INT64),
    ],
    online=True,
    batch_source=driver_hourly_stats,
    tags={},
)
```

The preceding block contains a `FeatureView`. The definition contains three features, `conv_rate`, `acc_rate`, and `avg_daily_trips`, and uses the `driver_id` entity defined in the second part of the file and the `driver_hourly_stats` batch source defined in the first part of the file. Apart from these, there are additional variables: `ttl`, `online`, and `tags`. `ttl` defines how long the features live. For instance, if you set `ttl` to 60 seconds, it will appear in the retrieval for only 60 seconds from the event time. After that, it is considered as an expired feature. The `online` variable indicates if the online store is enabled for `FeatureView` or not. `Tags` are used to store additional information about `FeatureView` such as the team, owner, and more, which may be usable in feature discovery.

In short, the `example.py` file consists of the entities, feature views, and data sources of the `demo` project. This is just a starter template for a demo. We can add additional entities, feature views, and data sources.

Now that we understand the fundamentals and basic project structure, let's familiarize ourselves with Feast APIs.

Feast usage

In this section, let's continue in the same notebook in which we initialized the `demo` project previously, register the feature view and entities, and use the Feast API to retrieve features.

Register feature definitions

The following code block registers all the entities and feature views defined in the `example.py` file:

```
%cd demo
!feast apply
```

The preceding code produces the following output:

```
/content/demo
Created entity driver_id
Created feature view driver_hourly_stats

Created sqlite table demo_driver_hourly_stats
```

The output message is straightforward except the last line, where it says **Created sqlite table demo_driver_hourly_stats**. This comes up if you have `online=True` set in the `FeatureView`. The `apply` command creates the `registry.db` and `online_store.db` files, which have been set in `feature_store.yaml`.

Now that entities and feature views have been registered, we can connect to the feature store and browse through the existing definitions.

Browsing the feature store

The following code connects to the feature store and lists all the entities:

```
from feast import FeatureStore
store = FeatureStore(repo_path=".")
for entity in store.list_entities():
    print(entity.to_dict())
```

The preceding code block looks for the `feature_store.yaml` file in the current directory and uses the `store.list_entities()` API to get all the entities. Similarly, the `store.list_feature_views()` API can be used to get all the available feature views. I will leave that as an exercise for you.

Let's add a new entity and feature view to the feature store.

Adding an entity and FeatureView

To add a new entity and feature view, we need a feature dataset. For now, let's produce a synthetic dataset using the `numpy` library and use that as the new features for which the entity and feature view need to be defined.

The following code generates the synthetic feature data:

```
import pandas as pd
import numpy as np
from pytz import timezone, utc
from datetime import datetime, timedelta
import random
days = [datetime.utcnow().
replace(hour=0, minute=0, second=0, microsecond=0).
replace(tzinfo=utc) \
        - timedelta(day) for day in range(10)][::-1]

customers = [1001, 1002, 1003, 1004, 1005]
customer_features = pd.DataFrame(
    {
        "datetime": [day for day in days for customer in
customers], # Datetime is required
        "customer_id": [customer for day in days for customer
in customers], # Customer is the entity
        "daily_transactions": [np.random.rand() * 10 for _
in range(len(days) * len(customers))], # Feature 1
        "total_transactions": [np.random.randint(100) for _
in range(len(days) * len(customers))], # Feature 2
    }
)
customer_features.to_parquet("/content/demo/data/customer_
features.parquet")
customer_features.head(5)
```

The preceding code generates a dataset with four columns and writes the dataset to `/content/demo/data/`. If you are running this on a local system, set the path accordingly for the `customer_features.to_parquet` API call, which is highlighted in the preceding code block.

The preceding code produces the dataset as shown in *Figure 3.8*:

	datetime	customer_id	daily_transactions	total_transactions
0	2022-02-11 00:00:00+00:00	1001	2.398850	44
1	2022-02-11 00:00:00+00:00	1002	6.776920	29
2	2022-02-11 00:00:00+00:00	1003	5.944877	73
3	2022-02-11 00:00:00+00:00	1004	2.245862	27
4	2022-02-11 00:00:00+00:00	1005	0.839079	82

Figure 3.8 – Synthetic customer data

The definitions of `Entity` and `FeatureView` for the dataset in *Figure 3.4* can be added to the existing `example.py` file, or you can create a new Python file and add the lines in the following code block.

The following code block defines the required `Entity`, `DataSource`, and `FeatureView` for the dataset in *Figure 3.8*:

```
from google.protobuf.duration_pb2 import Duration

from feast import Entity, Feature, FeatureView, FileSource,
ValueType

#Customer data source
customer_features = FileSource(
    path="/content/demo/data/customer_features.parquet",
    event_timestamp_column="datetime"
)

#Customer Entity
customer = Entity(name="customer_id",
                  value_type=ValueType.INT64,
                  description="customer id",)

# Customer Feature view
customer_features_view = FeatureView(
    name="customer_features",
```

```
    entities=["customer_id"],
    ttl=Duration(seconds=86400 * 1),
    features=[
        Feature(name="daily_transactions",
                dtype=ValueType.FLOAT),
        Feature(name="total_transactions",
                dtype=ValueType.INT64),
    ],
    online=True,
    batch_source=customer_features,
    tags={},
)
```

Like the `example.py` file we encountered, this file has the definition for the `customer_features` data source, the `customer` entity, and `customer_features_view`. Upload the newly created file or updated `example.py` file to the project root directory (the same directory as that of the existing `example.py` file).

> **Important Note**
>
> Don't remove `example.py` or replace the contents, but append new entities to the file or upload the new file. After running `feast apply`, you should have two entities, `driver_id` and `customer_id`, and two feature views, `driver_hourly_stats` and `customer_features`.

After uploading/copying the file to the root directory, run the following command to apply new definitions:

```
!feast apply
```

The preceding code block produces the following output:

```
Created entity customer_id
Created feature view customer_features

Created sqlite table demo_customer_features
```

Similar to the output of the previous `apply` command, the output is straightforward. If you browse through the feature store again, you will see the updated definitions. We will leave that as an exercise for you.

Generate training data

After running the `apply` command in the previous section, the feature store contains two entities: `driver_id` and `customer_id`, and two feature views: `driver_hourly_stats` and `customer_features`. We can generate training data by querying the historical store for either or both of the feature views using the corresponding entities. In this example, we will query for the `driver_hourly_stats` feature view. Feel free to try out the `get_historical_features` API on `customer_features`.

To generate the training data, an entity DataFrame is required. The entity DataFrame must have the following two columns:

- `entity_id`: This is the id of the entity defined in the feature store. For instance, to fetch the driver features, you need the `driver_id` column and the list of values for which the historical features are required.
- `event_timestamp`: A timestamp for each `driver_id` for the point-in-time join.

The following code block produces an entity DataFrame to fetch driver features:

```
from datetime import datetime, timedelta
import pandas as pd
from feast import FeatureStore
# The entity DataFrame is the DataFrame we want to enrich with
feature values
entity_df = pd.DataFrame.from_dict(
    {
        "driver_id": [1001, 1002, 1003],
        "event_timestamp": [
            datetime.now() - timedelta(minutes=11),
            datetime.now() - timedelta(minutes=36),
            datetime.now() - timedelta(minutes=73),
        ],
    }
)
entity_df.head()
```

The preceding code produces the following entity DataFrame:

	driver_id	event_timestamp
0	1001	2022-02-20 01:37:36.523322
1	1002	2022-02-20 01:12:36.523340
2	1003	2022-02-20 00:35:36.523343

Figure 3.9 – Entity DataFrame

Once you have the entity DataFrame, it is straightforward to fetch the data from the historical store. All that is required to do is connect to feature store and invoke the `store.get_historical_features()` API with the entity DataFrame created in the preceding code block and the list of required features.

The following code block connects to the feature store and fetches historical features for the entities:

```
store = FeatureStore(repo_path=".")

training_df = store.get_historical_features(
    entity_df=entity_df,
    features=[
        "driver_hourly_stats:conv_rate",
        "driver_hourly_stats:acc_rate",
        "driver_hourly_stats:avg_daily_trips",
    ],
).to_df()

training_df.head()
```

You may notice that one of the inputs to the API is a list of features. The format of the elements in the list is `<FeatureViewName>:<FeatureName>`. For instance, to fetch the `conv_rate` feature, which is part of the `driver_hourly_stats` FeatureView, the element in the list would be `driver_hourly_stats:conv_rate`.

The preceding code block produces the following output:

	event_timestamp	driver_id	conv_rate	acc_rate	avg_daily_trips
0	2022-02-20 00:35:36.523343+00:00	1003	0.459515	0.242431	363
1	2022-02-20 01:12:36.523340+00:00	1002	0.241556	0.996971	575
2	2022-02-20 01:37:36.523322+00:00	1001	0.049006	0.739369	991

Figure 3.10 – Get the historical features output

Load features to the online store

The historical data source is used for generating a training dataset, which can also be used for prediction in batch models. However, we already know that for online models, low-latency feature serving is required. To enable that, it is required to fetch the latest features from the historical data source and load the features into the online store. This can be done with a single command in Feast.

The following command loads the latest features to the online store:

```
!feast materialize-incremental {datetime.now().isoformat()}
```

The command takes a timestamp as one of the inputs, fetches the latest features at the time of the input timestamp, and loads the features to the online store. In this example, it is a SQLite database.

The preceding line of code outputs the following information:

```
Materializing 2 feature views to 2022-02-20 02:13:03+00:00 into the sqlite online store.

driver_hourly_stats from 2022-02-19 02:13:05+00:00 to 2022-02-20 02:13:03+00:00:
100%|████████████████████████████████████████████████| 5/5 [00:00<00:00, 375.83it/s]
customer_features from 2022-02-19 02:13:05+00:00 to 2022-02-20 02:13:03+00:00:
100%|████████████████████████████████████████████████| 5/5 [00:00<00:00, 444.15it/s]
```

Figure 3.11 – Feast materializing the output

Now that the features are available in the online store, they can be fetched during model prediction at low latency. The online store can be queried using `store.get_online_features()` and passing the features list in the same format as that of the list passed for querying historical data.

> **Important Note**
>
> The `feast materialize-incremental` command will sync all the existing feature views to the online store (in this case, SQLite). In the output shown in *Figure 3.11*, you can see two feature views: `driver_hourly_stats` and `customer_features`. You can query either of them. In this example, we are querying `driver_hourly_stats`.

The following code block fetches `conv_rate` and `avg_daily_trips` for drivers with `id` values of `1001` and `1004`:

```
store = FeatureStore(repo_path=".")
feature_vector = store.get_online_features(
    features=[
        "driver_hourly_stats:conv_rate",
        "driver_hourly_stats:avg_daily_trips",
    ],
    entity_rows=[
        {"driver_id": 1004},
        {"driver_id": 1005},
    ],
).to_dict()
feature_vector
```

The preceding code block produces the following output. If the value for a specific entity row doesn't exist, it will return `NULL` values:

```
{'avg_daily_trips': [34, 256],
 'conv_rate': [0.9326972365379333, 0.07134518772363663],
 'driver_id': [1004, 1005]}
```

Now that we have learned the Feast fundamentals, it is time to understand briefly what's going on behind the scenes to make it work. In the next section, let's look at the Feast components and set the stage for incorporating Feast in a project.

Feast behind the scenes

The following diagram shows different components that make up the architecture of Feast:

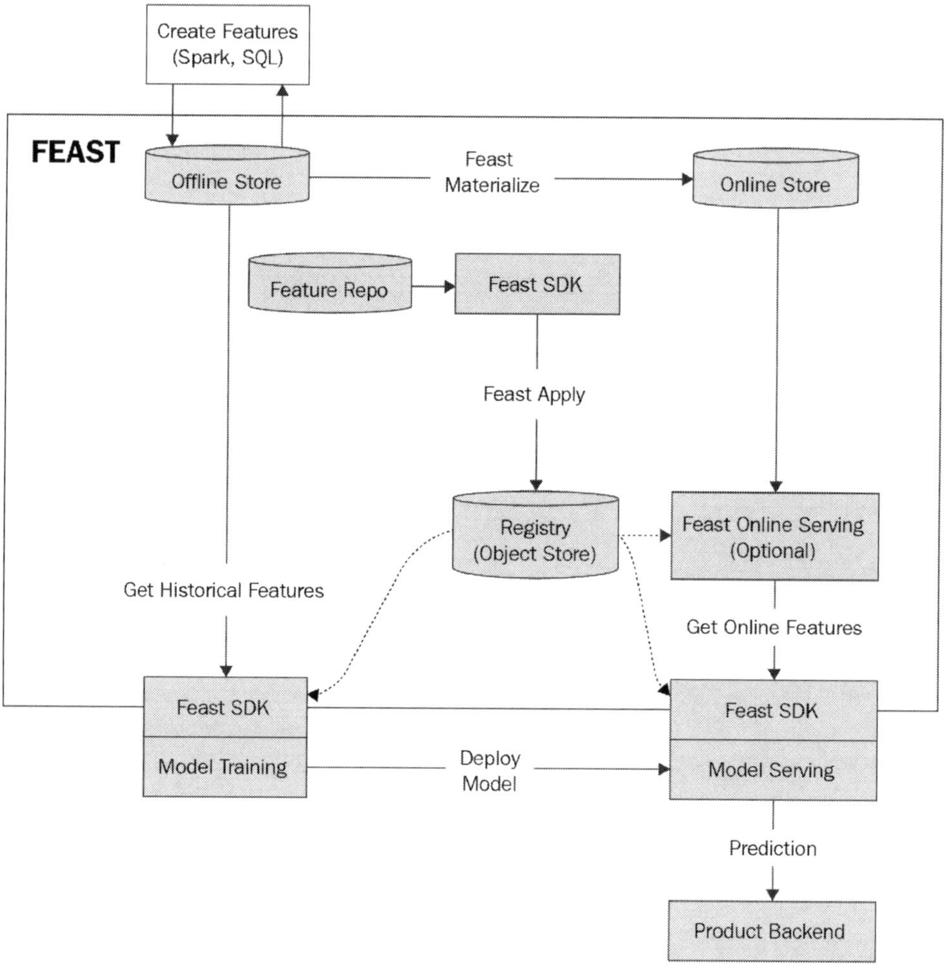

Figure 3.12 – Feast architecture (v0.18)

As seen in the preceding diagram, there are a lot of components involved in Feast. Let's break it down one by one:

- **Feature Repo**: A feature repository is a set of configuration files defining the infrastructure and feature definitions. In the demo project, *Figure 3.6* shows an example feature repo. The `data` folder is optional; the `feature_store.yml` file that defines the feature store configuration and the `example.py` file that defines the feature definitions constitute a feature repo.

- **Feast SDK**: The Feast SDK is the development kit with which users can interact with Feast. It is used for creating and updating feature definitions (`feast apply`), loading features from the offline to the online store (`feast materialize`), and providing a great set of APIs for users to browse through Feast and query online and offline stores. We used some of the Feast SDK APIs in the usage section.
- **Feast Registry**: The Feast registry uses the object store to persist the feature definitions, which can be browsed through using the Feast SDK.
- **Online store**: The online store is a low-latency database used for serving the latest features for model prediction. Users can load the latest features or query the online store using the Feast SDK. A streaming source can also be used for loading features into the online store.
- **Offline store**: The offline store is used for the storage and retrieval of historical data. It is also used for model training and batch scoring. In Feast, data in the offline store is user-managed.

Data flow in Feast

The following steps give an example of the data flow in Feast:

1. Data engineers build ETL/data pipelines to generate features and load them to an offline store supported by Feast.
2. Feature definitions are created, the Feast store configuration is defined, and the `feast apply` command is run.

> **Important Note**
> Feature store configuration involves defining the infrastructure details, hence it might also involve the creation of the infrastructure as well.

3. Using the Feast SDK, the data scientist/data engineer connects to the Feast repo and generates training data for the model. The model is trained, and if it doesn't meet the acceptance criteria, new features may be generated by adding an additional data pipeline.
4. Steps *1-3* will be executed again.

> **Important Note**
> In *step 2*, only new entities and feature definitions need to be added.

5. Features are loaded from the offline to the online store using the `feast materialize` command. This command may be run on schedule to load the latest features using an orchestration tool such as **Airflow**.
6. The trained model is packaged along with the Feast SDK code to fetch the required feature for model scoring during prediction. The packaged model is deployed to production.
7. During prediction, the model fetches the required features using the Feast SDK, runs the prediction, and returns the results.
8. The offline store can be monitored for data drift to determine whether it's time to retrain the model.

Let's summarize what we learned in this chapter next and move on to using Feast in our actual project next.

Summary

In this chapter, we discussed the terminology used in the feature store world, specifically terminology that relate to *Feast*. However, keep in mind that many of the existing feature stores use similar terminology, so if you are familiar with one, it is easy to understand the others. We also discussed how the *point-in-time join* works in Feast, along with the Feast fundamentals such as installation, initialization, project structure, and API usage. Finally, we explored the components of Feast and how the operationalization of a model works with Feast.

In the next chapter, we'll use Feast in the model we built in *Chapter 1, An Overview of the Machine Learning Life Cycle*, learn how it changes the way data scientists and engineers work, and see how it opens the door to new opportunities in feature sharing, monitoring, and easy productionization of our ML models.

Further reading

- *Introduction to Feast*: `https://docs.feast.dev/`
- *Overview of Feast*: `https://github.com/feast-dev/feast/blob/v0.18.1/examples/quickstart/quickstart.ipynb`

4
Adding Feature Store to ML Models

In the last chapter, we discussed **Feast** installation in your local system, common terminology in Feast, what the project structure looks like, API usage with an example, and a brief overview of the Feast architecture.

So far in the book, we have been talking about issues with feature management and how a feature store can benefit data scientists and data engineers. It is time for us to get our hands dirty with an ML model and add Feast to the ML pipeline.

In this chapter, we will revisit the **Customer Lifetime Value** (**LTV/CLTV**) ML model built in *Chapter 1, An Overview of the Machine Learning Life Cycle*. We will use AWS cloud services instead of the local system to run the examples in this chapter. As mentioned in *Chapter 3, Feature Store Fundamentals, Terminology, and Usage*, installation for AWS is different from that of a local system, so we will have to create a few resources. I will be using some Free Tier services and some that are featured services (free for the first 2 months of use with limits). Also, the terms and API usage examples we looked at in *Chapter 3, Feature Store Fundamentals, Terminology, and Usage*, will be very useful as we try to include Feast in the ML pipeline.

The goal of this chapter is to learn what it takes to include a feature store in a project and how it differs from the traditional ML model building that we did in *Chapter 1, An Overview of the Machine Learning Life Cycle*. We will learn about Feast installation, how to build a feature engineering pipeline for the LTV model, how to define feature definitions, and we will also look at feature ingestion in Feast.

We will discuss the following topics in order:

- Creating Feast resources in AWS
- Feast initialization for AWS
- Exploring the ML life cycle with Feast

Technical requirements

To follow the code examples in the chapter, all you need is familiarity with Python and any notebook environment, which could be a local setup such as Jupyter or an online notebook environment such as Google Collab, Kaggle, or SageMaker. You will also need an AWS account with full access to resources such as Redshift, S3, Glue, DynamoDB, the IAM console, and more. You can create a new account and use all the services for free during the trial period. You can find the code examples for the book at the following GitHub link:

`https://github.com/PacktPublishing/Feature-Store-for-Machine-Learning/tree/main/Chapter04`

The following GitHub link points to the feature repository:

`https://github.com/PacktPublishing/Feature-Store-for-Machine-Learning/tree/main/customer_segmentation`

Creating Feast resources in AWS

As discussed in the previous chapter, Feast aims to provide a quick setup for beginners to try it out; however, for team collaboration and to run a model in production, it requires a better setup. In this section, we will set up a Feast environment in the AWS cloud and use it in model development. In the previous chapter, we also discussed that Feast provides multiple choices when picking an online and offline store. For this exercise, Amazon S3 with Redshift will be used as an offline/historical store and DynamoDB will be used as an online store. So, we need a few resources on AWS before we can start using the feature store in our project. Let's create the resources one after another.

Amazon S3 for storing data

As mentioned in the AWS documentation, **Amazon Simple Storage Service (Amazon S3)** *is an object storage service offering industry-leading scalability, data availability, security, and performance*. Feast provides the capability to use S3 to store and retrieve all data and metadata. You could also use version control systems such as GitHub or GitLab to collaborate on the metadata and sync to S3 during deployment. To create an S3 bucket in AWS, log in to your AWS account, navigate to the S3 service using the search box, or visit `https://s3.console.aws.amazon.com/s3/home?region=us-east-1`. A web page will be displayed, as shown in *Figure 4.1*.

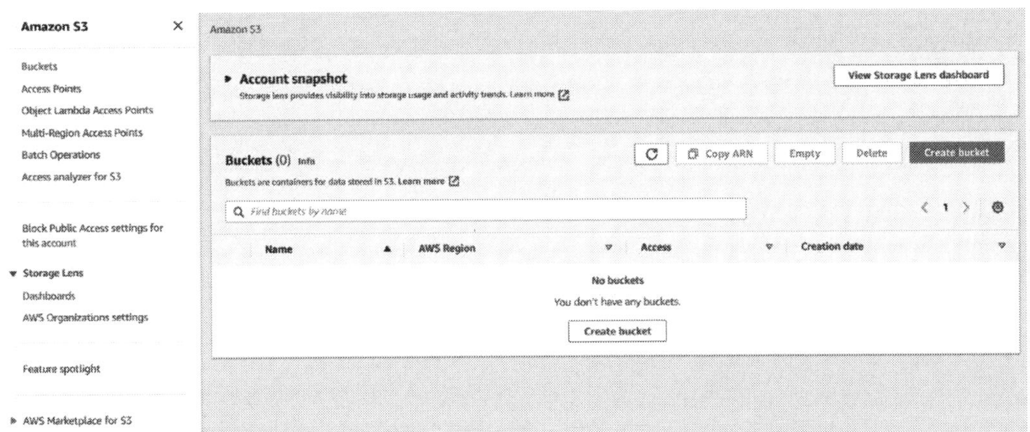

Figure 4.1 – AWS S3 home page

If you already have the buckets, you will see them on the page. I am using a new account, hence I don't see any buckets yet. To create a new bucket, click on **Create bucket** in the top right. You will see a page similar to the one in *Figure 4.2*. Choose a bucket name, leave everything else as the default, and scroll all the way down to click on **Create bucket**. I am going to name it `feast-demo-mar-2022`. One thing to keep in mind is that S3 bucket names are unique across accounts. If bucket creation fails with an error, **Bucket with the same name already exists**, try adding a few random characters to the end.

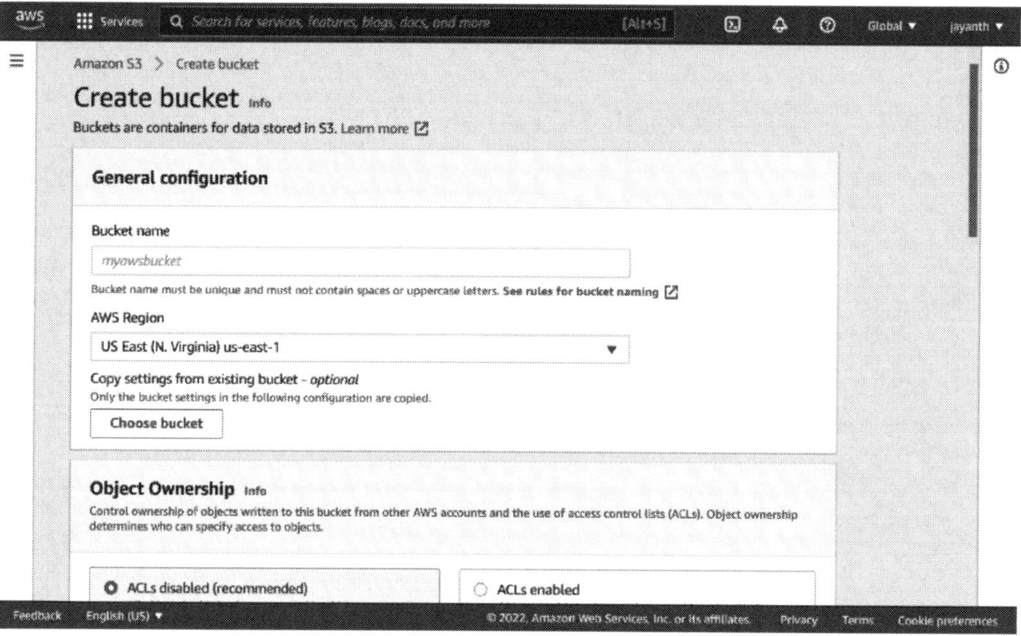

Figure 4.2 – S3 Create bucket

After successful bucket creation, you will see a screen similar to *Figure 4.3*.

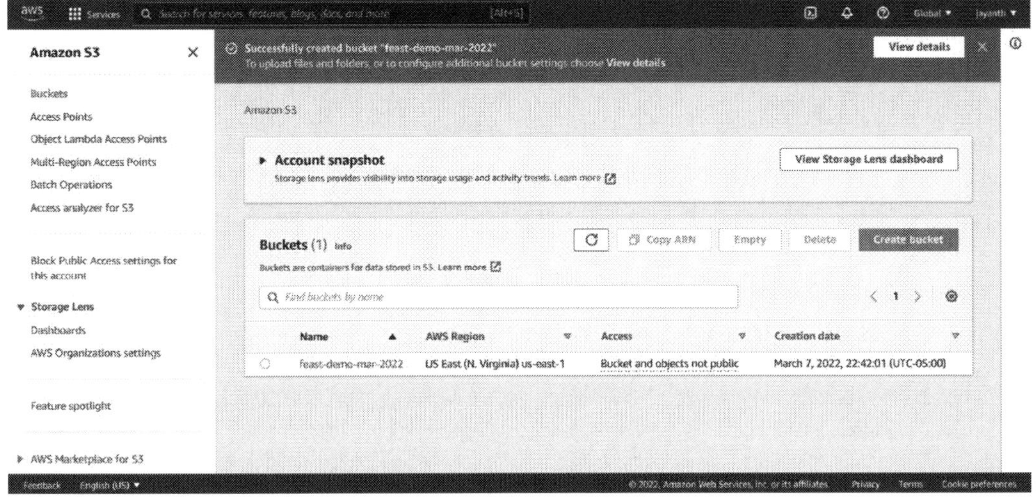

Figure 4.3 – After S3 bucket creation

AWS Redshift for an offline store

As mentioned in the AWS documentation, *Amazon Redshift uses SQL to analyze structured and semi-structured data across data warehouses, operational databases, and data lakes, using AWS-designed hardware and machine learning to deliver the best price performance at any scale*. As mentioned earlier, we will use a Redshift cluster for querying historical data. We need to create a cluster since we don't have one already. Before we create a cluster, let's create an **Identity and Access Management** (**IAM**) role. This is a role that Redshift will assume on our behalf to query the historical data in S3.

Let's start by creating an IAM role:

1. To create an IAM role, navigate to the AWS IAM console using the search or visit the URL `https://us-east-1.console.aws.amazon.com/iamv2/home?region=us-east-1#/roles`. A web page similar to the one in *Figure 4.4* will be displayed.

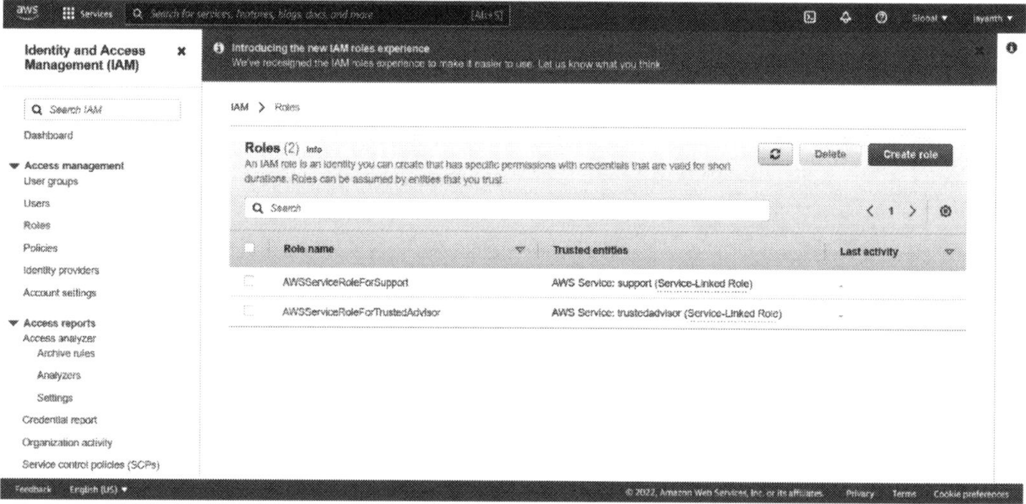

Figure 4.4 – IAM home page

2. To create a new role, click on the **Create role** button in the top-right corner. The following page will be displayed.

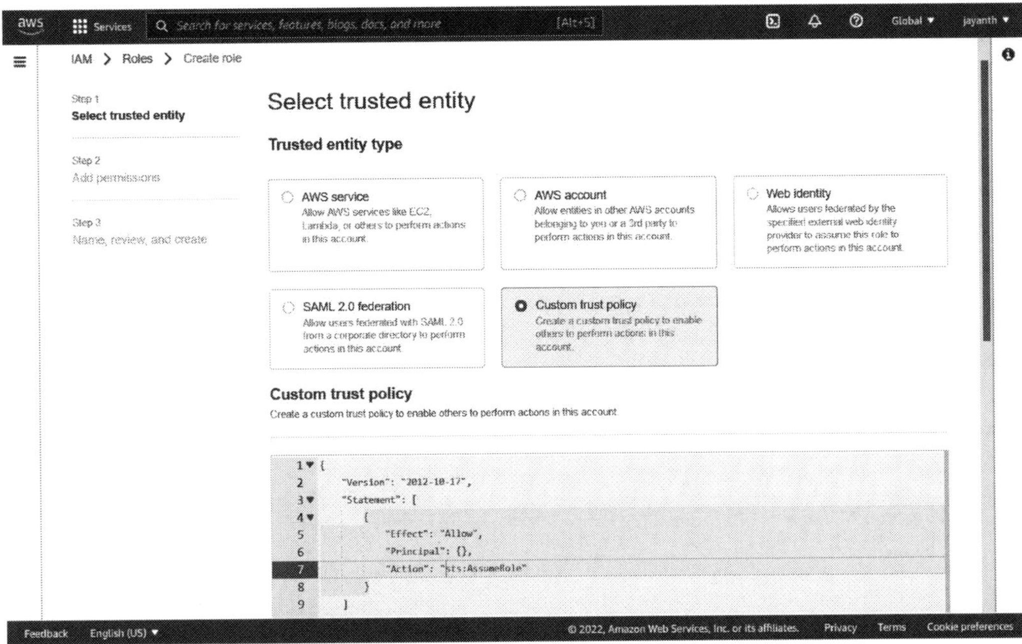

Figure 4.5 – IAM Create role

3. From the options available on the page, select **Custom trust policy**, copy the following code block, and replace the policy in the JSON in the textbox:

```
{
    "Version": "2012-10-17",
    "Statement": [
        {
            "Effect": "Allow",
            "Principal": {
                "Service": "redshift.amazonaws.com"
            },
            "Action": "sts:AssumeRole"
        }
    ]
}
```

4. Scroll all the way to the bottom and click on **Next**. On the next page, you will see a list of IAM policies that can be attached to the role, as shown in *Figure 4.6*.

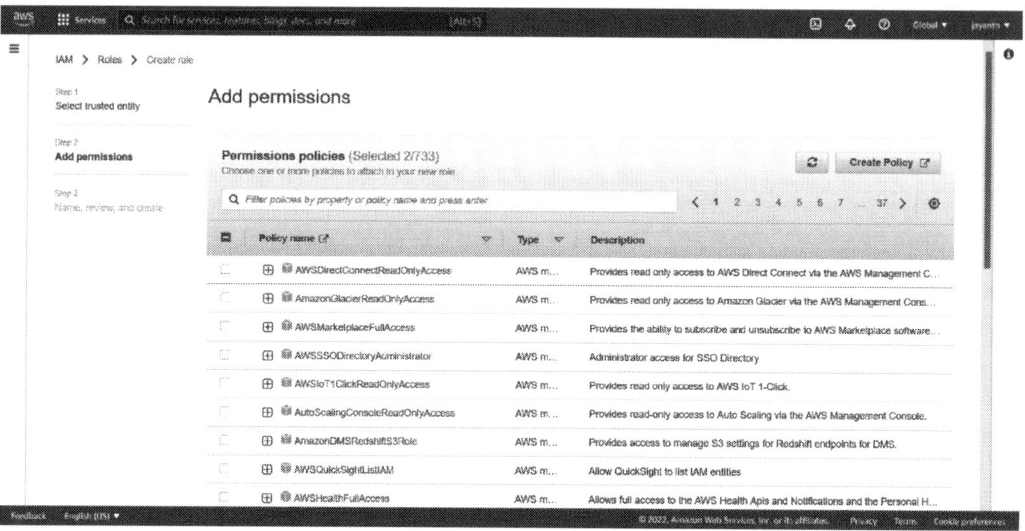

Figure 4.6 – IAM permissions for the role

5. We need **S3** access, since the data will be stored in S3 as Parquet files, and **AWS Glue** access. The data stored in S3 will be loaded as an external schema into Redshift using AWS Glue Data Catalog/Lake Formation. Follow along here and you will understand what it means to load data as an external schema. For S3 access, search for **AmazonS3FullAccess** and select the corresponding checkbox, then search for **AWSGlueConsoleFullAccess** and select the corresponding checkbox. Scroll all the way down and click on **Next**.

> **Important Note**
>
> We are providing full access to S3 and Glue on all the resources here, but it is recommended to restrict access to specific resources. I will leave that as an exercise since it is out of scope for this chapter.

The following page will be displayed after you click on **Next**.

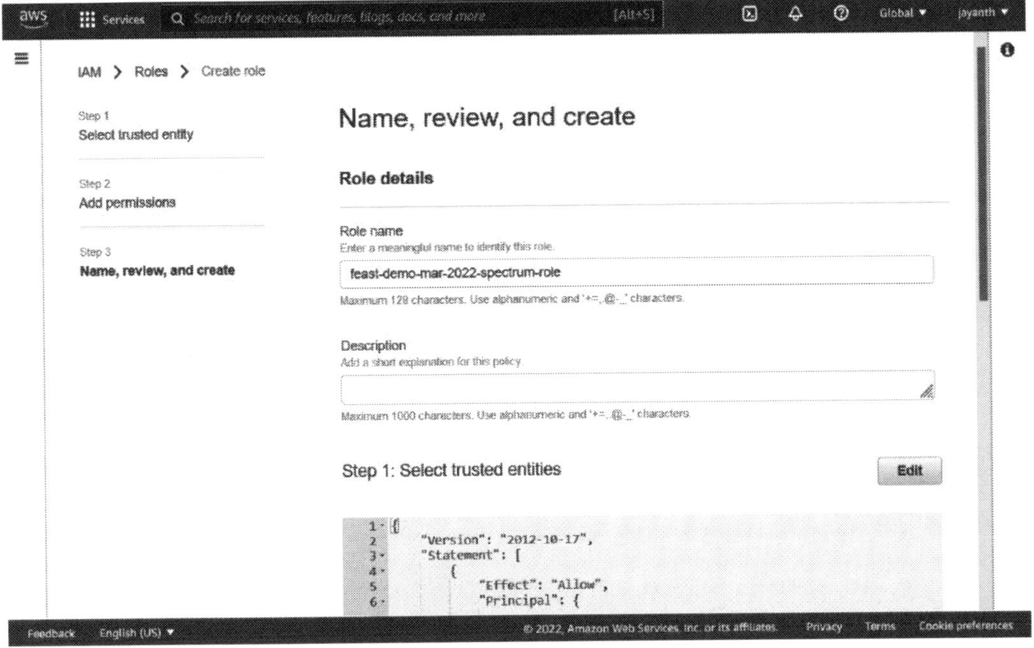

Figure 4.7 – IAM review

6. On this page, provide a name for the role. I have named the role `feast-demo-mar-2022-spectrum-role`. Review the details of the role and click on **Create role**. On successful creation, you will find the role on the IAM console page.

7. Now that we have the IAM role ready, the next step is to create a **Redshift** cluster and assign the created IAM role to it. To create the Redshift cluster, navigate to the Redshift home page using the search bar or visit the link `https://us-east-1.console.aws.amazon.com/redshiftv2/home?region=us-east-1#clusters`. The following page will be displayed.

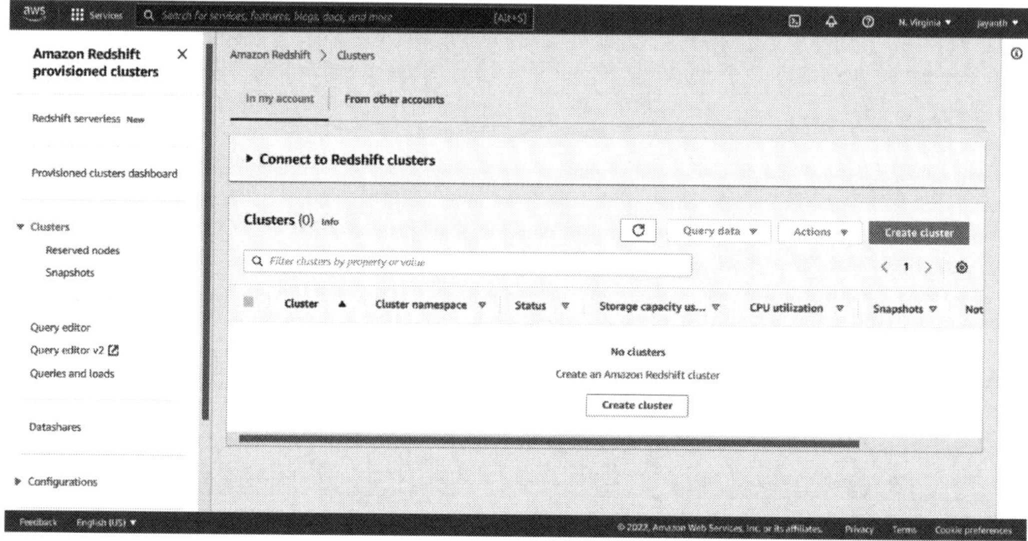

Figure 4.8 – Redshift home page

8. On the page in *Figure 4.8*, click on **Create cluster**. The following page will be displayed.

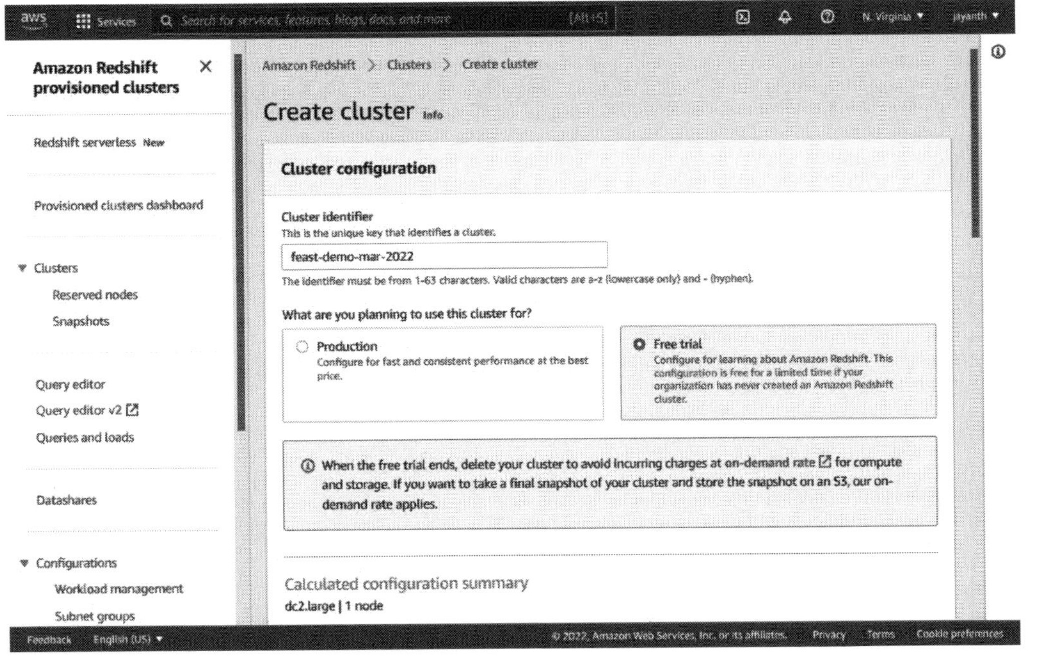

Figure 4.9 – Create a Redshift cluster

9. From the web page displayed in *Figure 4.9*, I am picking **Free trial** for the demo, but this can be configured based on the dataset size and load. After picking **Free trial**, scroll all the way down and pick a password. The following figure shows the lower half of the window when you scroll down.

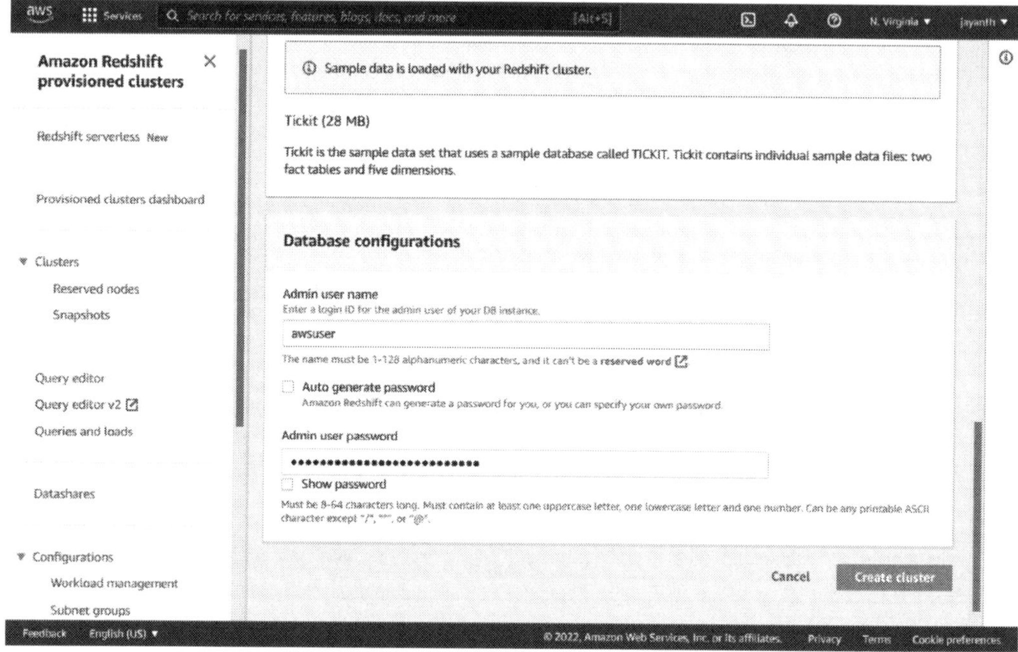

Figure 4.10 – Create cluster lower half

10. Once you've picked a password, click on **Create cluster** at the bottom. Cluster creation takes a few minutes. Once the cluster creation is complete, you should see the newly created cluster in the AWS Redshift console. One last thing that is pending is associating the IAM role that we created earlier with the Redshift cluster. Let's do that now. Navigate to the newly created cluster. You will see a web page similar to the one in *Figure 4.11*.

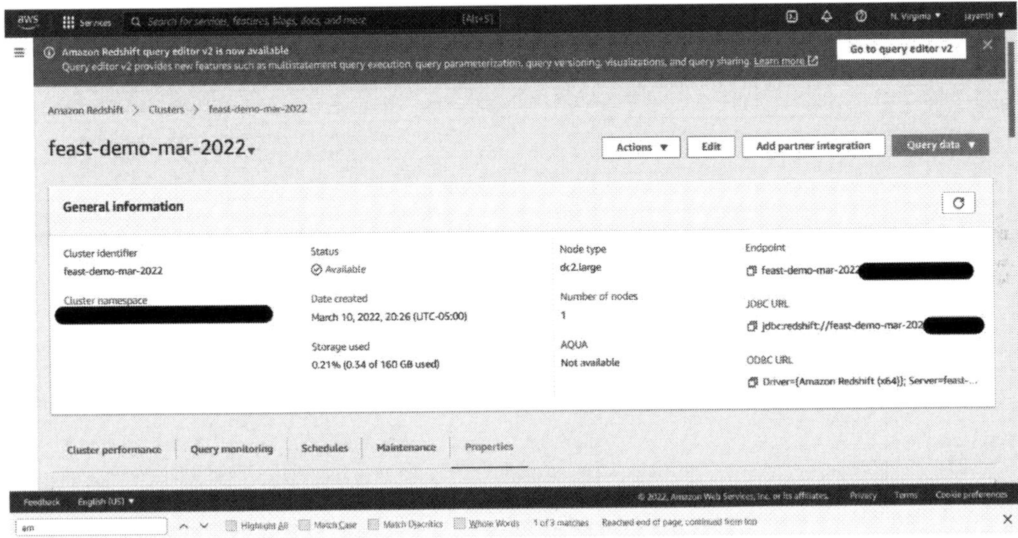

Figure 4.11 – Redshift cluster page

11. On the cluster home page, select the **Properties** tab and scroll down to **Associated IAM roles**. You will see the options displayed in *Figure 4.12*.

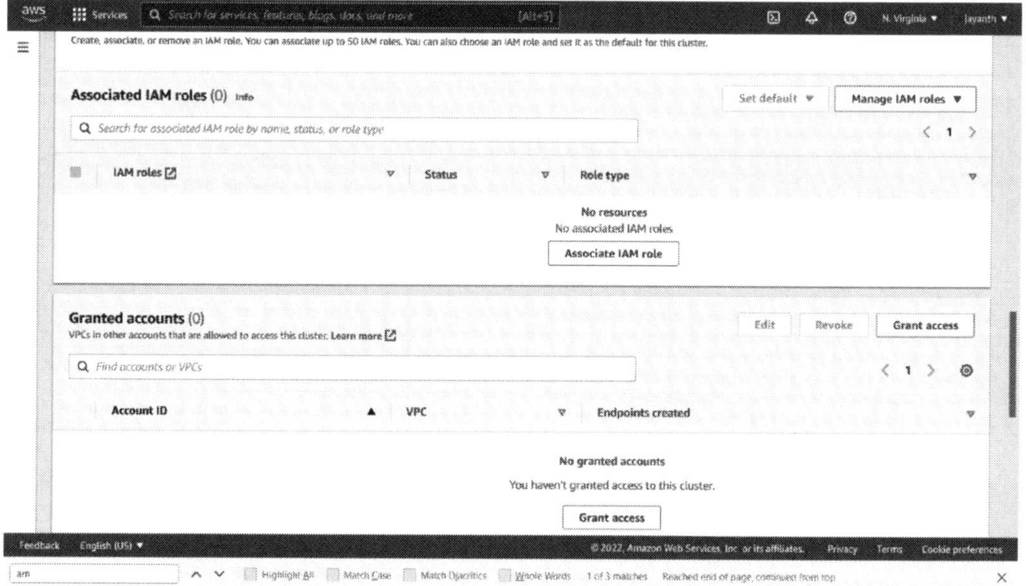

Figure 4.12 – Redshift Properties tab

12. From the web page, click on the **Associate IAM role** button. The IAM role that was created earlier will be displayed as shown in *Figure 4.13*. From the options, pick the IAM role you created earlier and click on the **Associate IAM roles** button. Please note, I named the IAM role `feast-demo-mar-2022-spectrum-role`, hence I am associating that role. Once you click on the button, the cluster will be updated with the new role. It may take a few minutes again. Once the cluster is ready, we are done with the required infrastructure for now. We will add the external data catalog when the features are ready to be ingested.

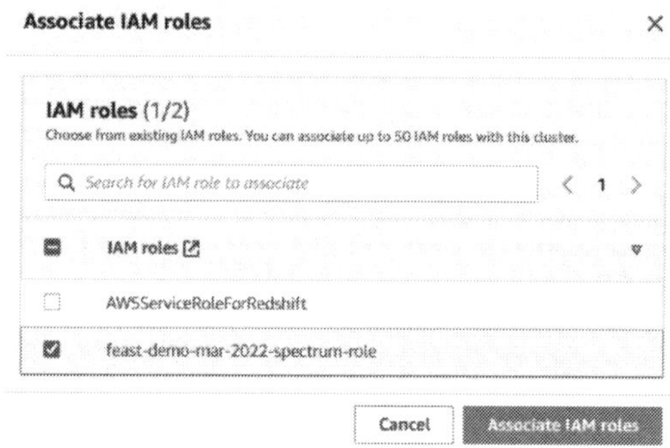

Figure 4.13 – Redshift Associate IAM roles

We need an IAM user to access these resources and perform operations on them. Let's create that next.

Creating an IAM user to access the resources

There are different ways to provide access to the users for the resources. If you are part of the organization, then the IAM roles can be integrated with Auth0 and active directories. Since that is out of scope here, I will be creating an IAM user and will give the required permissions for the user to access the resources created earlier:

1. Let's create the IAM user from the AWS console. The IAM console can be accessed using the search or visiting `https://console.aws.amazon.com/iamv2/home#/users`. The IAM console looks as shown in *Figure 4.14*.

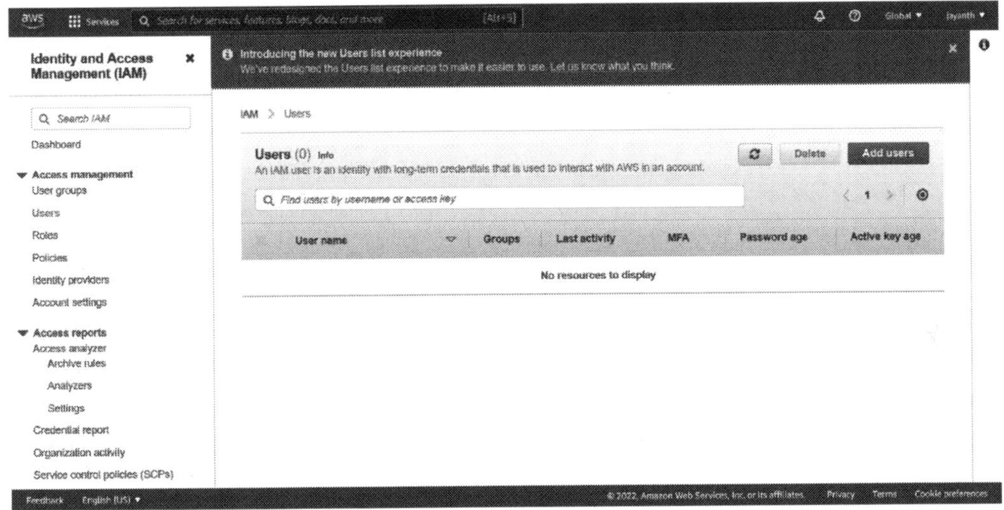

Figure 4.14 – IAM user page

2. On the IAM user page, click on the **Add users** button in the top right. The following web page will be displayed.

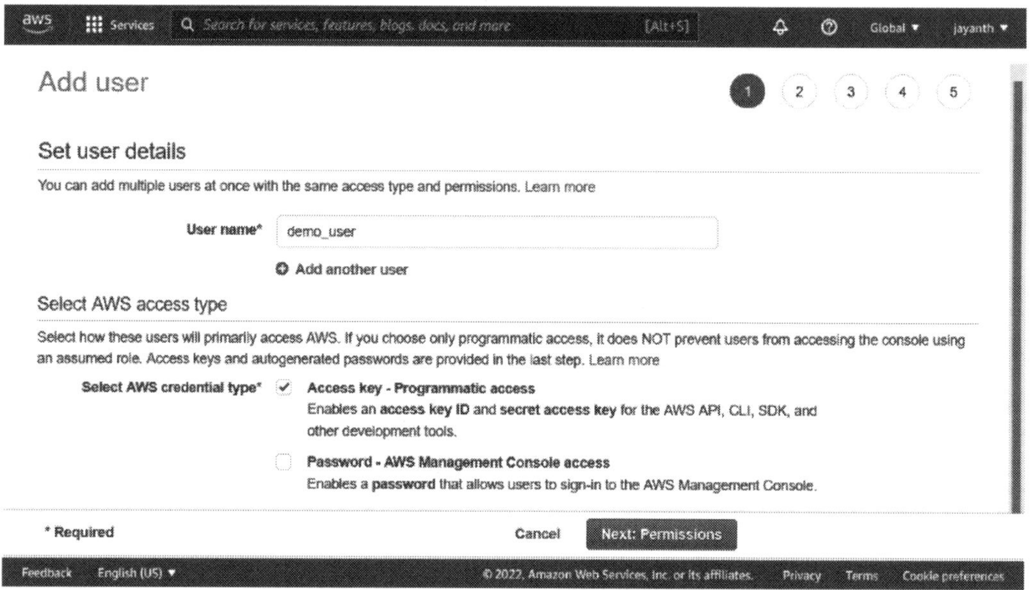

Figure 4.15 – IAM Add user

3. On the web page, provide a user name and select **Access key - Programmatic access**, then click on **Next: Permissions** at the bottom. The following web page will be displayed.

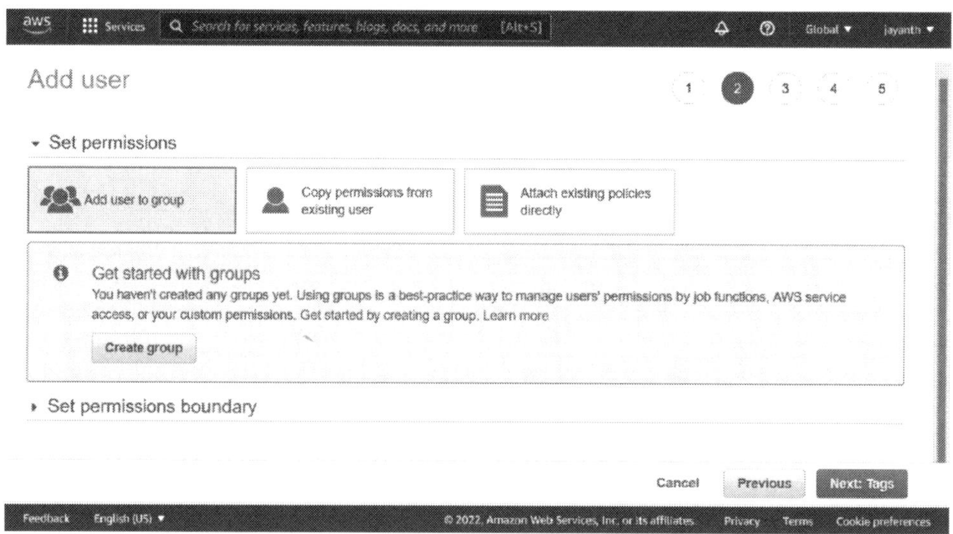

Figure 4.16 – IAM permissions

4. On the displayed web page, click on **Attach existing policies directly** and from the list of available policies, search for and attach the following policies: **AmazonRedshiftFullAccess**, **AmazonS3FullAccess**, and **AmazonDynamoDBFullAccess**.

> **Important Note**
>
> We are attaching full access here without restricting the user to specific resources. It is always a good practice to restrict access based on the resources and only provide required permissions.

5. Click **Next: Tags** and feel free to add tags and again click on **Next: Review**. The review page looks like the following:

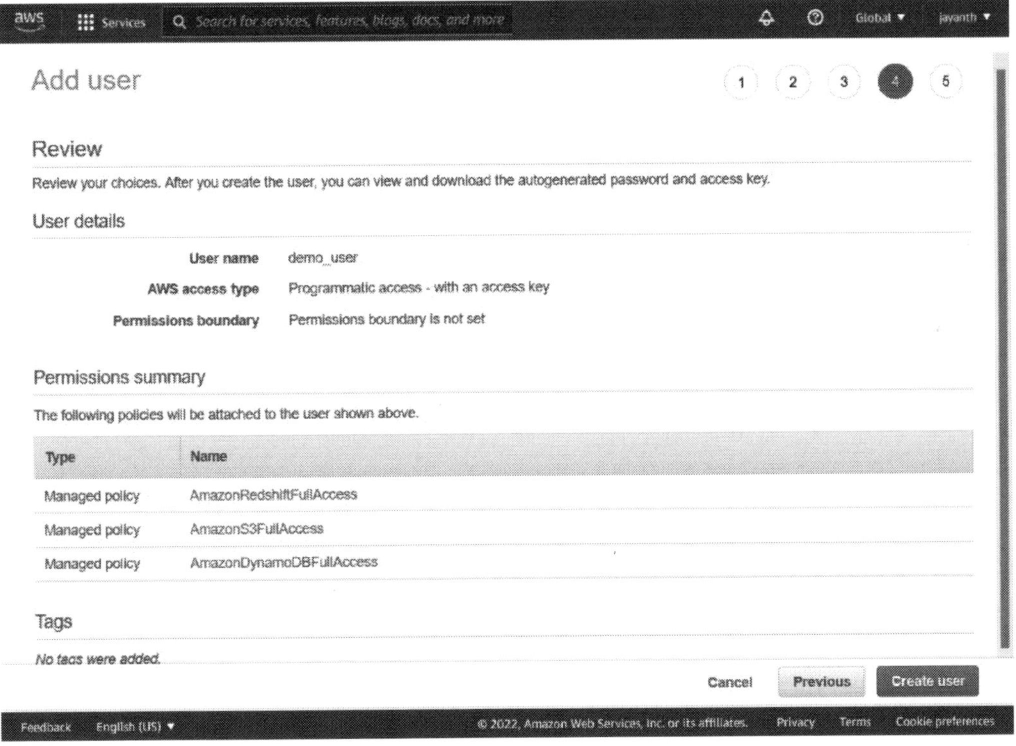

Figure 4.17 – IAM user review

6. From the review page, click on the **Create user** button. The web page in *Figure 4.18* will be displayed.

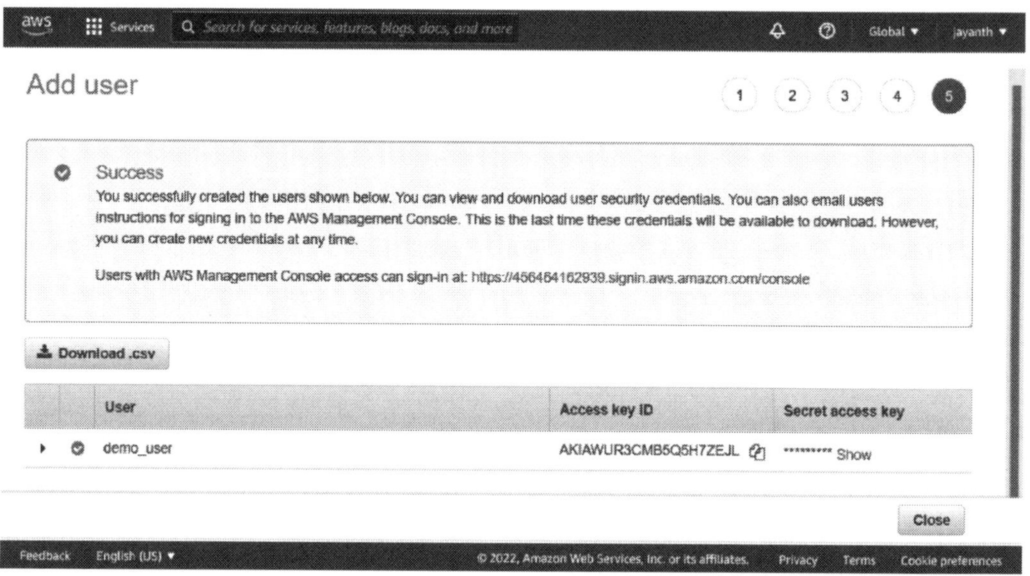

Figure 4.18 – IAM user credentials

7. On the web page, click on the **Download.csv** button and save the file in a secure location. It contains the **Access key ID** and **Secret access key** for the user we just created. The secret will be lost if you don't download and save it from this page. However, you can go into the user from the IAM user page and manage the secret (delete the existing credentials and create new credentials).

Now that the infrastructure is ready, let's initialize the Feast project.

Feast initialization for AWS

We have the infrastructure required for running Feast now. However, we need to initialize a Feast project before we can start using it. To initialize a Feast project, we need to install the Feast library as we did in *Chapter 3, Feature Store Fundamentals, Terminology, and Usage*. However, this time, we also need to install the AWS dependencies. Here is the link to the notebook: `https://github.com/PacktPublishing/Feature-Store-for-Machine-Learning/blob/main/Chapter04/ch4_Feast_aws_initialization.ipynb`.

The following command installs Feast with the required AWS dependencies:

```
!pip install feast[aws]
```

Once the dependencies are installed, we need to initialize the Feast project. Unlike the initialization we did in the last chapter, here, Feast initialization needs additional inputs such as Redshift ARN, database name, S3 path, and so on. Let's look at how the initialization differs here. Before we initialize the project, we need the following details:

- **AWS Region**: The Region where your infrastructure is running. I have created all the resources in **us-east-1**. If you have created them in a different Region, use that.
- **Redshift Cluster ID**: The cluster identifier of the Redshift cluster that was created earlier. It can be found on the home page.
- **Redshift Database Name**: The database name in Redshift. I am calling the database `dev`.
- **Redshift User Name**: The default user is `awsuser`. If you gave a different user name during cluster creation, use that here.
- **Redshift S3 Staging Location**: The location that can be used for staging temporary files. I will be using the same S3 bucket that I created earlier with a different prefix: `s3://feast-demo-mar-2022/staging`. Also create the staging folder in the bucket.
- **Redshift IAM Role for S3**: The ARN of the IAM role that we created earlier. It can be found on the IAM role details page. It will be in the following format: `arn:aws:iam::<account_number>:role/feast-demo-mar-2022-spectrum-role`.

Once you have the values for the mentioned parameters, the new project can be initialized in two ways. One is using the following command:

```
feast init -t aws customer_segmentation
```

The preceding command initializes the Feast project. During initialization, the command will ask you for the mentioned arguments.

The second way is to edit the `feature_store.yaml` file:

```
project: customer_segmentation
registry: data/registry.db
provider: aws
online_store:
```

```
    type: dynamodb
    region: us-east-1
offline_store:
    type: redshift
    cluster_id: feast-demo-mar-2022
    region: us-east-1
    database: dev
    user: awsuser
    s3_staging_location: s3://feast-demo-mar-2022/staging
    iam_role: arn:aws:iam::<account_number>:role/feast-demo-mar-
2022-spectrum-role
```

Whichever method you choose for initializing the project, make sure that you provide the appropriate values for the parameters. I have highlighted the parameter that may need to be replaced for the Feast functionalities to work without issues. If you are using the first method, the `init` command will give the option to choose whether to load example data or not. Choose `no` to upload the example data.

Now that we have our feature repository initialized for the project, let's apply our initial feature set, which is basically empty. The following code block removes the unwanted files that get created if you use `feast init` for the initialization of the project:

```
%cd customer_segmentation
!rm -rf driver_repo.py test.py
```

If you don't run the preceding commands, it will create the feature definitions for the entity and feature views in the `driver_repo.py` file.

The following code block creates feature and entity definitions defined in the project. In this project, there are none so far:

```
!feast apply
```

When the preceding command is run, it displays the message **No changes to registry**, which is correct since we don't have any feature definitions yet.

The folder structure of `customer_segmentation` should look like *Figure 4.19*.

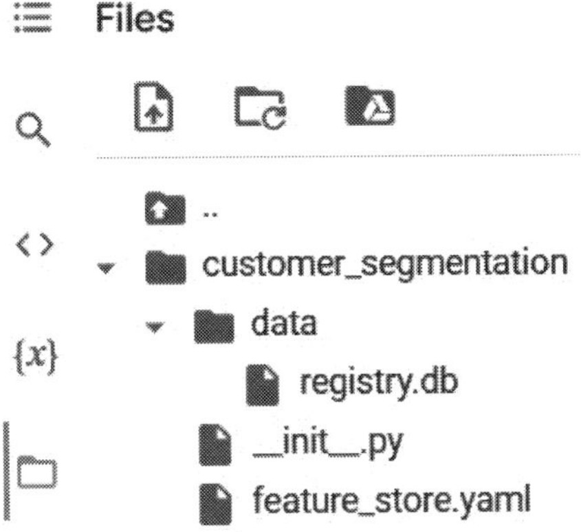

Figure 4.19 – Project folder structure

The feature repository is ready for use now. This can be checked into *GitHub* or *GitLab* for versioning and collaboration.

> **Important Note**
> Also note that all the preceding steps can be automated using infrastructure as code frameworks such as Terraform, the AWS CDK, Cloud Formation, or others. Depending on the team structure followed in the organization, it will be the responsibility of the data engineer or platform/infrastructure team to create the required resources and share the repository details that can be used by data scientists or engineers.

In the next section, let's look at how the ML life cycle changes with the feature store.

Exploring the ML life cycle with Feast

In this section, let's discuss what ML model development looks like when you are using a feature store. We went through the ML life cycle in *Chapter 1, An Overview of the Machine Learning Life Cycle*. This makes it easy to understand how it changes with a feature store and enables us to skip through a few steps that will be redundant.

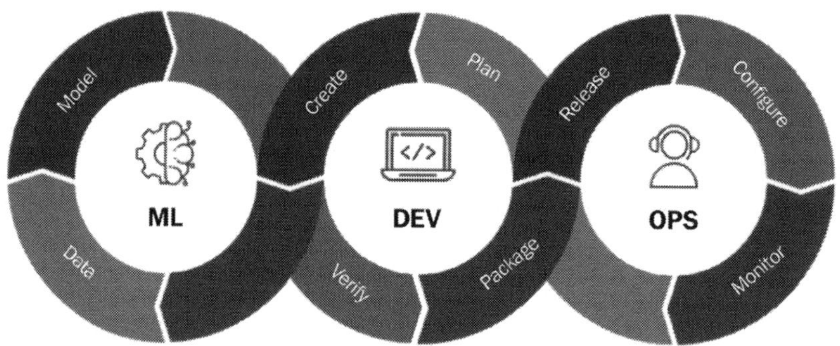

Figure 4.20 – ML life cycle

Problem statement (plan and create)

The problem statement remains the same as it was in *Chapter 1, An Overview of the Machine Learning Life Cycle*. Let's assume that you own a retail business and would like to improve the customer experience. First and foremost, you want to find your customer segments and customer lifetime value.

Data (preparation and cleaning)

Unlike in *Chapter 1, An Overview of the Machine Learning Life Cycle*, before exploring the data and figuring out the access and more, here the starting point for model building is the feature store. Here is the link to the notebook:

`https://github.com/PacktPublishing/Feature-Store-for-Machine-Learning/blob/main/Chapter04/ch4_browse_feast_for_features.ipynb`

Let's start with the Feature Store:

1. So, let's open up a notebook and install Feast with AWS dependencies:

```
!pip install feast[aws]
```

2. If the feature repository created in the last section was pushed into source control such as GitHub or GitLab, let's clone the repository. The following code clones the repository:

```
!git clone <repo_url>
```

3. Now that we have the feature repository, let's connect to Feast/the feature store and check what's available:

```
# change directory
%cd customer_segmentation

"""import feast and load feature store object with the
path to the directory which contains feature_story.
yaml."""
from feast import FeatureStore
store = FeatureStore(repo_path=".")
```

The preceding code block connects to the Feast feature repository. The `repo_path="."` parameter indicates that `feature_store.yaml` is in the current working directory.

4. Let's check whether the feature store contains any **entities** or **feature views** that can be used in the model instead of exploring the data and regenerating the features that already exist:

```
#Get list of entities and feature views
print(f"List of entities: {store.list_entities()}")
print(f"List of FeatureViews: {store.list_feature_
views()}")
```

The preceding code block lists the **entities** and **feature views** that exist in the current feature repository we are connected to. The code block outputs two empty lists as follows:

```
List of entities: []
List of FeatureViews: []
```

> **Important Note**
>
> You may be wondering *What about the features created by other teams? How can I get access to them and check what's available?* There are ways to manage that. We will get to that a little later.

Since the entities and feature views are empty, there is nothing that can be used. The next step is to perform data exploration and feature engineering.

We will be skipping over the data exploration stage as we have already done it in *Chapter 1, An Overview of the Machine Learning Life Cycle*. Also, the steps for generating the features would be the same. Hence I will not be expanding on feature engineering. Instead, I will use the same code and briefly mention what the code does. Refer to *Chapter 1, An Overview of the Machine Learning Life Cycle*, for a detailed description of how features are generated.

Model (feature engineering)

In this section, we will generate the features required for the model. Just the way we did in *Chapter 1, An Overview of the Machine Learning Life Cycle*, we will use 3 months of data to generate RFM features and 6 months of data to generate the labels for the dataset. We will go through the steps in the same order as we did in *Chapter 1, An Overview of the Machine Learning Life Cycle*. Here is the link to the feature engineering notebook:

`https://github.com/PacktPublishing/Feature-Store-for-Machine-Learning/blob/main/Chapter04/ch4_feature_engineering.ipynb.`

Let's start with feature engineering:

1. The following code block reads the dataset and filters out the data that doesn't belong to `United Kingdom`:

```
%pip install feast[aws]==0.19.3 s3fs
import pandas as pd
from datetime import datetime, timedelta, date
from sklearn.cluster import Kmeans

##Read the data and filter out data that belongs to
country other than UK
retail_data = pd.read_csv('/content/OnlineRetail.csv',
encoding= 'unicode_escape')
retail_data['InvoiceDate'] = pd.to_datetime(retail_
data['InvoiceDate'], errors = 'coerce')
uk_data = retail_data.query("Country=='United Kingdom'").
reset_index(drop=True)
```

2. Once we have the filtered data, the next step is to create two DataFrames, one for 3 months and one for 6 months.

The following code block creates two different DataFrames, one for the data between `2011-03-01 00:00:00.054000` and `2011-06-01 00:00:00.054000`, the second one for the data between `2011-06-01 00:00:00.054000` and `2011-12-01 00:00:00.054000`:

```
## Create 3months and 6 months DataFrames
t1 = pd.Timestamp("2011-06-01 00:00:00.054000")
t2 = pd.Timestamp("2011-03-01 00:00:00.054000")
t3 = pd.Timestamp("2011-12-01 00:00:00.054000")
uk_data_3m = uk_data[(uk_data.InvoiceDate < t1) & (uk_
data.InvoiceDate >= t2)].reset_index(drop=True)
uk_data_6m = uk_data[(uk_data.InvoiceDate >= t1) & (uk_
data.InvoiceDate < t3)].reset_index(drop=True)
```

3. The next step is to generate RFM features from the 3 months DataFrame. The following code block generates RFM values for all customers:

```
## Calculate RFM values.
Uk_data_3m['revenue'] = uk_data_3m['UnitPrice'] * uk_
data_3m['Quantity']
max_date = uk_data_3m['InvoiceDate'].max() +
timedelta(days=1)
rfm_data = uk_data_3m.groupby(['CustomerID']).agg({
    'InvoiceDate': lambda x: (max_date - x.max()).days,
    'InvoiceNo': 'count',
    'revenue': 'sum'})
rfm_data.rename(columns={'InvoiceDate': 'Recency',
                         'InvoiceNo': 'Frequency',
                         'revenue': 'MonetaryValue'},
                inplace=True)
```

Now that we have generated RFM values for all the customers, the next step is to generate an R group, an F group, and an M group for each of the customers ranging from 0 to 3. Once we have the RFM groups for the customers, they will be used to calculate the RFM score by summing the individual group values for the customer.

4. The following code block generates RFM groups for the customers and calculates the RFM score:

```
## Calculate RFM groups of customers
r_grp = pd.qcut(rfm_data['Recency'],
                q=4, labels=range(3,-1,-1))
f_grp = pd.qcut(rfm_data['Frequency'],
                q=4, labels=range(0,4))
m_grp = pd.qcut(rfm_data['MonetaryValue'],
                q=4, labels=range(0,4))
rfm_data = rfm_data.assign(R=r_grp.values).assign(F=f_
grp.values).assign(M=m_grp.values)
rfm_data['R'] = rfm_data['R'].astype(int)
rfm_data['F'] = rfm_data['F'].astype(int)
rfm_data['M'] = rfm_data['M'].astype(int)
rfm_data['RFMScore'] = rfm_data['R'] + rfm_data['F'] +
rfm_data['M']
```

5. With the RFM score calculated, it is time to group customers into low-, mid-, and high-value customers.

   The following code block groups customers into these groups:

```
# segment customers.
Rfm_data['Segment'] = 'Low-Value'
rfm_data.loc[rfm_data['RFMScore']>4,'Segment'] =
'Mid-Value'
rfm_data.loc[rfm_data['RFMScore']>6,'Segment'] = 'High-
Value'
rfm_data = rfm_data.reset_index()
```

6. Now we have the RFM features ready. Let's keep those aside and calculate the revenue using the 6-month DataFrame that was created in an earlier step.

   The following code block calculates the revenue from every customer in the 6-months dataset:

```
# Calculate revenue using the six month dataframe.
Uk_data_6m['revenue'] = uk_data_6m['UnitPrice'] * uk_
data_6m['Quantity']
revenue_6m = uk_data_6m.groupby(['CustomerID']).agg({
        'revenue': 'sum'})
```

```
revenue_6m.rename(columns={'revenue': 'Revenue_6m'},
                  inplace=True)
revenue_6m = revenue_6m.reset_index()
```

7. The next step is to merge the 6-months dataset with revenue into the RFM features DataFrame. The following code block merges both the DataFrames in the `CustomerId` column:

```
# Merge the 6m revenue DataFrame with RFM data.
Merged_data = pd.merge(rfm_data, revenue_6m, how="left")
merged_data.fillna(0)
```

8. Since we are treating the problem as a classification problem, let's generate the customer LTV labels to use the **k-means** clustering algorithm. Here, we will be using the 6-months revenue to generate the labels. Customers will be grouped into three groups, namely **LowLTV**, **MidLTV**, and **HighLTV**.

   The following code block generates the LTV groups for the customers:

```
# Create LTV cluster groups
merged_data = merged_data[merged_
data['Revenue_6m']<merged_data['Revenue_6m'].
quantile(0.99)]
kmeans = Kmeans(n_clusters=3)
kmeans.fit(merged_data[['Revenue_6m']])
merged_data['LTVCluster'] = kmeans.predict(merged_
data[['Revenue_6m']])
```

9. Now we have the final dataset, let's look at what the feature set that we have generated looks like. The following code block converts categorical values into integer values:

```
Feature_data = pd.get_dummies(merged_data)
feature_data['CustomerID'] = feature_data['CustomerID'].
astype(str)
feature_data.columns = ['customerid', 'recency',
'frequency', 'monetaryvalue', 'r', 'f', 'm', 'rfmscore',
'revenue6m', 'ltvcluster', 'segmenthighvalue',
'segmentlowvalue', 'segmentmidvalue']
feature_data.head(5)
```

The preceding code block produces the following feature set:

	customerid	recency	frequency	monetaryvalue	r	f	m	rfmscore	revenue6m	ltvcluster	segmenthighvalue	segmentlowValue	segmentmidvalue
0	12747.0	7	35	1082.09	3	2	3	8	1666.11	1	1	0	0
1	12748.0	1	582	4336.73	3	3	3	9	18679.01	2	1	0	0
2	12749.0	8	54	782.10	3	3	3	9	2323.04	1	1	0	0
4	12823.0	63	1	459.00	0	0	2	2	765.00	1	0	1	0
7	12836.0	28	62	814.71	1	3	3	7	951.46	1	1	0	0

Figure 4.21 – Final feature set for the model

In *Chapter 1, An Overview of the Machine Learning Life Cycle*, the next step that was performed was model training and scoring. This is where we'll diverge from that. I am assuming this will be our final feature set. However, during the model development, the feature set evolves over time. We will discuss how to handle these changes in later chapters.

Now that we have a feature set, the next thing is to create entities and feature views in Feast.

Creating entities and feature views

In the previous chapter, *Chapter 3, Feature Store Fundamentals, Terminology, and Usage*, we defined **entities** and **feature views**. An entity is defined as a collection of semantically related features. Entities are domain objects to which features can be mapped. A feature view is defined as feature view is like a database table. It represents the structure of the feature data at its source. A feature view consists of entities, one or more features, and a data source. A feature view is generally modeled around a domain object similar to database objects. Since creating and applying a feature definition is a one-time activity, it is better to keep it in a separate notebook or Python file. Here is a link to the notebook:

`https://github.com/PacktPublishing/Feature-Store-for-Machine-Learning/blob/main/Chapter04/ch4_create_apply_feature_definitions.ipynb`

Let's open a notebook, install the libraries, and clone the feature repository as mentioned before:

```
!pip install feast[aws]==0.19.3
!git clone <feature_repo>
```

Now that we have cloned the feature repository, let's create the entity and feature views. Going by the definition of entity and feature views, the job is to identify the entities, features, and feature views in the feature set in *Figure 4.21*. Let's start with the entities. The only domain object that can be found in *Figure 4.21* is `customerid`:

1. Let's start by defining the customer entity. The following code block defines the customer entity for Feast:

```
# Customer ID entity definition.
from feast import Entity, ValueType
customer = Entity(
    name='customer',
    value_type=ValueType.STRING,
    join_key='customeriD',
    description="Id of the customer"
)
```

   The preceding entity definition has a few required attributes, such as `name`, `value_type`, and `join_key`, and others are optional. There are additional attributes that can be added if the users want to provide more information. The most important attribute is `join_key`. The value of this attribute should match the column name in the feature DataFrame.

   We have figured out the entity in the feature set. The next job is to define the feature views. Before we define feature views, a thing to keep in mind is to define the feature views as if you are a consumer who didn't generate the feature set. What I mean by that is do not name the feature views `customer_segmentation_features` or `LTV_features` and push all of them to a single table. Always try to break them into logical groups that are meaningful when other data scientists browse through them.

2. With that in mind, let's look at the feature set and decide how many logical groups can be formed here and what features go into what groups. From *Figure 4.21*, it can be grouped into either one or two groups. The two groups I see are RFM features for the customers and revenue features. Since RFM also has revenue details, I would rather group them into one group instead of two as there are no clear subgroups here. I will call it `customer_rfm_features`.

   The following code block defines the feature view:

```
from feast import ValueType, FeatureView, Feature,
RedshiftSource
```

```
from datetime import timedelta

# Redshift batch source
rfm_features_source = RedshiftSource(
    query="SELECT * FROM spectrum.customer_rfm_features",
    event_timestamp_column="event_timestamp",
    created_timestamp_column="created_timestamp",
)

# FeatureView definition for RFM features.
rfm_features_features = FeatureView(
    name="customer_rfm_features",
    entities=["customer"],
    ttl=timedelta(days=3650),
    features=[
        Feature(name="recency", dtype=ValueType.INT32),
        Feature(name="frequency", dtype=ValueType.INT32),
        Feature(name="monetaryvalue",
        dtype=ValueType.DOUBLE),
        Feature(name="r", dtype=ValueType.INT32),
        Feature(name="f", dtype=ValueType.INT32),
        Feature(name="m", dtype=ValueType.INT32),
        Feature(name="rfmscore", dtype=ValueType.INT32),
        Feature(name="revenue6m", dtype=ValueType.
DOUBLE),
        Feature(name="ltvcluster", dtype=ValueType.
INT32),
        Feature(name="segmenthighvalue",
        dtype=ValueType.INT32),
        Feature(name="segmentlowvalue",
        dtype=ValueType.INT32),
        Feature(name="segmentmidvalue",
        dtype=ValueType.INT32),
    ],
    batch_source=rfm_features_source,
)
```

The preceding code block has two definitions. The first one is the batch source definition. Depending on the offline store that is being used, the definition of the batch source differs. In the previous chapter, we used `FileSource` in the example. Since we are using Redshift to query the offline store, `RedshiftSource` has been defined. The input to the object is query, which is a simple `SELECT` statement. The source can be configured to have complex SQL queries with joins, aggregation, and more. However, the output should match the column names defined in `FeatureView`. The other input to the source is `created_timestamp_column` and `event_timestamp_column`. These columns are missing in *Figure 4.21*. The columns represent what their headings state, the time when the event occurred, and when the event was created. These columns need to be added to the data before we ingest it.

`FeatureView` represents the table structure of the data at the source. As we looked at it in the last chapter, it has `entities`, `features`, and the `batch_source`. In *Figure 4.21*, the entity is `customer`, that was defined earlier. The rest of the columns are the features and the batch source, which is the `RedshiftSource` object. The feature name should match the column name and `dtype` should match the value type of the columns.

3. Now that we have the feature definition for our feature set, we must register the new definitions to be able to use them. To register the definitions, let's copy the entity and feature definitions into a Python file and add this file to our feature repository folder. I will be naming the file `rfm_features.py`. After adding the file to the repository, the folder structure looks like the following figure.

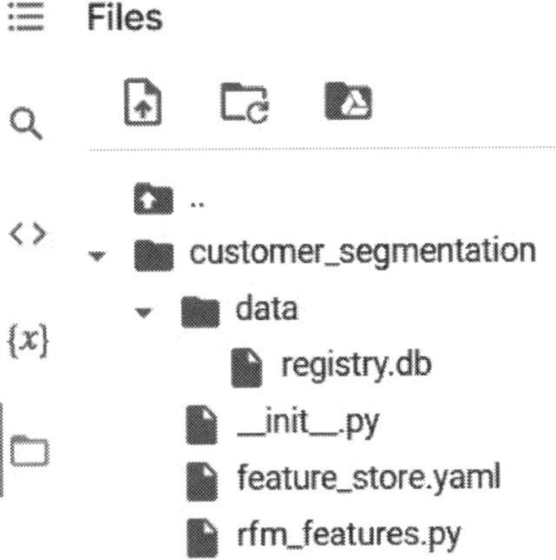

Figure 4.22 – Project with feature definitions file

Before registering the definition using the `apply` command, let's map the external schema on Redshift.

Creating an external catalog

If you recall correctly, during the Redshift resource creation, I mentioned that the data in Amazon S3 will be added as an external mapping using Glue/Lake Formation. What that means is data will not be ingested into Redshift directly; instead, the dataset will be in S3. The structure of the dataset will be defined in the Lake Formation catalog, which you will see in a moment. Then, the database will be mapped as an external schema on Redshift. Hence, the ingestion will push data into S3 directly and the query will be executed using the Redshift cluster.

Now that we understand the workings of ingestion and querying, let's create the database and catalog for our feature set in Lake Formation:

1. To create a database, visit the AWS Lake Formation page via a search or using this URL: `https://console.aws.amazon.com/lakeformation/home?region=us-east-1#databases`.

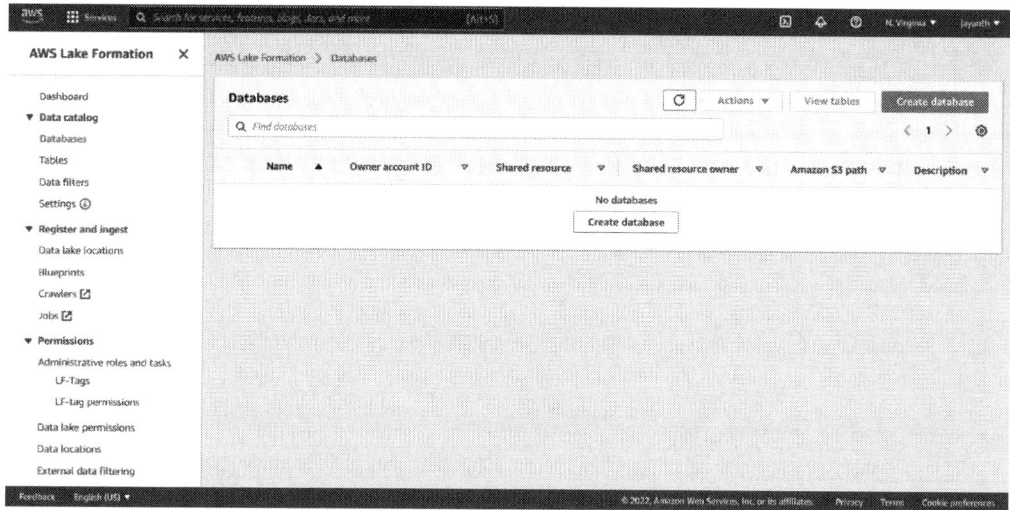

Figure 4.23 – Databases in AWS Lake Formation

Figure 4.23 displays the list of databases in AWS Lake Formation.

2. On the web page, click on **Create database**. The following web page will appear. If you see any popups in the transition, asking you to get started with Lake Formation, it can either be canceled or accepted.

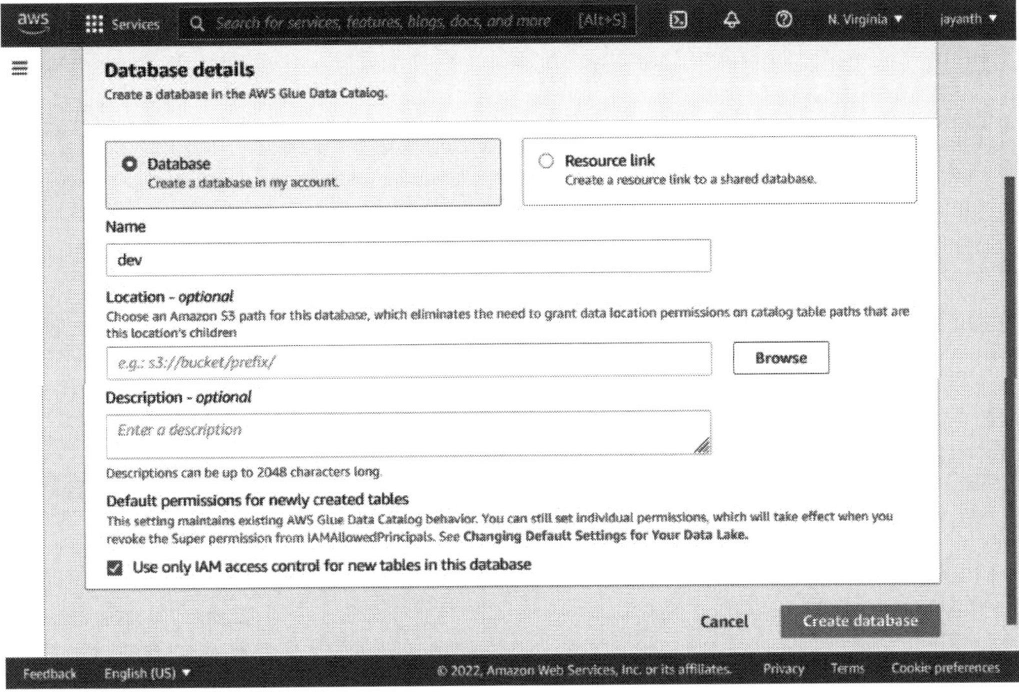

Figure 4.24 – Lake formation Create database

3. From the web page displayed above, give the database a name. I am calling it `dev`. Leave everything else as the default and click on **Create database**. The database will be created, and it will redirect to the database details page. As databases are groupings of tables together, you can think of this database as a grouping for all the feature views in the project. Once you have the database, the next step is to create the table. As you might have already realized, the table we create here corresponds to the feature view. In the current exercise, there is just one feature view. Hence, a corresponding table needs to be created.

> **Note**
>
> As and when you add a new feature view, a corresponding table needs to be added to the database in Lake Formation.

4. To create a table in the database, click on **Tables** from the page in *Figure 4.23* or visit this URL: `https://console.aws.amazon.com/lakeformation/home?region=us-east-1#tables`.

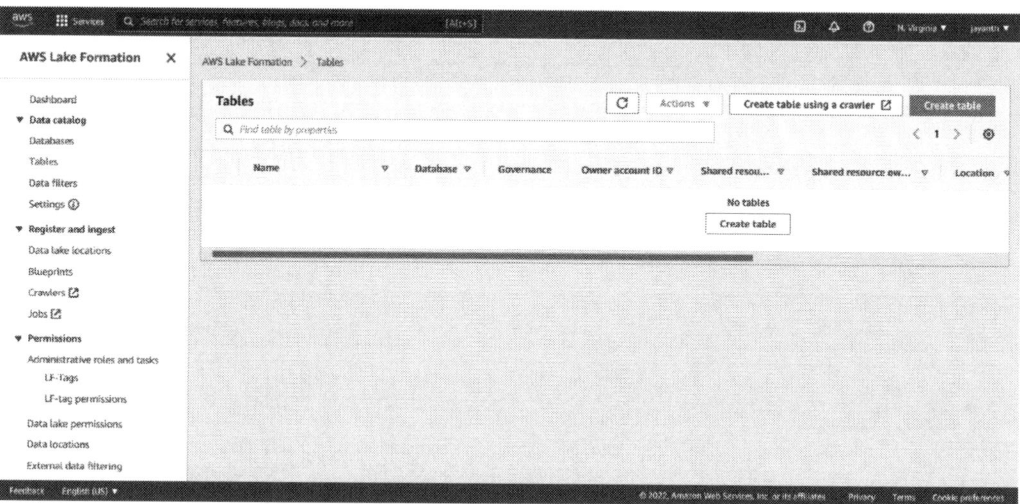

Figure 4.25 – Lake Formation tables

5. From the web page in *Figure 4.25*, click on the **Create table** button at the top right. The following web page will be displayed:

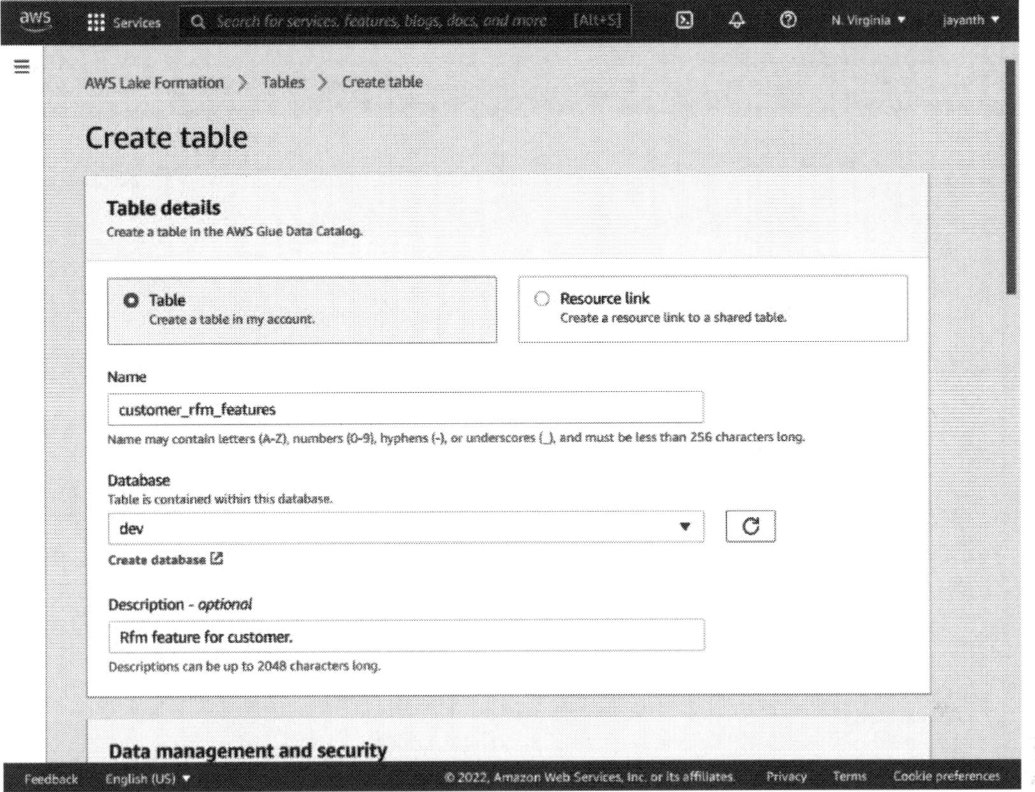

Figure 4.26 – Lake Formation Create table 1

6. For the **Name** parameter, I have set `customer_rfm_features` and I have selected the database that was created earlier (`dev`). A description is optional. Once these details are filled in, scroll down. The following options will be seen in the next part of the **Create table** page.

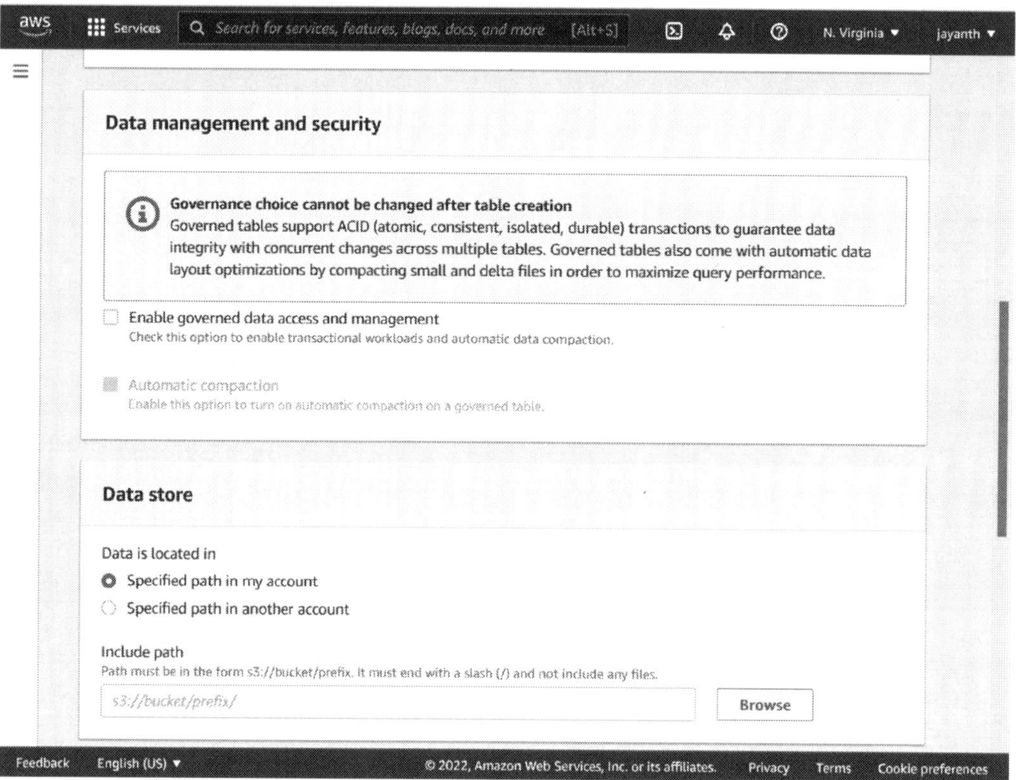

Figure 4.27 – Lake Formation Create table 2

7. The data store is one of the important properties here. It stands for the location of data in S3. So far, we haven't pushed any data to S3 yet. We will be doing that soon. Let's define where data for this table will be pushed to. I am going to use the S3 bucket we created earlier, hence the location will be `s3://feast-demo-mar-2022/customer-rfm-features/`.

> **Important Note**
>
> Create the `customer-rfm-features` folder in the S3 path.

8. After selecting the S3 path, scroll down to the last part of the page – the following options will be displayed.

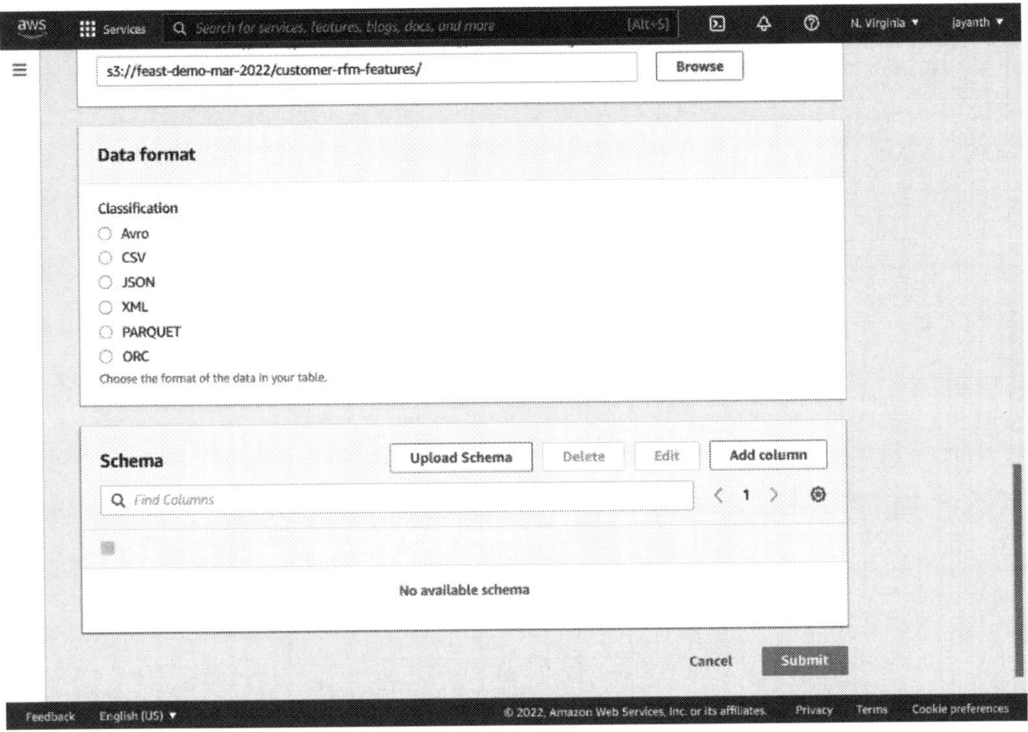

Figure 4.28 – Lake Formation Create table 3

Figure 4.28 shows the last part of the table creation. The **Data format** section is asking for the file format of the data. We will be selecting **PARQUET** for this exercise. Feel free to experiment with others. Whatever format is selected here, all the ingested data files should be of the same format, else it might not work as expected.

9. The last section is the **Schema** definition of the dataset. You can either click on the **Add column** button and add the columns individually or can click on the **Upload Schema** button to upload a JSON defining all the columns at once. Let's use the **Add column** button and add all the columns in order. Once all the columns are added along with the data types, the columns should look like the following:

#	Column Name	Data type	Partition key	Comment	LF-Tags
1	customerid	string	-	-	-
2	recency	bigint	-	-	-
3	frequency	bigint	-	-	-
4	monetaryvalue	double	-	-	-
5	r	bigint	-	-	-
6	f	bigint	-	-	-
7	m	bigint	-	-	-
8	rfmscore	bigint	-	-	-
9	revenue6m	double	-	-	-
10	ltvcluster	int	-	-	-
11	segmenthighvalue	int	-	-	-
12	segmentlowvalue	int	-	-	-
13	segmentmidvalue	int	-	-	-
14	event_timestamp	timestamp	-	-	-
15	created_timestamp	timestamp	-	-	-

Figure 4.29 – Column list in Create table

As can be seen from *Figure 4.29*, all the columns have been added, along with the entity `customerid` and the two timestamp columns: `event_timestamp` and `created_timestamp`. Once the columns are added, click on the **Submit** button at the bottom.

10. Now, the only thing that is pending is to map this table in the Redshift cluster that has been created. Let's do that next. To create the mapping of the external schema, visit the Redshift cluster page and select the cluster that was created earlier. A web page similar to the one in *Figure 4.30* will be displayed.

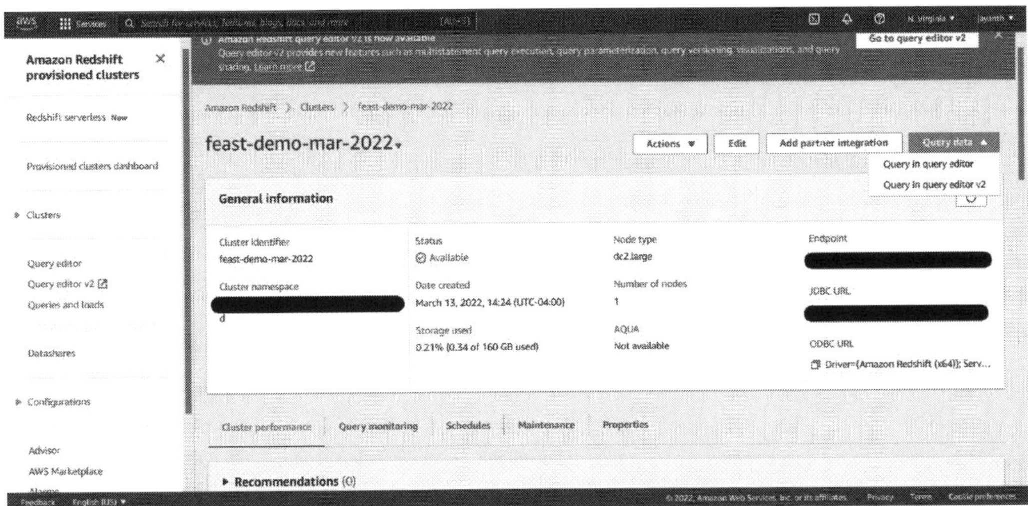

Figure 4.30 – Redshift cluster details page

11. From the web page displayed in *Figure 4.30*, click on **Query data** in the top right of the page. Among the options in the dropdown, pick **Query in query editor v2**. It will open up a query editor as shown in the following figure:

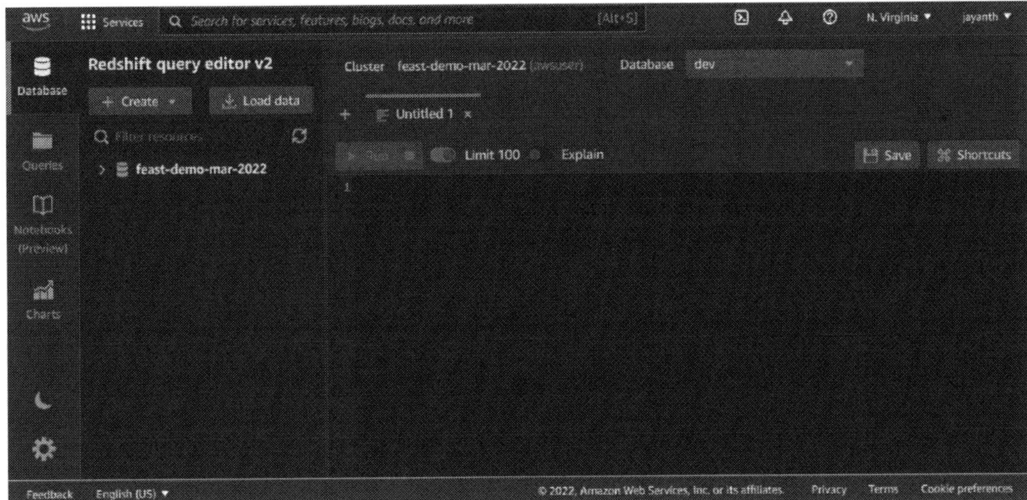

Figure 4.31 – Redshift query editor v2

12. Select the cluster from the left panel and also the database if not selected by default. In the query editor shown in *Figure 4.31*, run the following query to map the external database into a schema called `spectrum`:

```
create external schema spectrum
from data catalog database dev
iam_role '<redshift_role_arn>'
create external database if not exists;
```

13. In the preceding code block, replace <redshift_role_arn> with the **ARN** of the role that was created and associated with Redshift. The ARN can be found in the IAM console on the role details page, similar to the one in *Figure 4.32*.

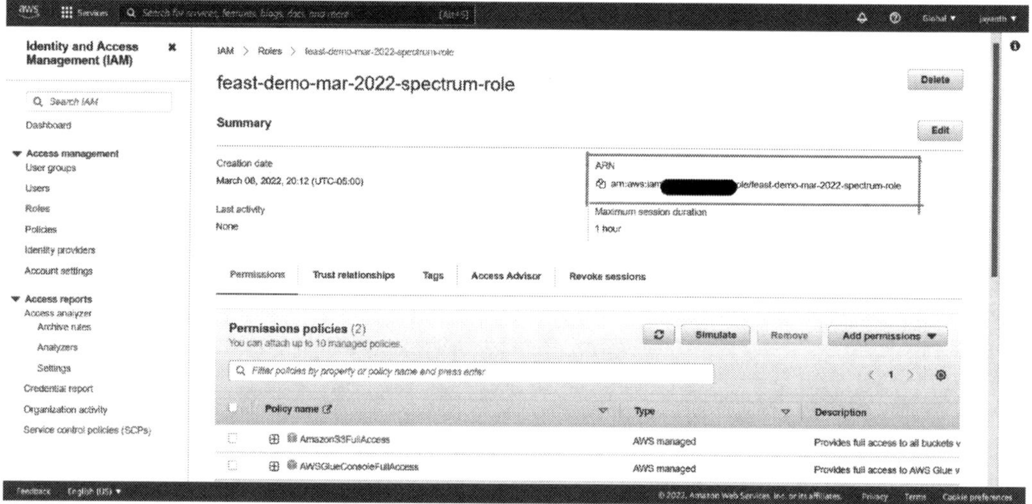

Figure 4.32 – IAM role details page

On successful execution of the query, you should be able to see the output `spectrum` schema under the database after refreshing the page as shown in *Figure 4.33*.

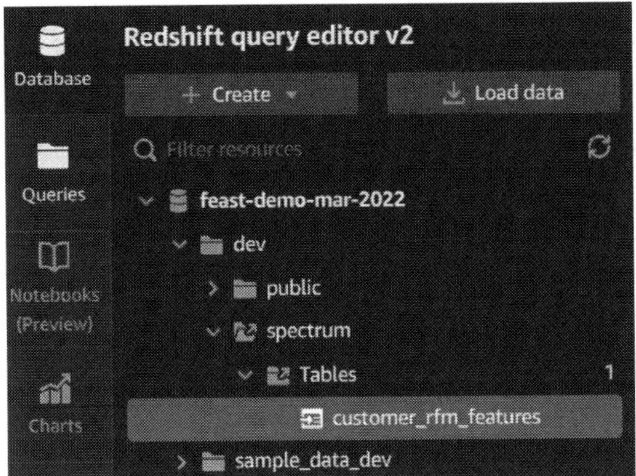

Figure 4.33 – Redshift spectrum schema

14. You can also verify the mapping by executing the following SQL `SELECT` query:

```
SELECT * from spectrum.customer_rfm_features limit 5
```

The preceding SQL query will return an empty table in the result as the data is not ingested yet.

We have completed the mapping of the external table now. All we are left with is to apply the feature set and ingest the data. Let's do that next.

> **Important Note**
> It might seem like a lot of work to add a feature store in an ML pipeline, however, that is not true. Since we are doing it for the first time, it just seems like that. Also, all the steps from resource creation to mapping the external table can be automated using infrastructure as code. Here is a link to an example that automates infrastructure creation (`https://github.com/feast-dev/feast-aws-credit-scoring-tutorial`). Apart from that, if you use managed feature stores such as Tecton, SageMaker, or Databricks, the infrastructure is managed and all you will have to do is to create features, ingest them, and use them without worrying about the infrastructure. We will do a comparison of Feast with other feature stores in *Chapter 7, Feast Alternatives and ML Best Practices*.

Applying definitions and ingesting data

So far, we have performed data cleaning, feature engineering, defined the entities and feature definitions, and also created and mapped the external table to Redshift. Now, let's apply the feature definitions and ingest the data. Continue in the same notebook that we created in the *Creating entities and feature views* section (`https://github.com/PacktPublishing/Feature-Store-for-Machine-Learning/blob/main/Chapter04/ch4_create_apply_feature_definitions.ipynb`).

To apply a feature set, we need the IAM user credentials that was created earlier. Recall that, during the creation of the IAM user, the credential files were available for download. The file contains `AWS_ACCESS_KEY_ID` and `AWS_SECRET_ACCESS_KEY`. Once you have it handy, replace `<aws_key_id>` and `<aws_secret>` in the following code block:

```
import os
os.environ["AWS_ACCESS_KEY_ID"] = "<aws_key_id>"
os.environ["AWS_SECRET_ACCESS_KEY"] = "<aws_secret>"
os.environ["AWS_DEFAULT_REGION"] = "us-east-1"
```

> **Important Note**
>
> It is never a good idea to set the credentials in the notebook as a raw string. Depending on the tools that are available to the user, it is a good practice to use a secret manager to store secrets.

After setting the environment variable, all you have to do is to run the following code block to apply the defined feature set:

```
%cd customer_segmentation/
!feast apply
```

The preceding code block registers the new feature definitions and also creates the AWS DynamoDB tables for all the feature views in the definition. The output of the preceding code block is displayed in *Figure 4.34*.

```
/content/customer_segmentation
/usr/local/lib/python3.7/dist-packages/scipy/fft/__init__.py:97: DeprecationWarning: The module
  from numpy.dual import register_func
/usr/local/lib/python3.7/dist-packages/scipy/sparse/sputils.py:17: DeprecationWarning: `np.typeDi
  supported_dtypes = [np.typeDict[x] for x in supported_dtypes]
/usr/local/lib/python3.7/dist-packages/feast/infra/offline_stores/redshift_source.py:55: Deprecat
  DeprecationWarning,
03/14/2022 03:01:38 AM INFO:Found credentials in environment variables.
Created data source
Created entity customer
Created feature view customer_rfm_features

Deploying infrastructure for customer_rfm_features
```

Figure 4.34 – Feast apply output

To verify that DynamoDB tables are created for the feature views, navigate to the DynamoDB console, using the search or visit `https://console.aws.amazon.com/dynamodbv2/home?region=us-east-1#tables`. You should see the `customer_rfm_features` table as shown in *Figure 4.35*.

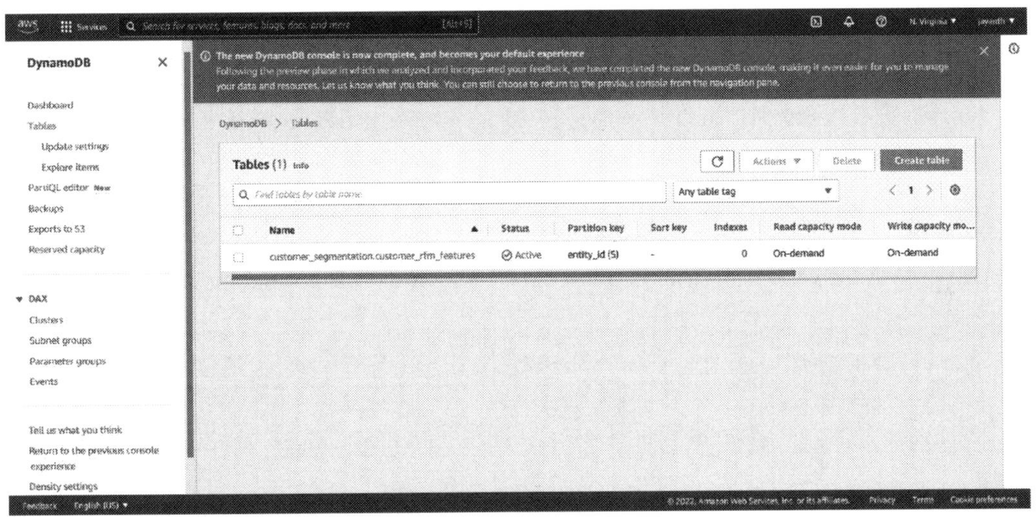

Figure 4.35 – DynamoDB tables

Now that feature definitions have been applied, to ingest the feature data, let's pick up the feature engineering notebook created in the *Model (feature engineering)* section (`https://github.com/PacktPublishing/Feature-Store-for-Machine-Learning/blob/main/Chapter04/ch4_feature_engineering.ipynb`) and continue in that (the last command of feature engineering produced *Figure 4.21*). To ingest the data, the only thing we have to do is write the features DataFrame to the S3 location that is mapped in *Figure 4.28*. I mapped the data store location as `s3://feast-demo-mar-2022/customer-rfm-features/`. Let's write the DataFrame to the location as Parquet.

The following code block ingests the data in the S3 location:

```
import os
from datetime import datetime
os.environ["AWS_ACCESS_KEY_ID"] = "<aws_key_id>"
os.environ["AWS_SECRET_ACCESS_KEY"] = "<aws_secret>"
os.environ["AWS_DEFAULT_REGION"] = "us-east-1"
file_name = f"rfm_features-{datetime.now()}.parquet"
feature_data["event_timestamp"] = datetime.now()
feature_data["created_timestamp"] = datetime.now()
s3_url = f's3://feast-demo-mar-2022/customer-rfm-features/
{file_name}'
feature_data.to_parquet(s3_url)
```

The preceding code block sets the AWS credentials of the IAM user, adds the missing columns, `event_timestamp` and `created_timestamp`, and finally writes the Parquet file to the S3 location. To verify that the file is written successfully, navigate to the S3 location and verify that the file exists. To make sure that the file is in the correct format, let's navigate to the Redshift query editor in *Figure 4.32* and run the following query:

```
SELECT * from spectrum.customer_rfm_features limit 5
```

The preceding command should result in success, with the output as shown in *Figure 4.36*.

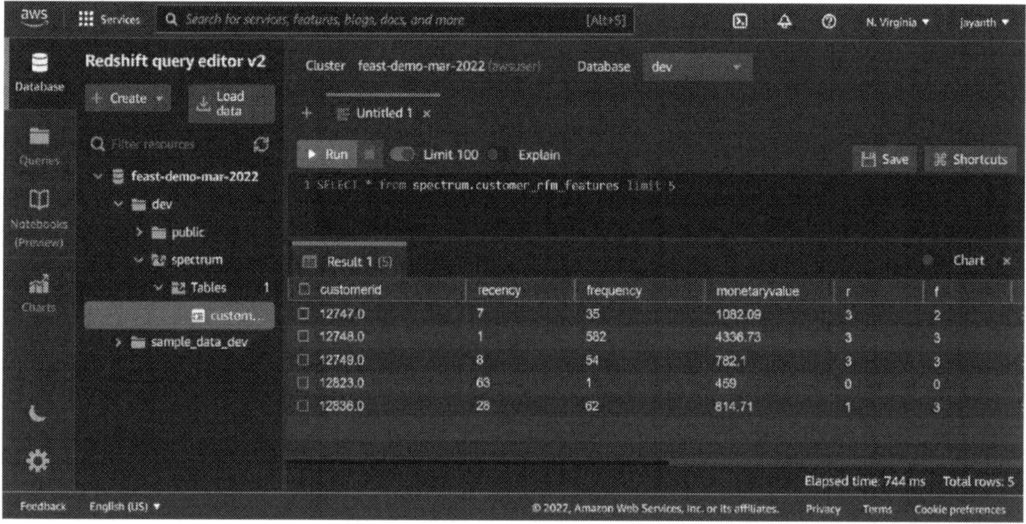

Figure 4.36 – Redshift query after ingesting the data

Before we move on to the next stage of ML, let's just run a couple of APIs, look at what our feature repository looks like, and verify that the query to the historical store works okay. For the following code, let's use the notebook we used to create and apply feature definitions (`https://github.com/PacktPublishing/Feature-Store-for-Machine-Learning/blob/main/Chapter04/ch4_create_apply_feature_definitions.ipynb`).

The following code connects to the feature store and lists the available entities and feature views:

```
"""import feast and load feature store object with the path to
the directory which contains feature_story.yaml."""
from feast import FeatureStore
store = FeatureStore(repo_path=".")
#Get list of entities and feature views
print("----------------------Entity--------------------")
for entity in store.list_entities():
  print(f"entity: {entity}")
print("------------------Feature Views----------------")
for feature_view in store.list_feature_views():
  print(f"List of FeatureViews: {feature_view}")
```

The preceding code block prints the `customer` entity and `customer_rfm_features` feature view. Let's query the offline store for a few entities and see if it works as expected.

To query offline data, we need entity IDs and timestamp columns. The entity ID column is a list of customer IDs and the timestamp column is used for performing point-in-time join queries on the dataset. The following code creates an entity DataFrame for the query:

```
import pandas as pd
from datetime import datetime, timedelta
entity_df = pd.DataFrame.from_dict(
    {
        "customerid": ["12747.0", "12748.0", "12749.0"],
        "event_timestamp": [datetime.now()]*3
    }
)
entity_df.head()
```

The preceding code block produces an entity DataFrame like the one in *Figure 4.37*.

	CustomerID	event_timestamp
0	12747.0	2022-03-15 00:58:45.594038
1	12748.0	2022-03-15 00:58:45.594038
2	12749.0	2022-03-15 00:58:45.594038

Figure 4.37 – Entity DataFrame

With the sample entity DataFrame, let's query the historical data. The following code fetches a subset of features from the historical store:

```
job = store.get_historical_features(
    entity_df=entity_df,
    features=[
              "customer_rfm_features:recency",
              "customer_rfm_features:frequency",
              "customer_rfm_features:monetaryvalue",
              "customer_rfm_features:r",
              "customer_rfm_features:f",
              "customer_rfm_features:m"]
    )
df = job.to_df()
df.head()
```

The following code block may take a couple of minutes to run but finally outputs the following results:

	customerid	event_timestamp	recency	frequency	monetaryvalue	r	f	m
0	12747.0	2022-03-15 00:58:45.594038	7	35	1082.09	3	2	3
1	12749.0	2022-03-15 00:58:45.594038	8	54	782.10	3	3	3
2	12748.0	2022-03-15 00:58:45.594038	1	582	4336.73	3	3	3

Figure 4.38 – Historical retrieval job output

Now we can say that our feature engineering pipeline is ready. The next steps that are required are to train the model, perform validation, and, if happy with the performance of the model, deploy the pipeline into production. We will look at training, validation, deployment, and model scoring in the next chapter. Let's briefly summarize what we have learned next.

Summary

In this chapter, we started with the goal of adding the Feast feature store to our ML model development. We accomplished that by creating the required resources on AWS, adding an IAM user to access those resources. After creating the resources, we went through the steps of the ML life cycle again from the problem statement to feature engineering and feature ingestion. We also verified that created feature definitions and ingested data could be queried through the API.

Now that we have set the stage for the next steps of the ML life cycle – model training, validation, deployment, and scoring, in the next chapter, we will learn how the addition of the feature store right from the beginning makes the model production-ready when the development is complete.

References

- Feast documentation: `https://docs.feast.dev/`
- Credit scoring with Feast on AWS: `https://github.com/feast-dev/feast-aws-credit-scoring-tutorial`

5
Model Training and Inference

In the last chapter, we discussed **Feast deployment** in the AWS cloud and set up S3 as an offline store and DynamoDB as an online store for the model. We also revisited the few stages of the ML life cycle using the **Customer Lifetime Value** (**LTV/CLTV**) model built in *Chapter 1, An Overview of the Machine Learning Life Cycle*. During the processing of model development, we performed data cleaning and feature engineering and produced the feature set for which the feature definitions were created and applied to Feast. In the end, we ingested the features into Feast successfully and we were also able to query the ingested data.

In this chapter, we will continue with the rest of the ML life cycle, which will involve model training, packaging, batch, and online model inference using the feature store. The goal of this chapter is to continue using the feature store infrastructure that was created in the previous chapter and go through the rest of the ML life cycle. As we go through this process, it will provide an opportunity to learn how using the feature store in ML development can improve the time to production of the model, decouples different stages of the ML life cycle, and helps in collaboration. We will also look back at *Chapter 1, An Overview of the Machine Learning Life Cycle*, and compare the different stages as we go through these steps. This chapter will help you understand how to use the feature store for model training, followed by model inference. We will also learn what use case the online store serves and use cases served by the offline store.

We will discuss the following topics in order:

- Model training with the feature store
- Model packaging
- Batch model inference with Feast
- Online model inference with Feast
- Handling changes to the feature set during development

Prerequisites

To run through the examples and to get a better understanding of this chapter, the resources created in *Chapter 4, Adding Feature Store to ML Models*, are required. In this chapter, we will use the resources created in the previous chapter and also use the feature repository created in the chapter. The following GitHub link points to the feature repository I created: `https://github.com/PacktPublishing/Feature-Store-for-Machine-Learning/tree/main/customer_segmentation`.

Technical requirements

To follow the code examples in the chapter, all you need is familiarity with Python and any notebook environment, which could be a local setup such as Jupyter or an online notebook environment such as Google Colab, Kaggle, or SageMaker. You will also need an AWS account with full access to resources such as Redshift, S3, Glue, DynamoDB, the IAM console, and more. You can create a new account and use all the services for free during the trial period. In the last part, you will need an IDE environment to develop the REST endpoints for the online model. You can find the code examples of the book at the following GitHub link: `https://github.com/PacktPublishing/Feature-Store-for-Machine-Learning/tree/main/Chapter05`.

Model training with the feature store

In *Chapter 1, An Overview of the Machine Learning Life Cycle*, after feature engineering, we jumped right into model training in the same notebook. Whereas in *Chapter 4, Adding Feature Store to ML Models*, the generated features were ingested into the feature store. This is one of the standardizations that the feature store helps with in the ML life cycle. By ingesting features into the feature store, a discoverable, sharable, reusable, and versioned dataset/feature set was created.

Now let's assume that two data scientists, Ram and Dee, are working on the same model. Both can use this feature set without having to do anything extra. Not only that, if the background data gets refreshed every day, then all that needs to be done is to run the feature engineering notebook once a day when data scientists comes in, and the latest features will be available for consumption. An even better thing to do is schedule the feature engineering notebook using an orchestration framework such as **Airflow**, **AWS Step Functions**, or even **GitHub** workflows. Once that is done, the latest features are available for experimentation for both Dee and Ram when they come to work.

As we have been discussing, one of the biggest advantages that data engineers and scientists get out of feature stores is collaboration. Let's try and see how our two data scientists, Dee and Ram, can collaborate/compete in model building. Every day when Dee and Ram come into work, assuming that the scheduled feature engineering has run successfully, they start with the model training. The other important thing to note here is, for model training, the source is the feature store. Data scientists don't need to go into raw data sources to generate features unless they are not happy with the model produced by the existing features. In which case, data scientists would go into data exploration again, generate additional feature sets, and ingest them into the feature store. The ingested features are again available for everybody to use. This will go on until the team/data scientist is happy with the model's performance.

Before we split the workflow of two data scientists, Dee and Ram, let's run through the common steps of their model training notebook. Let's open a new Python notebook, call it `model-training.ipynb`, and generate training data. The offline store will be used for generating training datasets as it stores the historical data and versions the data with a timestamp. In Feast, the interface to data stores is through an API, as we looked at in *Chapter 3, Feature Store Fundamentals, Terminology, and Usage.* and in *Chapter 4, Adding Feature Store to ML Models*. Hence, to generate the training dataset, we will be using `get_historical_features`. One of the inputs of the `get_historical_features` API is entity IDs. Usually, in enterprises, entity IDs can be fetched from the raw data source. The typical raw sources include databases, data warehouses, object stores, and more. The queries to fetch entities could be as simple as `select unique {entity_id} from {table};`. Let's do something similar here. Our raw data source is the CSV file. Let's use that to fetch the entity IDs. Before we go further, let's install the required packages:

1. The following code block installs the required packages for the model training:

```
!pip install feast[aws]==0.19.3 pandas xgboost
```

2. After installing the required packages, if you haven't already cloned the feature repository, please do so, since we need to connect to the feature store to generate the training dataset. The following code clones the repository:

```
!git clone <repo_url>
```

3. Now that we have the feature repository, let's connect to Feast/the feature store and make sure that everything works as expected before we move on:

```
# change directory
%cd customer_segmentation

"""import feast and load feature store object with the
path to the directory which contains feature_story.
yaml."""
from feast import FeatureStore
store = FeatureStore(repo_path=".")
for entity in store.list_entities():
  print(f"entity: {entity}")
```

The preceding code block connects to the Feast feature repository The `repo_path="."` parameter indicates that `feature_store.yaml` is in the current working directory. It also lists the available entities in the `customer_segmentation` feature repository

Now that we are able to connect to the feature repository let's create the list of entity IDs that are required for training the model. To get the list of entity IDs, in this case, `CustomerId`, let's use the raw dataset and filter out the entity IDs from it.

> **Important Note**
>
> We are using the same raw dataset that was used in *Chapter 4, Adding Feature Store to ML Models*. Here is the URL of the dataset: `https://www.kaggle.com/datasets/vijayuv/onlineretail`.

4. The following code block loads the raw data:

```
import pandas as pd

##Read the OnlineRetail.csv
retail_data = pd.read_csv('/content/OnlineRetail.csv',
                          encoding= 'unicode_escape')
```

```
retail_data['InvoiceDate'] = pd.to_datetime(
  retail_data['InvoiceDate'], errors = 'coerce')
```

Important Note

You might question why we need raw data here. Feast allows queries on entities. Hence, we need the entity IDs for which the features are needed.

5. Let's filter out the customer IDs that are of interest, similar to the filtering done during feature creation. The following code block selects the dataset that doesn't belong to the United Kingdom and also the customer IDs that exists in the three months dataset (the reason for picking the customers in the three months dataset is, after generating the RFM feature, we performed a left join on the dataset in the feature engineering notebook).

   The following code block performs the described filtering:

   ```
   ## filter data for United Kingdom
   uk_data = retail_data.query("Country=='United Kingdom'").
   reset_index(drop=True)
   t1 = pd.Timestamp("2011-06-01 00:00:00.054000")
   t2 = pd.Timestamp("2011-03-01 00:00:00.054000")
   uk_data_3m = uk_data[(uk_data.InvoiceDate < t1) & (uk_
   data.InvoiceDate >= t2)].reset_index(drop=True)
   ```

   From `uk_data_3m`, we need to fetch the unique `CustomerId`. The additional column required in the entity data is the timestamp to perform point-in-time joins. For now, I'm going to use the latest timestamp for all the entity IDs.

6. The following code block creates the entity DataFrame required for querying the historical store:

   ```
   from datetime import datetime
   entity_df = pd.DataFrame(data = {
       "customerid": [str(item) for item in uk_data_3m.
   CustomerID.unique().tolist()],
       "event_timestamp": datetime.now()
   })
   entity_df.head()
   ```

The preceding code block produces the following output:

	CustomerID	event_timestamp
0	14620.0	2022-03-26 16:24:21.490847
1	14740.0	2022-03-26 16:24:21.490847
2	13880.0	2022-03-26 16:24:21.490847
3	16462.0	2022-03-26 16:24:21.490847
4	17068.0	2022-03-26 16:24:21.490847

Figure 5.1 – Entity DataFrame for generating the training dataset

As you can see in *Figure 5.1*, the entity DataFrame contains two columns:

- **CustomerID**: A list of customers for whom the features need to be fetched.
- **event_timestamp**: The timestamp for a point-in-time join. The latest features for a given customer are at the given `event_timestamp`.

Now that the common steps in Dee and Ram's model training notebook are complete, let's split their workflow and look at how they can collaborate.

Dee's model training experiments

Continuing from the last step (feel free to copy the code blocks and run them in a different notebook and name it as `dee-model-training.ipynb`), it is time to pick the feature set required for training the model:

1. To pick the features, Dee would run the following command to look at the available features in the existing feature view:

```
feature_view = store.get_feature_view("customer_rfm_
features")
print(feature_view.to_proto())
```

The preceding command outputs the feature view. The following block displays a part of the output that includes features and entities that are part of the feature view:

```
name: "customer_rfm_features"
entities: "customer"
features {
  name: "recency"
  value_type: INT32
```

```
  }
  features {
    name: "frequency"
    value_type: INT32
  }
  features {
    name: "monetaryvalue"
    value_type: DOUBLE
  }
  …

meta {
  created_timestamp {
    seconds: 1647301293
    nanos: 70471000
  }
  last_updated_timestamp {
    seconds: 1647301293
    nanos: 70471000
  }
}
```

From the feature set, let's assume that Dee wants to leave out frequency-related features and see how the performance of the model is affected. Hence, she picks all other features for the query and leaves out *frequency* and *F*, which indicates frequency group.

2. The following code block queries the historical/offline store to fetch the required features using the entity DataFrame shown in *Figure 5.1*:

```
import os
from datetime import datetime
os.environ["AWS_ACCESS_KEY_ID"] = "<aws_key_id>"
os.environ["AWS_SECRET_ACCESS_KEY"] = "<aws_secret>"
os.environ["AWS_DEFAULT_REGION"] = "us-east-1"
job = store.get_historical_features(
    entity_df=entity_df,
    features=[
```

```
                "customer_rfm_features:recency",
                "customer_rfm_features:monetaryvalue",
                "customer_rfm_features:r",
                "customer_rfm_features:m",
                "customer_rfm_features:rfmscore",
                "customer_rfm_features:segmenthighvalue",
                "customer_rfm_features:segmentlowvalue"
                "customer_rfm_features:segmentmidvalue",
                "customer_rfm_features:ltvcluster"
                ]
    )
feature_data = job.to_df()
feature_data = feature_data.dropna()
feature_data.head()
```

The previous code block outputs the DataFrame shown as follows:

	customerid	event_timestamp	recency	monetaryvalue	r	m	rfmscore	segmenthighvalue	segmentlowvalue	segmentmidvalue	ltvcluster
0	12748.0	2022-03-26 18:05:06.863532	1.0	4336.73	3.0	3.0	9.0	1.0	0.0	0.0	1.0
2	12839.0	2022-03-26 18:05:06.863532	7.0	303.58	3.0	1.0	6.0	0.0	0.0	1.0	2.0
4	12878.0	2022-03-26 18:05:06.863532	45.0	854.99	1.0	3.0	6.0	0.0	0.0	1.0	0.0
5	12891.0	2022-03-26 18:05:06.863532	29.0	204.00	1.0	0.0	1.0	0.0	1.0	0.0	0.0
6	12916.0	2022-03-26 18:05:06.863532	10.0	1441.13	3.0	3.0	8.0	1.0	0.0	0.0	0.0

Figure 5.2 – Training dataset for Dee's model

> **Important Note**
>
> Replace `<aws_key_id>` and `<aws_secret>` in the preceding code block with the user credentials created in *Chapter 4, Adding Feature Store to ML Models*.

3. Now that Dee has the training dataset generated, the next step is model training. Let's build the XGBoost model with the same parameters that were used in *Chapter 1, An Overview of the Machine Learning Life Cycle*. The following code block splits the dataset into training and testing:

```
from sklearn.metrics import classification_
report,confusion_matrix
import xgboost as xgb
from sklearn.model_selection import KFold, cross_val_
score, train_test_split
```

```
#Drop prediction column along with event time and
customerId columns from X
X = feature_data.drop(['ltvcluster', 'customerid',
                      'event_timestamp'], axis=1)
y = feature_data['ltvcluster']
X_train, X_test, y_train, y_test = \
train_test_split(X, y, test_size=0.1)
```

4. The following code block uses the training and test dataset created in the previous example and trains an `XGBClassifier` model:

```
xgb_classifier = xgb.XGBClassifier(max_depth=5,
objective='multi:softprob')
#model training
xgb_model = xgb_classifier.fit(X_train, y_train)
#Model scoring
acc = xgb_model.score(X_test,y_test)
print(f"Model accuracy: {acc}")
```

The preceding code block prints the accuracy of the model:

```
Model accuracy: 0.8840579710144928
```

5. The following code block runs the `predict` function on the test dataset and prints the classification report:

```
#Run prediction on the test dataset
y_pred = xgb_model.predict(X_test)
print(classification_report(y_test, y_pred))
```

The preceding code block produces the following output:

```
              precision    recall  f1-score   support

         0.0       0.93      0.95      0.94       119
         1.0       0.67      0.67      0.67         3
         2.0       0.50      0.44      0.47        16

    accuracy                           0.88       138
   macro avg       0.70      0.68      0.69       138
weighted avg       0.88      0.88      0.88       138
```

Figure 5.3 – Classification report of Dee's model

Not only this but Dee can also try out different feature sets and algorithms. For now, let's assume Dee is happy with her model. Let's move on and look at what Ram does.

Ram's model training experiments

Again, we'll continue in the notebook from the step after *Figure 5.1* (feel free to copy the code blocks, run them in a different notebook, and name it as `ram-model-training.ipynb`). It's time to pick the feature set required for training the model. To pick the features, Ram would follow similar steps as Dee did. Let's assume that Ram thinks differently – instead of dropping out one specific category, he drops the features with actual values and just uses the R, F, and M categorical features and segments categorical features. According to Ram, these categorical variables are some transformations of the actual values:

1. The following code block produces the features set required by Ram to train the model:

```
import os
from datetime import datetime
os.environ["AWS_ACCESS_KEY_ID"] = "<aws_key_id>"
os.environ["AWS_SECRET_ACCESS_KEY"] = "<aws_secret>"
os.environ["AWS_DEFAULT_REGION"] = "us-east-1"
job = store.get_historical_features(
    entity_df=entity_df,
    features=[
              "customer_rfm_features:r",
              "customer_rfm_features:m",
              "customer_rfm_features:f",
              "customer_rfm_features:segmenthighvalue",
              "customer_rfm_features:segmentlowvalue",
              "customer_rfm_features:segmentmidvalue",
              "customer_rfm_features:ltvcluster"
              ]
    )
feature_data = job.to_df()
feature_data = feature_data.dropna()
feature_data.head()
```

> **Important Note**
>
> Replace <`aws_key_id`> and <`aws_secret`> in the preceding code block with the user credentials created in *Chapter 4, Adding Feature Store to ML Models*.

The preceding code block produces the following output:

	customerid	event_timestamp	r	m	f	segmenthighvalue	segmentlowvalue	segmentmidvalue	ltvcluster
0	12748.0	2022-03-26 23:53:55.691200	3.0	3.0	3.0	1.0	0.0	0.0	1.0
2	12839.0	2022-03-26 23:53:55.691200	3.0	1.0	2.0	0.0	0.0	1.0	2.0
4	12878.0	2022-03-26 23:53:55.691200	1.0	3.0	2.0	0.0	0.0	1.0	0.0
5	12891.0	2022-03-26 23:53:55.691200	1.0	0.0	0.0	0.0	1.0	0.0	0.0
6	12916.0	2022-03-26 23:53:55.691200	3.0	3.0	2.0	1.0	0.0	0.0	0.0

Figure 5.4 – Training dataset for Ram's model

2. The next step is similar to what Dee performed, which is to train the model and look at its classification report. Let's do that.

   The following code block trains the model on the feature set in *Figure 5.4*:

```
from sklearn.metrics import classification_
report,confusion_matrix
from sklearn.linear_model import LogisticRegression
from sklearn.model_selection import KFold, cross_val_
score, train_test_split

X = feature_data.drop(['ltvcluster', 'customerid',
                       'event_timestamp'], axis=1)
y = feature_data['ltvcluster']
X_train, X_test, y_train, y_test = \
train_test_split(X, y, test_size=0.1)
model =  (random_state=0).fit(X_train, y_train)
acc = model.score(X_test,y_test)
print(f"Model accuracy: {acc}")
```

   The preceding code block prints the model accuracy after training and scoring the model on the test set. The code is similar to what Dee was using, but instead of `XGBClassifier` uses `LogisticRegression`. The code block produces the following output:

```
Model accuracy: 0.8623188405797102
```

3. Let's print the classification report on the test dataset so that we can compare Ram and Dee's models. The following code block produces the classification report for the model:

```
y_pred = model.predict(X_test)
print(classification_report(y_test, y_pred))
```

The preceding code block produces the following output:

```
              precision    recall  f1-score   support

         0.0       0.86      1.00      0.93       119
         1.0       0.00      0.00      0.00         1
         2.0       0.00      0.00      0.00        18

    accuracy                           0.86       138
   macro avg       0.29      0.33      0.31       138
weighted avg       0.74      0.86      0.80       138
```

Figure 5.5 – Classification report of Ram's model

Ram and Dee can now compare each other's work by looking at the experiments each of them has run. Not only these two experiments but they can run multiple experiments and come up with the best model after all the comparisons. Not only that, but they can also automate the experimentation by writing code to try out all combinations of feature sets and look at and explore more data or work on some other aspect while these experiments are run.

One other thing I suggest here is to use one of the experiment tracking tools/software. There are many out there on the market. Some of them come with the notebook infrastructure that you use. For example, **Databricks** offers **MLflow**, **SageMaker** has its own, and there are also third-party experiment tracking tools such as **Neptune**, **ClearML**, and others. More tools for experiment tracking and comparison can be found in the following blog: `https://neptune.ai/blog/best-ml-experiment-tracking-tools`.

Let's assume that Dee and Ram, after all the experimentation, conclude that `XGBClassifier` performed better and decide to use that model. Let's look at model packaging in the next section.

Model packaging

In the previous section, we built two versions of the model. In this section, let's package one of the models and save it for model scoring and deployment. As mentioned in the previous section, let's package the `XGBClassifier` model. Again, for packaging, there are different solutions and tools available. To avoid setting up another tool, I will be using the `joblib` library to package the model:

1. Continuing in the same notebook that produced the `XGBClassifier` model, the following code block installs the `joblib` library:

```
#install job lib library for model packaging
!pip install joblib
```

2. After installing the `joblib` library, the next step is to package the model object using it. The following code block packages the model and writes the model to a specific location on the filesystem:

```
import joblib
joblib.dump(xgb_model, '/content/customer_segment-v0.0')
```

The preceding code block creates a file in the `/content` folder. To verify that, run an `ls` command and check whether the file exists. Let's also verify whether the model can be loaded and if we can run the `predict` function on it.

3. The following code block loads the model from the location `/content/customer_segment-v0.0` and runs predictions on a sample dataset:

```
loaded_model = joblib.load('/content/customer_
segment-v0.0')
prediction = loaded_model.predict(X_test.head())
prediction.tolist()
```

The preceding code block should run without any errors and print the following prediction output:

```
[0.0, 0.0, 0.0, 2.0, 0.0]
```

4. Now that we have the packaged model, the next step is to register it in the model repository. Again, there are a bunch of tools available to use to manage the model, such as MLflow, SageMaker, and others. I would highly recommend using one of them as they handle a lot of use cases for sharing, deployment, standard versioning, and more. For simplicity, I will use an S3 bucket as the model registry here and upload the trained model to it.

The following code uploads the packaged model into the S3 bucket:

```
import boto3
s3_client = boto3.client('s3')
s3_client.upload_file(
   '/content/customer_segment-v0.0',
   "feast-demo-mar-2022",
   "model-repo/customer_segment-v0.0")
```

The preceding code block uploads the file S3 bucket, `feast-demo-mar-2022`, into the following prefix: `model-repo/customer_segment-v0.0`. Please verify this by visiting the AWS console to make sure the model is uploaded to the specified location.

So far, we are done with model training and experimentation and have registered a candidate model in the model registry (S3 bucket). Let's create the model prediction notebook for a batch model use case in the next section.

Batch model inference with Feast

In this section, let's look at how to run prediction for batch models. To perform prediction for a batch model, we need two things: one is a model and the other is a list of customers and their feature set for prediction. In the previous section, we created and registered a model in the model registry (which is S3). Also, the required features are available in the feature store. All we need is the list of customers for whom we need to run the predictions. The list of customers can be generated from the raw dataset as we did before, during model training. However, for the purpose of this exercise, we will take a small subset of customers and run predictions on them.

Let's create a model prediction notebook and load the model that is registered in the model registry:

1. The following code block installs the required dependencies for the prediction notebook:

   ```
   !pip install feast[aws]==0.19.3 pandas xgboost joblib
   ```

2. After installing the dependencies, the other required step is to fetch the feature repository if you haven't already. This is one of the common requirements in all the notebooks that use Feast. However, the process may not be the same in other feature stores. One of the reasons for this being Feast is SDK/CLI oriented. Other feature stores, such as SageMaker and Databricks, might just need the credentials to access it. We will look at an example in a later chapter.

3. Assuming that you have cloned the Feast repository that was created in the previous chapter (which was also used during the model creation), the next step is to fetch the model from the model registry S3.

   The following code block downloads the model from the S3 location (the same location to which the model was uploaded):

```
import boto3
import os
#aws Credentials
os.environ["AWS_ACCESS_KEY_ID"] = "<aws_key_id>"
os.environ["AWS_SECRET_ACCESS_KEY"] = "<aws_secret>"
os.environ["AWS_DEFAULT_REGION"] = "us-east-1"

#Download model from s3
model_name = "customer_segment-v0.0"
s3 = boto3.client('s3')
s3.download_file("feast-demo-mar-2022",
                 f"model-repo/{model_name}",
                 model_name)
```

   After executing the preceding code block, you should see a file named `customer_segment-v0.0` in the current work directory. You can verify it using the `ls` command or through the folder explorer.

> **Important Note**
>
> Replace `<aws_key_id>` and `<aws_secret>` in the preceding code block with the user credentials created in *Chapter 4, Adding Feature Store to ML Models.*

4. The next step is to get the list of customers who need to be scored. As mentioned before, this can be fetched from the raw data source, but for the purpose of the exercise, I will be hardcoding a sample list of customers. To mimic fetching the customers from the raw data source, I will be invoking a function that returns the list of customers.

   The following code block displays the mock function to fetch customers from the raw data source:

```
def fetch_customers_from_raw_data():
    ## todo: code to fetch customers from raw data
```

```
    return ["12747.0", "12841.0", "12849.0",
            "12854.0", "12863.0"]

customer_to_be_scored=fetch_customers_from_raw_data()
```

5. Now that we have the list of customers to be scored, the next step is to fetch the features for these customers. There are different ways to do it. One way is to use the online store and the other is to use the offline store. For batch models, since latency is not a requirement, the most cost-efficient way is to use the offline store; it's just that offline stores need to be queried for the latest features. This can be done by using the `event_timestamp` column. Let's use the offline store and query the required features for the given customer list. To do that, we need the entity DataFrame. Let's create that next.
6. The following code block creates the required entity DataFrame to fetch the latest features:

```
import pandas as pd
from datetime import datetime

entity_df = pd.DataFrame(data={
    "customerid": customer_to_be_scored,
    "event_timestamp": datetime.now()
})
entity_df.head()
```

The preceding code block outputs the following entity DataFrame:

	CustomerID	event_timestamp
0	12747.0	2022-03-27 05:00:50.309139
1	12841.0	2022-03-27 05:00:50.309139
2	12849.0	2022-03-27 05:00:50.309139
3	12854.0	2022-03-27 05:00:50.309139
4	12863.0	2022-03-27 05:00:50.309139

Figure 5.6 – Entity DataFrame for prediction

To fetch the latest features for any customer, you need to set `event_timestamp` to `datetime.now()`. Let's use the entity DataFrame in *Figure 5.4* to query the offline store.

7. The following code block fetches the features for the given entity DataFrame:

```
%cd customer_segmentation

from feast import FeatureStore
store = FeatureStore(repo_path=".")
job = store.get_historical_features(
    entity_df=entity_df,
    features=[
                "customer_rfm_features:recency",
                "customer_rfm_features:monetaryvalue",
                "customer_rfm_features:r",
                "customer_rfm_features:m",
                "customer_rfm_features:rfmscore",
                "customer_rfm_features:segmenthighvalue",
                "customer_rfm_features:segmentlowvalue",
                "customer_rfm_features:segmentmidvalue"
            ]
    )
pred_feature_data = job.to_df()
pred_feature_data = pred_feature_data.dropna()
pred_feature_data.head()
```

The preceding code block produces the following output:

	customerid	event_timestamp	recency	monetaryvalue	r	m	rfmscore	segmenthighvalue	segmentlowvalue	segmentmidvalue
0	12747.0	2022-03-27 05:00:50.309139	7	1082.09	3	3	8	1	0	0
1	12863.0	2022-03-27 05:00:50.309139	7	-17.00	3	0	3	0	1	0
2	12854.0	2022-03-27 05:00:50.309139	50	401.82	1	2	5	0	0	1
3	12849.0	2022-03-27 05:00:50.309139	77	704.50	0	2	4	0	1	0
4	12841.0	2022-03-27 05:00:50.309139	31	548.34	1	2	6	0	0	1

Figure 5.7 – Features for prediction

8. Now that we have the features for prediction, the next step is to load the downloaded model and run the prediction for the customers using the features in *Figure 5.5*. The following code block does just that:

```
import joblib
## Drop unwanted columns
features = pred_feature_data.drop(
    ['customerid', 'event_timestamp'], axis=1)
loaded_model = joblib.load('/content/customer_
segment-v0.0')
prediction = loaded_model.predict(features)
```

9. The last step after running the prediction is to store the prediction results in a database or object store for later consumption. In this exercise, I will be writing the prediction results to an S3 bucket. Feel free to sink the results into other data stores.
10. The following code block saves the prediction results along with the features in an S3 location:

```
file_name = f"customer_ltv_pred_results_{datetime.now()}.
parquet"
pred_feature_data["predicted_ltvcluster"] = prediction.
tolist()
s3_url = f's3://feast-demo-mar-2022/prediction_results/
{file_name}'
pred_feature_data.to_parquet(s3_url)
```

With that last code block, we are done with the implementation of a batch model. The question in your mind will be *how has the introduction of the feature store changed the ML life cycle so far?*. The early adoption of it decoupled the steps of feature engineering, model training, and model scoring. Any of them can be run independently without having to disturb the other parts of the pipeline. That's a huge benefit. The other part is deployment. The notebook we created in step one is concrete and does a specific job such as feature engineering, model training, and model scoring.

Now, to productionize the model, all we need to do is schedule the feature engineering notebook and model scoring notebook using an orchestration framework and the model will be running at full scale. We will look at the productionization of the model in the next chapter.

In the next section, let's look at what needs to be done for the online model use case.

Online model inference with Feast

In the last section, we discussed how to use Feast in batch model inference. Now, it's time to look at the online model use case. One of the requirements of online model inference is that it should return results in low latency and also be invoked from anywhere. One of the common paradigms is to expose the model as a REST API endpoint. In the *Model packaging* section, we logged the model using the `joblib` library. That model needs to be wrapped with the RESTful framework to be deployable as a REST endpoint. Not only that but the features also need to be fetched in real time when the inference endpoint is invoked. Unlike in *Chapter 1, An Overview of the Machine Learning Life Cycle*, where we didn't have the infrastructure for serving features in real time, here, we already have that in place thanks to Feast. However, we need to run the command to sync offline features to the online store using the Feast library. Let's do that first. Later, we will look into packaging.

Syncing the latest features from the offline to the online store

To load features from the offline to the online store, we need the Feast library:

1. Let's open a notebook and install the required dependencies:

```
!pip install feast[aws]==0.19.3
```

2. After installing the required dependencies, clone the feature store repository As mentioned before, this is a requirement for all notebooks. Assuming you have cloned the repository in the current working directory, the following command will load the latest features from the offline to the online store:

```
%cd customer_segmentation/
from datetime import datetime
import os
#aws Credentials
os.environ["AWS_ACCESS_KEY_ID"] = "<aws_key_id>"
os.environ["AWS_SECRET_ACCESS_KEY"] = "<aws_secret>"
os.environ["AWS_DEFAULT_REGION"] = "us-east-1"

# Command to sync offline features into online.
!feast materialize-incremental {datetime.now().
isoformat()}
```

The preceding command outputs the progress as shown in the following screenshot:

```
/content/customer_segmentation
/usr/local/lib/python3.7/dist-packages/scipy/fft/__init__.py:97: DeprecationWarning: The module numpy.dual
  from numpy.dual import register_func
/usr/local/lib/python3.7/dist-packages/scipy/sparse/sputils.py:17: DeprecationWarning: `np.typeDict` is a
  supported_dtypes = [np.typeDict[x] for x in supported_dtypes]
/usr/local/lib/python3.7/dist-packages/feast/infra/offline_stores/redshift_source.py:55: DeprecationWarning:
  DeprecationWarning,
Materializing 1 feature views to 2022-03-27 18:09:10+00:00 into the dynamodb online store.

customer_rfm_features from 2012-03-29 18:09:12+00:00 to 2022-03-27 18:09:10+00:00:
03/27/2022 06:09:12 PM INFO:Found credentials in environment variables.
100%|████████████████████████████████████████| 1377/1377 [00:02<00:00, 603.48it/s]
/usr/local/lib/python3.7/dist-packages/feast/infra/offline_stores/redshift_source.py:55: DeprecationWarning:
  DeprecationWarning,
```

Figure 5.8 – Sync the offline to the online store

3. After loading the offline data into the online store, let's run a query on the online store and make sure that it works as expected. To query the online store, initialize the feature store object and invoke the `get_online_features` API, as shown in the following code block:

```
import pandas as pd
from feast import FeatureStore
store = FeatureStore(repo_path=".")

feature_vector = store.get_online_features(
    features=[
        "customer_rfm_features:recency",
        "customer_rfm_features:monetaryvalue",
        "customer_rfm_features:r",
        "customer_rfm_features:m",
    ],
    entity_rows=[
        {"customer": "12747.0"},
        {"customer": "12841.0"},
{"customer": "abcdef"},
    ],
).to_dict()
df = pd.DataFrame(feature_vector)
df.head()
```

The preceding code block fetches the data from the online store (**DynamoDB**) at low latency. When you run the preceding block, you will notice how quickly it responds compared to the historical store queries. The output of the code block is as shown in the following screenshot:

	customerid	monetaryvalue	r	recency	m
0	12747.0	1082.09	3.0	7.0	3.0
1	12841.0	548.34	1.0	31.0	2.0
2	abcdef	NaN	NaN	NaN	NaN

Figure 5.9 – Query the online store

In *Figure 5.7*, the last row contains `NaN` values. That is an example of how Feast would respond if any of the given entity IDs don't exist in the online store. In this example, the customer with the ID `abcdef` doesn't exist in the feature store, hence it returns `NaN` values for the corresponding row.

Now that the online store is ready with the latest features, let's look into packaging the model as a RESTful API next.

Packaging the online model as a REST endpoint with Feast code

This part is more about software engineering than data engineering or data science skills. There are many REST API frameworks for Python that are available out there, namely **Flask**, **Django**, **FastAPI**, and others, which can be used for the implementation. The implementation is straightforward. We will expose the `POST` method endpoint, which will take a list of customer IDs as input and return the prediction list:

1. The following code block shows the API contract that will be implemented:

```
POST /invocations
{
   "customer_list": ["id1", "id2", …]
}
Response: status 200
{
"predictions": [0, 1, …]
}
```

2. Now that we have the API contract, the next step is to choose the REST framework that we are going to use. There are different trade-offs in choosing one over the other among the existing REST frameworks. Since that is out of scope for this book, I will use `fastapi` (`https://fastapi.tiangolo.com/`) as it is an async framework. If you are familiar with other frameworks such as `flask` or `django`, feel free to use them. The prediction result will be the same irrespective of the framework you use. Whatever framework you choose, just remember that we will be dockerizing the REST API before deployment.

   To build the API, I will be using the PyCharm IDE. If you have another favorite IDE, feel free to use that. Also, for the development of the API and for running the API, we need the following libraries: `feast[aws]`, `uvicorn[standard]`, `fastapi`, `joblib`, and `xgboost`. You can install the libraries using the `pip install` command. I will leave it up to you since the steps to install differ based on the IDE and the platform you are using and also personal preferences. However, I will be using `virtualenv` to manage my Python environment.

   The folder structure of my project looks as shown in the following figure. If you haven't noticed already, the feature repository is also copied into the same folder as we need to initialize the feature store object and also the online store for features:

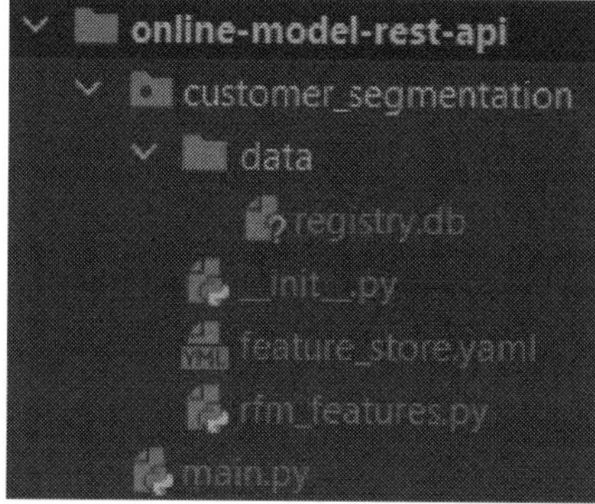

Figure 5.10 – Online model folder structure in the IDE

3. In the `main.py` file, let's define the APIs that we will be implementing. Copy the following code and paste it into the `main.py` file:

```
from fastapi import FastAPI

app = FastAPI()

@app.get("/ping")
def ping():
```

```
    return {"ping": "ok"}

@app.post("/invocations")
def inference(customers: dict):
    return customers
```

As you can see in the preceding code block, there are two APIs: `ping` and `inference`:

- `ping`: The `ping` API is a health check endpoint that will be required when deploying the application. The ping URL will be used by the infrastructure, such as ECS or Kubernetes, to check whether the application is healthy.
- `inference`: The `inference` API, on the other hand, will contain the logic for fetching the features for the given customers from the feature store, scoring against the model, and returning the results.

4. Once you've copied the preceding code and pasted it into `main.py` and saved, go to the terminal and run the following command:

```
cd <project_folder>
uvicorn main:app --reload
```

5. The preceding commands will run the FastAPI server in a local server and print output similar to the following code block:

```
$ uvicorn main:app --reload
INFO:     Will watch for changes in these directories:
['<folder path>']
INFO:     Uvicorn running on http://127.0.0.1:8000 (Press
CTRL+C to quit)
INFO:     Started reloader process [24664] using watchgod
WARNING:  The --reload flag should not be used in
production on Windows.
INFO:     Started server process [908]
INFO:     Waiting for application startup.
INFO:     Application startup complete.
```

> **Important Note**
>
> Make sure that you have activated the virtual environment in the terminal before running the command.

6. Once the application is run, visit the URL `http://127.0.0.1:8000/docs`. You should see a Swagger UI, as shown in the following screenshot:

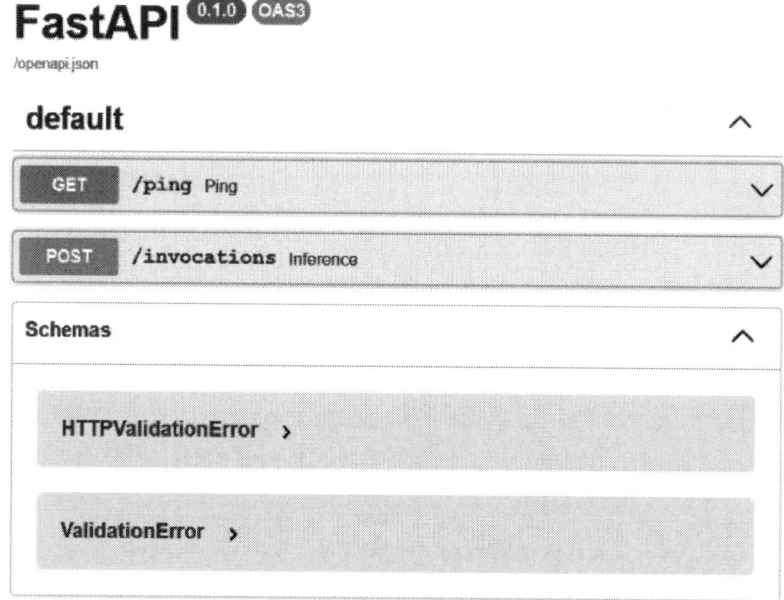

Figure 5.11 – Swagger UI for the API

We will be using the Swagger UI in *Figure 5.9* to invoke the APIs later. For now, feel free to play around, explore what is available, and invoke the APIs.

7. Now that we have the API structure set up, let's implement the `inference` API next. As mentioned, the `inference` API will read the features from the feature store and run predictions.

8. We also need to load the model from the model repository. In our case, the repository is S3. Hence, we need code to download the model from the S3 location and load the model into the memory. The following code block downloads the model from S3 and loads it into the memory. Please note that this is a one-time activity during the initial application load. Hence, let's add the following code outside the functions in the `main.py` file:

```
import boto3
Import joblib
model_name = "customer_segment-v0.0"
s3 = boto3.client('s3')
## download file from s3
s3.download_file(
    "feast-demo-mar-2022",
    f"model-repo/{model_name}",
    model_name)
## Load the model into memory.
loaded_model = joblib.load('customer_segment-v0.0')
```

9. Now that the model is loaded into the memory, the next step is to initialize the feature store object. The initialization can also be outside the method since it is a one-time activity:

```
#initialize the feature store object.
store = FeatureStore(repo_path=os.path.join(os.
getcwd(), "customer_segmentation"))
```

10. As the `customer_segmentation` feature repository is at the same level as that of `main.py` file, as shown in *Figure 5.8*, I have set `repo_path` appropriately. The remaining logic to fetch features from the online store, run prediction, and return results goes into the `inference` method definition. The following code block contains the same. Copy the method and replace it in the `main.py` file:

```
@app.post("/invocations")
def inference(customers: dict):
    ##Step1: list of features required for scoring the
model
    required_features = [
        "customer_rfm_features:recency",
        "customer_rfm_features:monetaryvalue",
```

```
        "customer_rfm_features:r",
        "customer_rfm_features:m",
        "customer_rfm_features:rfmscore",
        "customer_rfm_features:segmenthighvalue",
        "customer_rfm_features:segmentlowvalue",
        "customer_rfm_features:segmentmidvalue"
    ]
    ##step 2: get entity rows from the input
    entity_rows = [{"customer": cust_id} for cust_
id in customers["customer_list"]]
    ##Step 3: query online store
    feature_vector = store.get_online_features(
        features=required_features,
        entity_rows=entity_rows,
    ).to_dict()
    ##Step 4: convert features to dataframe and reorder
the feature columns in the same order that model expects.
    features_in_order = ['recency', 'monetaryvalue',
                         'r', 'm', 'rfmscore',
                         'segmenthighvalue',
                         'segmentlowvalue',
                         'segmentmidvalue']
    df = pd.DataFrame(feature_vector)
    features = df.drop(['customerid'], axis=1)
    features = features.dropna()
    features = features[features_in_order]
    ##Step 5: run prediction and return the list
    prediction = loaded_model.predict(features)
    return {"predictions": prediction.tolist()}
```

11. Now that the prediction logic is complete, let's run the application and try running the prediction. To run the application, the command is the same as the one used before:

```
export AWS_ACCESS_KEY_ID=<aws_key_id>
export AWS_SECRET_ACCESS_KEY=<aws_secret>
export AWS_DEFAULT_REGION=us-east-1
cd <project_folder>
uvicorn main:app --reload
```

> **Important Note**
>
> Replace `<aws_key_id>` and `<aws_secret>` in the preceding code block with the user credentials created in *Chapter 4, Adding Feature Store to ML Models*.

12. Once the application loads successfully, visit the Swagger UI URL (`http://localhost:8000/docs`). In the Swagger UI, expand the `invocations` API and click on **Try out**. You should see a screen similar to the one in *Figure 5.12*.

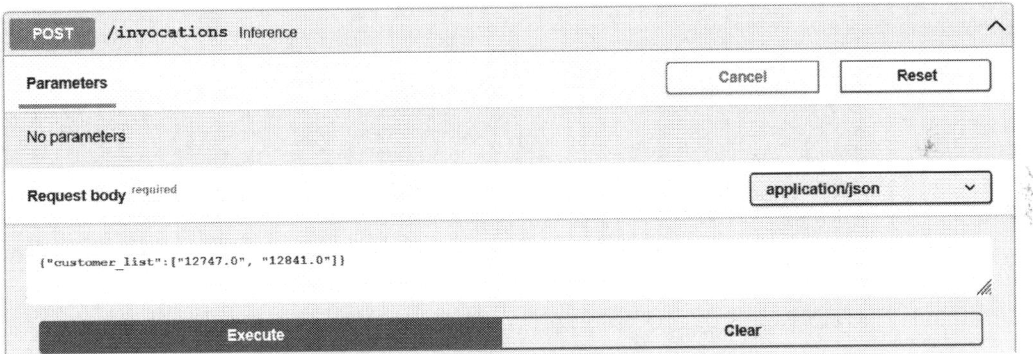

Figure 5.12 – Swagger UI invocation API

13. In the request body, provide the input as shown in *Figure 5.12* (the one in the following code block):

```
{"customer_list":["12747.0", "12841.0"]}
```

14. With this input, submit a request by clicking on **Execute**. The API should respond within milliseconds and the output will be visible when you scroll down on the screen. The following figure shows an example output:

Responses

Curl

```
curl -X 'POST' \
  'http://localhost:8000/invocations' \
  -H 'accept: application/json' \
  -H 'Content-Type: application/json' \
  -d '{"customer_list":["12747.0", "12841.0"]}'
```

Request URL

```
http://localhost:8000/invocations
```

Server response

Code Details

200

Response body

```
{
  "predictions": [
    0,
    0
  ]
}
```

Download

Response headers

```
content-length: 25
content-type: application/json
date: Sun,27 Mar 2022 23:28:41 GMT
server: uvicorn
```

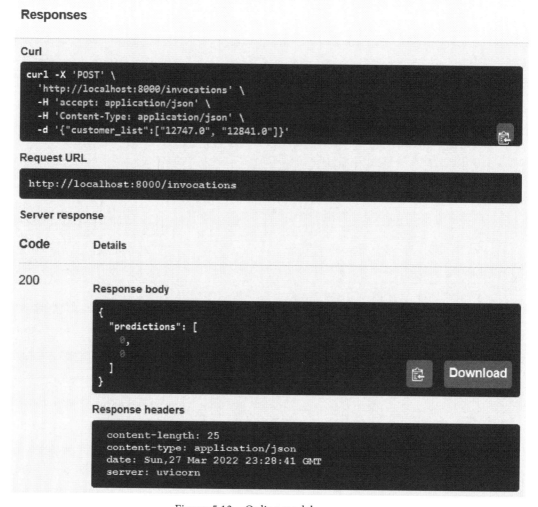

Figure: 5.13 – Online model response

That completes the steps of building a REST API for an online model with code to fetch features from Feast. Now that we have both the online and the batch model, in the next chapter, we will look at how to productionize these and how the transition from development to production is simple as we adopted the feature store and MLOps early.

One thing that we are yet to look into is how to change/update or add additional features. Let's look at this briefly before we move on.

Handling changes to the feature set during development

Model development is an evolving process. So are models – they evolve over time. Today, we may be using a few features for a specific model, but as and when we discover and try out new features, if the performance is better than the current model, we might end up including the new features in the model training and scoring. Hence, the feature set may change over time. What that means with the feature store is some of the steps we performed in *Chapter 4, Adding Feature Store to ML Models*, might need to be revisited. Let's look at what those steps are.

> **Important Note**
> The assumption here is feature definitions change during model development, not after production. We will look at how to handle changes to the feature set after the model goes into production in later chapters.

Step 1 – Change feature definitions

If the features or entities change during the model development, the first step is to update the feature definitions in the feature repository If you recall correctly, when the features were finalized, the first thing that we did was to create feature definitions. In the feature repository, the file `rfm_features.py` contains the definitions. After making the changes, run the `feast apply` command to update the feature definition in the resource. If you create or delete new entities or views, the corresponding online store resources (DynamoDB tables) will be created or deleted. You can verify that in the console. If there are minor changes such as changing the data type or feature name, the changes will be saved in the feature repository registry.

Step 2 – Add/update schema in the Glue/Lake Formation console

The second step is to define new tables in the Glue/Lake Formation database that we created. If the old tables are not required, you can delete them to avoid any confusion later. In case of the schema changes (if the feature name or data type changes), you need to update the existing schema to reflect the changes. If the schema is not updated with the changes, there will be errors when you query the historical store or try to load the latest feature from an offline to an online store. One other thing to note here is, when defining the schema, we set an S3 location for the feature views. Now that this location contains the old data, which works only with the old schema, you need to define a new path to which the data that adheres to the new schema will be written.

An alternate approach would be to define a brand new table with the new schema definitions and new S3 path for data and also update the Redshift source definitions in the feature repository with the new table name. If you do that, you can query the data in both old and new definitions. However, keep in mind that you may be managing two versions of the feature set, one with the older schema and one with the new schema. Also, there will be two DynamoDB tables.

Step 3 – Update notebooks with the changes

The last step is simple, which is to go update all the affected notebooks. In the feature engineering notebook, the update would be to write data into the new location, whereas in the model training and scoring notebook, it would be to update the feature name or fetch additional features during training and scoring respectively.

These are the three steps you need to perform every time there are updates to the feature definitions. With that, let's summarize what we learned in this chapter, and in the next chapter, we will look at how to productionize the online and batch models that we built in the chapter and what the challenges are beyond production.

Summary

In this chapter, our aim was to look at how model training and scoring change with the feature store. To go through the training and scoring stages of the ML life cycle, we used the resources that were created in the last chapter. In the model training phase, we looked at how data engineers and data scientists can collaborate and work towards building a better model. In model prediction, we discussed batch model scoring and how using an offline store is a cost-effective way of running a batch model. We also built a REST wrapper for the online model and added Feast code to fetch the features for prediction during runtime. At the end of the chapter, we looked at the required changes if there are updates to features during development.

In the next chapter, we will continue using the batch model and the online model that we built in this chapter, productionize them and look at what the challenges are once the models are in production.

Further reading

You can find more information on Feast in the following references:

- Feast: `https://docs.feast.dev/`
- Feast AWS credit scoring tutorial: `https://github.com/feast-dev/feast-aws-credit-scoring-tutorial`

6 Model to Production and Beyond

In the last chapter, we discussed model training and prediction for online and batch models with **Feast**. For the exercise, we used the Feast infrastructure that was deployed to the AWS cloud during the exercises in *Chapter 4, Adding Feature Stores to ML Models*. During these exercises, we looked at how Feast decouples feature engineering from model training and model prediction. We also learned how to use offline and online stores during batch and online prediction.

In this chapter, we will reuse the feature engineering pipeline and the model built in *Chapter 4, Adding Feature Stores to ML Models*, and *Chapter 5, Model Training and Inference*, to productionize the **machine learning** (**ML**) pipeline. The goal of this chapter is to reuse everything that we have built in the previous chapters, such as Feast infrastructure on AWS, feature engineering, model training, and model-scoring notebooks, to productionize the ML model. As we go through the exercises, it will give us an opportunity to look at how early adoption of Feast not only decoupled the ML pipeline stages but also accelerated the production readiness of the ML model. Once we productionize the batch and online ML pipelines, we will look at how the adoption of Feast opens up opportunities for other aspects of the ML life cycle, such as feature monitoring, automated model retraining, and also how it can accelerate the development of a future ML model. This chapter will help you understand how to productionize the batch and online models that use Feast, and how to use Feast for feature drift monitoring and model retraining.

We will discuss the following topics in order:

- Setting up Airflow for orchestration
- Productionizing a batch model pipeline
- Productionizing an online model pipeline
- Beyond model production

Technical requirements

To follow the code examples in the chapter, the resources created in *Chapter 4, Adding Feature Store to ML Models*, and *Chapter 5, Model Training and Inference*, are required. You will need familiarity with Docker and any notebook environment, which could be a local setup, such as Jupyter, or an online notebook environment, such as Google Colab, Kaggle, or SageMaker. You will also need an AWS account with full access to some of the resources, such as Redshift, S3, Glue, DynamoDB, and the IAM console. You can create a new account and use all the services for free during the trial period. You can find the code examples of the book and feature repository in the following GitHub links:

- `https://github.com/PacktPublishing/Feature-Store-for-Machine-Learning/tree/main/Chapter06`
- `https://github.com/PacktPublishing/Feature-Store-for-Machine-Learning/tree/main/customer_segmentation`

Setting up Airflow for orchestration

To productionize the online and batch model, we need a workflow orchestration tool that can run the ML pipelines for us on schedule. There are a bunch of tools available, such as Apache Airflow, AWS Step Functions, and SageMaker Pipelines. You can also run it as GitHub workflows if you prefer. Depending on the tools you are familiar with or offered at your organization, orchestration may differ. For this exercise, we will use Amazon **Managed Workflows for Apache Airflow** (**MWAA**). As the name suggests, it is an Apache Airflow-managed service by AWS. Let's create an Amazon MWAA environment in AWS.

> **Important Note**
>
> Amazon MWAA doesn't have a free trial. You can view the pricing for the usage at this URL: `https://aws.amazon.com/managed-workflows-for-apache-airflow/pricing/`. Alternatively, you can choose to run Airflow locally or on EC2 instances (EC2 has free tier resources). You can find the setup instructions to run Airflow locally or on EC2 here:
>
> Airflow local setup: `https://towardsdatascience.com/getting-started-with-airflow-locally-and-remotely-d068df7fcb4`
>
> Airflow on EC2: `https://christo-lagali.medium.com/getting-airflow-up-and-running-on-an-ec2-instance-ae4f3a69441`

S3 bucket for Airflow metadata

Before we create an environment, we need an S3 bucket to store the Airflow dependencies, **Directed Acyclic Graphs** (**DAGs**), and so on. To create an S3 bucket first, please follow the instructions in the *Amazon S3 for storing data* subsection of *Chapter 4, Adding Feature Store to ML Models*. Alternatively, you can also choose to use an existing bucket. We will be creating a new bucket with the name `airflow-for-ml-mar-2022`. In the S3 bucket, create a folder named `dags`. We will be using this folder to store all the Airflow DAGs.

The Amazon MWAA provides multiple different ways to configure additional plugins and Python dependencies to be installed in the Airflow environment. Since we need to install a few Python dependencies to run our project, we need to tell Airflow to install these required dependencies. One way of doing it is by using the `requirements.txt` file. The following code block shows the contents of the file:

```
papermill==2.3.4
boto3==1.21.41
ipython==8.2.0
ipykernel==6.13.0
apache-airflow-providers-papermill==2.2.3
```

Save the contents of the preceding code block in a `requirements.txt` file. We will be using `papermill` (`https://papermill.readthedocs.io/en/latest/`) to run the Python notebooks. You can also extract code and run the Python script using the `bash` or `python` operator available in Airflow.

> **Important Note**
>
> If you are running Airflow locally, make sure that the library versions are compatible with the Airflow version. The Amazon MWAA Airflow version at the time of writing is 2.2.2.

Once you have the `requirement.txt` file created, upload it into the S3 bucket we have created. We will be using it in the next section during the environment creation.

Amazon MWAA environment for orchestration

Now that we have the required resources for creating the Amazon MWAA environment, let's follow the following steps to create the environment:

1. To create a new environment, log in to your AWS account and navigate to the Amazon MWAA console using the search bar in the AWS console. Alternatively, visit `https://us-east-1.console.aws.amazon.com/mwaa/home?region=us-east-1#environments`. The following web page will be displayed:

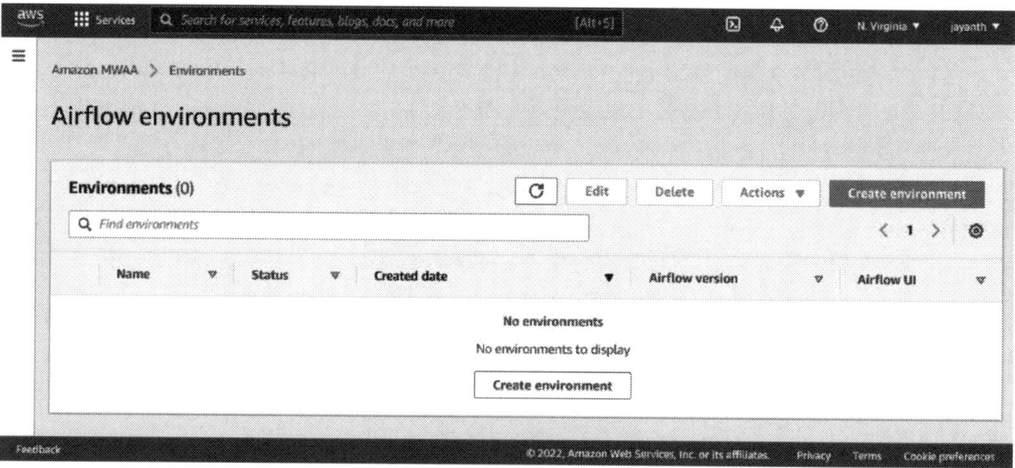

Figure 6.1 – The Amazon MWAA environments console

2. On the page displayed in *Figure 6.1*, click on the **Create environment** button, and the following page will be displayed:

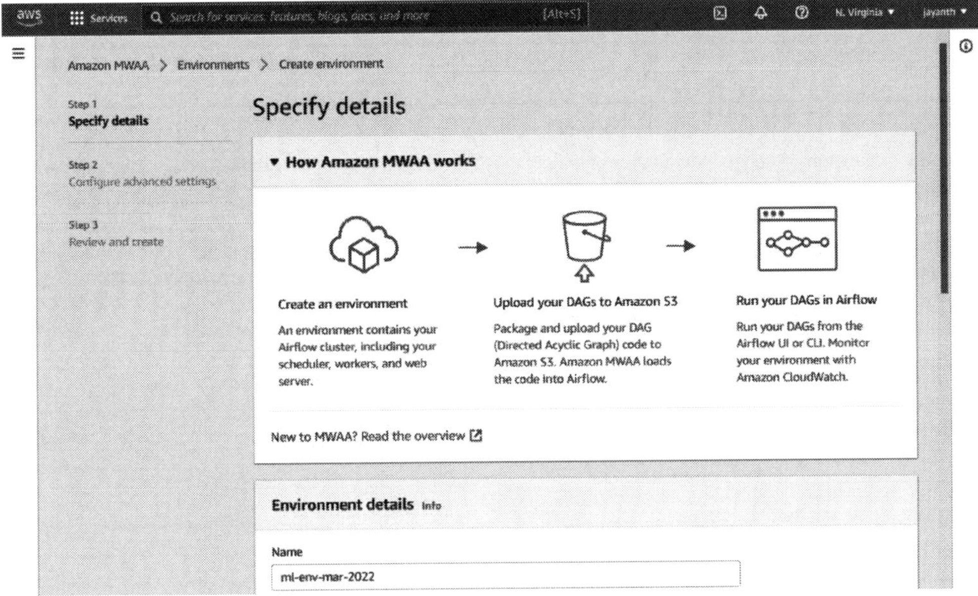

Figure 6.2 – Amazon MWAA environment details

3. Provide a name for the Amazon MWAA environment on the page displayed in *Figure 6.2*. Scroll down to the **DAG code in Amazon S3** section; you should see the following parameters on the screen:

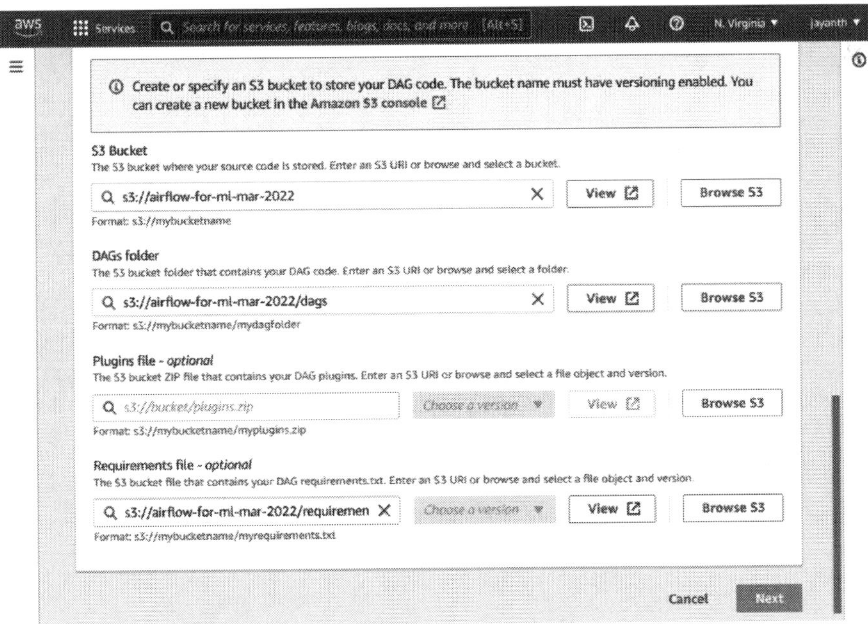

Figure 6.3 – Amazon MWAA – the DAG code in S3 section

4. On the screen displayed in *Figure 6.3*, enter the S3 bucket in the textbox or use the **Browse S3** button. Here, we will use the S3 bucket that we created earlier in the section. Once you select the S3 bucket, the other fields will appear. For **DAGs folder**, select the folder that we created earlier in the S3 bucket. Also, for the **Requirements file - optional** field, browse for the `requirements.txt` file that we uploaded or enter the path to the file. As we don't need any plugins to run the project, we can leave the optional **Plugins file** field blank. Click on the **Next** button:

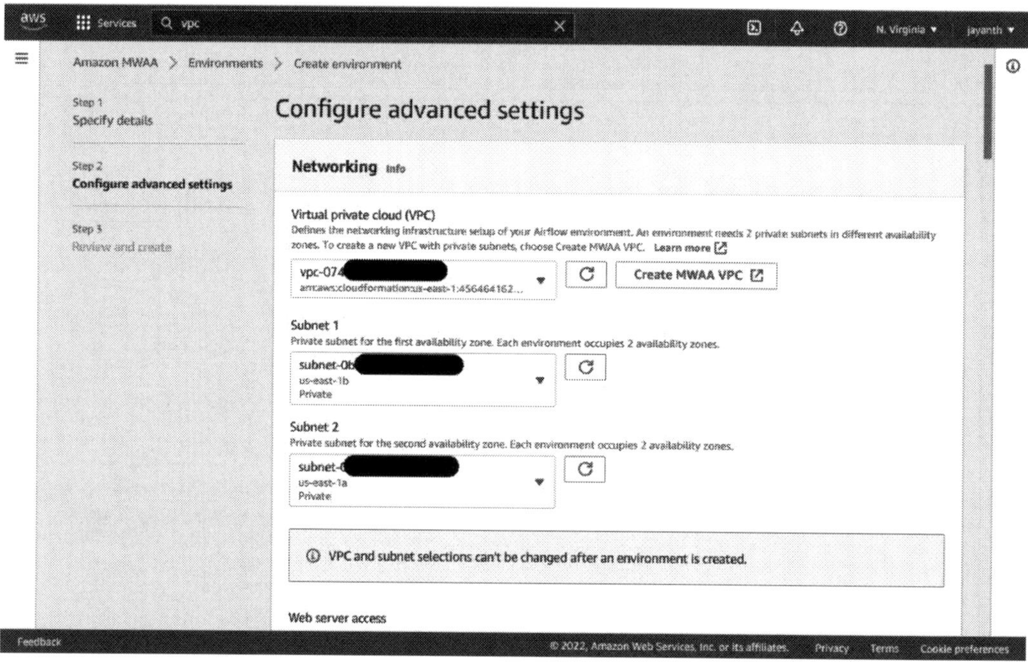

Figure 6.4 – Amazon MWAA advanced settings

5. The next page displayed is shown in *Figure 6.4*. For **Virtual private cloud (VPC)**, select the available default VPC from the dropdown. One caveat here is that the selected VPC should have at least two private subnets. If it doesn't have the private subnets, when you try to select **Subnet 1** and **Subnet 2**, you will notice that all the options are grayed out. If you run into this scenario, click on **Create MWAA VPC**. It will take you to the CloudFormation console; once you have filled in the form with all the parameters, follow through and click on **Create stack**. It will create a VPC that can be used by Amazon MWAA. Once the VPC is created, come back to this window and select the new VPC and subnets, and continue.

6. After selecting the VPC, for **Web server access**, select **Public network**; leave everything else to default, and scroll all the way down. In the **Permissions** section, you will notice that it says it will create a new role for Amazon MWAA. Make a note of the role name. We will have to add permissions to this role later. After that, click on **Next**.
7. On the next page, review all the input provided, scroll all the way down, and click on **Create environment**. It will take a few minutes to create the environment.
8. Once the environment is created, you should be able to see the environment in the **Available** state on the Amazon MWAA environments page. Pick the environment that we just created and click on the **Open Airflow UI** link. An Airflow home page will be displayed, similar to the one in the following figure:

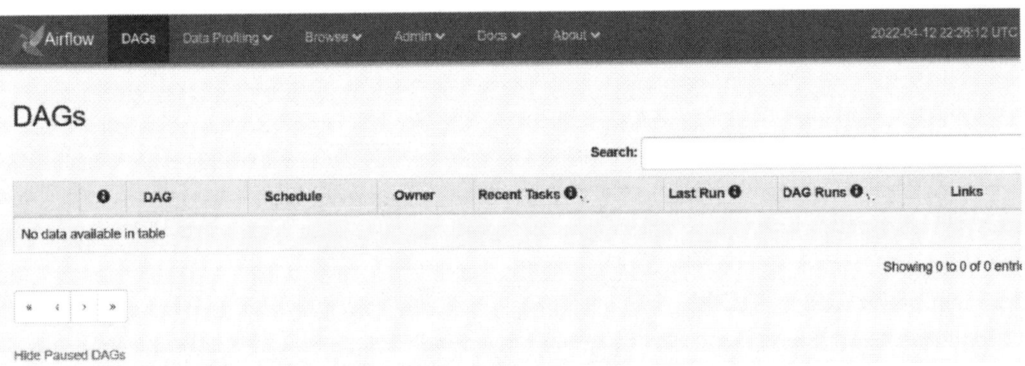

Figure 6.5 – The Airflow UI

9. To test whether everything is working fine, let's quickly create a simple DAG and look at how it works. The following code block creates a simple DAG with a dummy operator and a Python operator:

```
from datetime import datetime
from airflow import DAG
from airflow.operators.dummy_operator import
DummyOperator
from airflow.operators.python_operator import
PythonOperator

def print_hello():
    return 'Hello world from first Airflow DAG!'
dag = DAG('hello_world',
          description='Hello World DAG',
          schedule_interval='@daily',
```

```
            start_date=datetime(2017, 3, 20),
            catchup=False)

    start = DummyOperator(task_id="start", dag=dag)

    hello_operator = PythonOperator(
        task_id='hello_task',
        python_callable=print_hello,
        dag=dag)

    start >> hello_operator
```

10. The DAG defined in the preceding code is pretty simple; it has two tasks – `start` and `hello_operator`. The `start` task is a `DummyOperator`, does nothing, and is used for making the DAG look pretty on the UI. The `hello_operator` task just invokes a function that returns a message. In the last line, we define a dependency between the operators.
11. Copy the preceding code block, save the file as `example_dag.py`, and upload it to the `dags` folder in S3 that we created earlier. (My S3 location is `s3://airflow-for-ml-mar-2022/dags`.) Once you upload it, it should appear in the Airflow UI within seconds. The following figure displays the Airflow UI with the DAG:

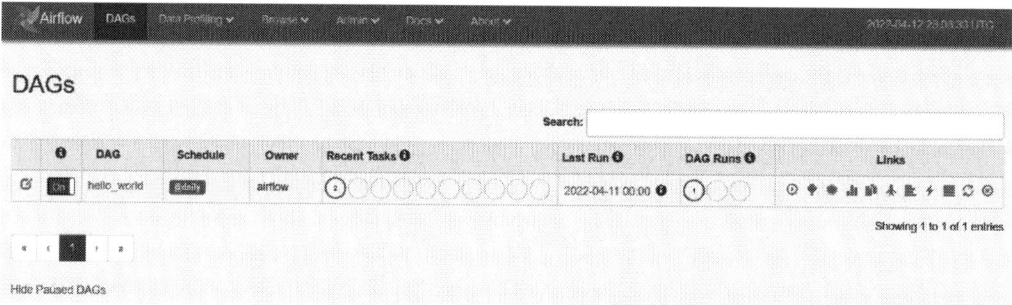

Figure 6.6 – The Airflow UI with the example DAG

12. By default, the DAGs are disabled; hence, when you visit the page, you may not see the exact page such as the one displayed in *Figure 6.6*. Enable the DAG by clicking on the toggle button in the left-most column. Once enabled, DAG will run for the first time and update the run results. You can also trigger the DAG using the icon in the **Links** column. Click on the **hello_world** hyperlink in the DAG column in the UI. You will see the details page of the DAG with different tabs. Feel free to play around and look at the different options available on the details page.

13. The following figure displays the graph view of the DAG:

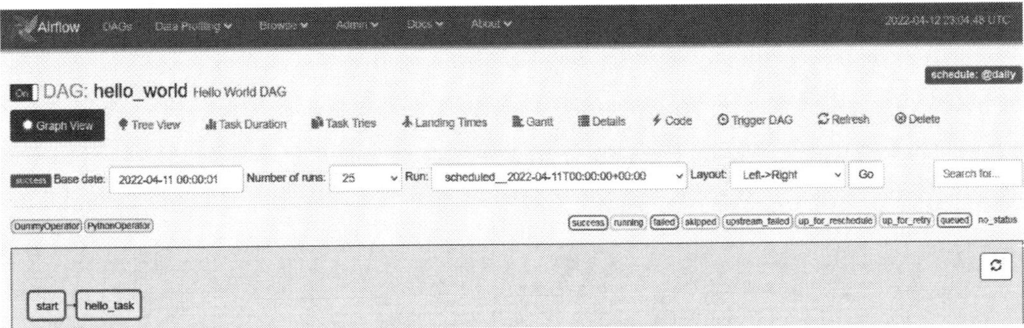

Figure 6.7 – The graph view of the DAG

14. Now that we have verified that Airflow is set up correctly, let's add the required permissions for Airflow to run the ML pipeline.
15. If you recall, during the last step of environment creation (the paragraph following *Figure 6.4*), we made note of the role name the Airflow environment is using to run the DAGs. Now, we need to add permissions to the role. To do so, navigate to the AWS IAM roles console page using the search function or visit `https://us-east-1.console.aws.amazon.com/iamv2/home?region=us-east-1#/roles`. In the console, you should see the IAM role that is associated with the Airflow environment. Select the IAM role; you should see the following page:

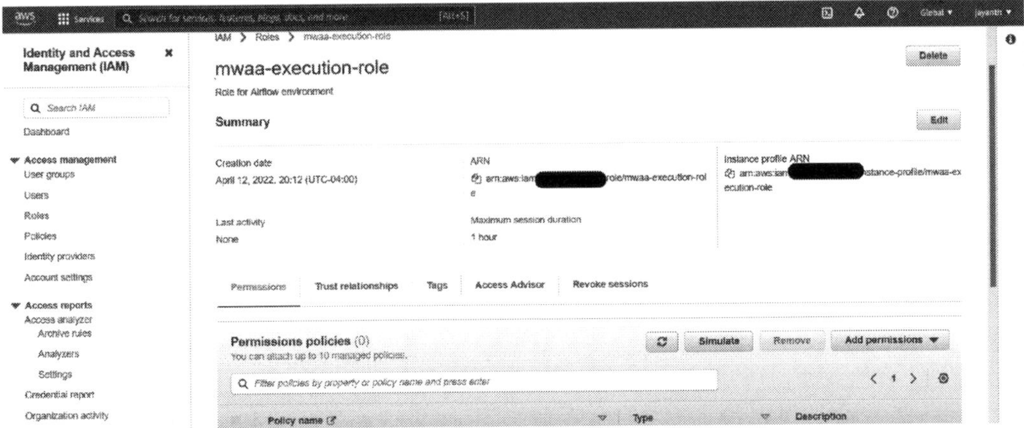

Figure 6.8 – The Amazon MWAA IAM role

> **Important Note**
>
> If you didn't make a note, you can find the role name in the environment details page on the AWS console.

16. In *Figure 6.8*, click on **Add permissions**; from the dropdown, select **Attach policies**, and you will be taken to the following page:

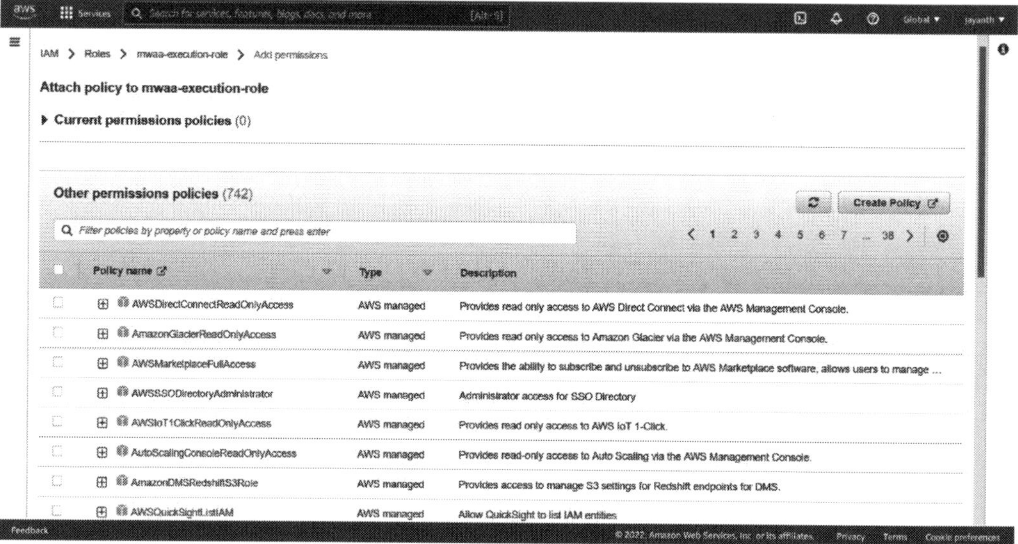

Figure 6.9 – IAM – Attach policies

17. On the web page, search and select the following policies – **AmazonS3FullAccess**, **AWSGlueConsoleFullAccess**, **AmazonRedshiftFullAccess**, and **AmazonDynamoDBFullAccess**. Once the policies are selected, scroll down and click on **Attach policies** to save the role with the new policies.

> **Important Note**
>
> It is never a good idea to assign full access to any of the resources without restrictions. When you run an enterprise application, it is recommended to restrict access based on the resources, such as read-only access to a specific S3 bucket and DynamoDB tables.
>
> If you are running Airflow locally, you can use the IAM user credential in the notebook.

Now that our orchestration system is ready, let's look at how to use it to productionize the ML pipeline.

Productionizing the batch model pipeline

In *Chapter 4, Adding Feature Store to ML Models*, for model training, we used the features ingested by the feature engineering notebook. We also created a model-scoring notebook that fetches features for a set of customers from Feast and runs predictions for it using the trained model. For the sake of the experiment, let's assume that the raw data freshness latency is a day. That means the features need to be regenerated once a day, and the model needs to score customers against those features once a day and store the results in an S3 bucket for consumption. To achieve this, thanks to our early organization and decoupling of stages, all we need to do is run the feature engineering and model scoring notebook/Python script once a day consecutively. Now that we also have a tool to perform this, let's go ahead and schedule this workflow in the Airflow environment.

The following figure displays how we will be operationalizing the batch model:

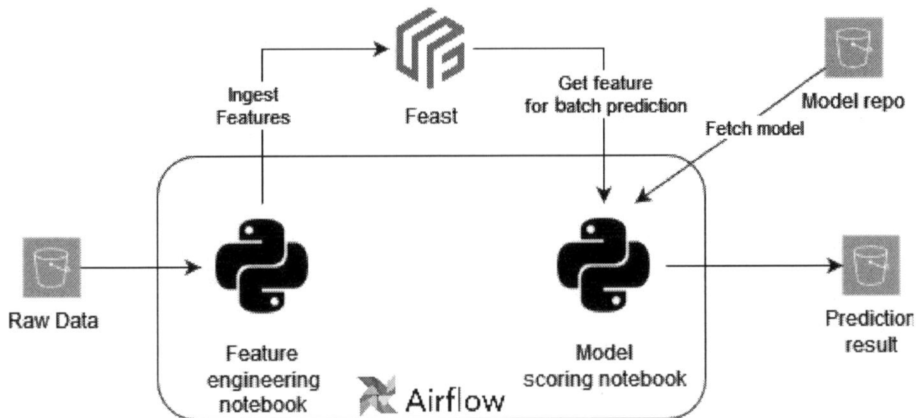

Figure 6.10 – Operationalization of the batch model

As you can see in the figure, to operationalize the workflow, we will use Airflow to orchestrate the feature-engineering and model-scoring notebooks. The raw data source for feature engineering, in our case, is the S3 bucket where `online-retail.csv` is stored. As we have already designed our scoring notebook to load the production model from the model repo (in our case, an S3 bucket) and store the prediction results in a S3 bucket, we will reuse the same notebook. One thing you might notice here is that we are not using the model-training notebook for every run; the reason is obvious – we want to run predictions against a version of the model that has been validated, tested, and also met our performance criteria on the test data.

Before scheduling this workflow, I have done minor changes to the feature-engineering notebook and model-prediction notebooks. The final notebooks can be found at the following GitHub URL: `https://github.com/PacktPublishing/Feature-Store-for-Machine-Learning/blob/main/Chapter06/notebooks/` (`ch6_feature_engineering.ipynb`, `ch6_model_prediction.ipynb`). To schedule the workflow, download the final notebooks from GitHub and upload them to an S3 bucket that we created earlier, as an Airflow environment will need to access these notebooks during runs. I will upload it to the following location: `s3://airflow-for-ml-mar-2022/notebooks/`.

> **Important Note**
>
> AWS secret access key and an S3 path – I have commented out AWS credentials in both the notebooks, as we are adding permissions to an Amazon MWAA IAM role. If you are running it in local Airflow, please uncomment and add secrets. Also, update the S3 URLs wherever necessary, as the S3 URLs point to the private buckets that I have created during the exercises.
>
> Feature repo – As we have seen before, we must clone the feature repo so that the Feast library can read the metadata. You can follow the same `git clone` (provided that `git` is installed) approach or set up a GitHub workflow to push the repo to S3 and download the same in the notebook. I have left both code blocks in the notebook with comments. You can use whichever is convenient.
>
> S3 approach – To use an S3 download approach, clone the repo in your local system and run the following commands in the Linux terminal to upload it to a specific S3 location:
>
> ```
> export AWS_ACCESS_KEY_ID=<aws_key>
> export AWS_SECRET_ACCESS_KEY=<aws_secret>
> AWS_DEFAULT_REGION=us-east-1
> aws s3 cp customer_segmentation s3://<s3_bucket>/customer_segmentation --recursive
> ```
>
> On successful upload, you should be able to see the folder contents in the S3 bucket.

Now that the notebooks are ready, let's write the Airflow DAG for the batch model pipeline. The DAG will have the following tasks in order – `start` (`dummy operator`), `feature_engineering` (`Papermill operator`), `model_prediction` (`Papermill operator`), and `end` (`dummy operator`).

The following code block contains the first part of the Airflow DAG:

```
from datetime import datetime
from airflow import DAG
from airflow.operators.dummy_operator import DummyOperator
from airflow.providers.papermill.operators.papermill import
PapermillOperator
import uuid
dag = DAG('customer_segmentation_batch_model',
          description='Batch model pipeline',
          schedule_interval='@daily',
          start_date=datetime(2017, 3, 20), catchup=False)
```

In the preceding code block, we have defined the imports and DAG parameters such as `name`, `schedule_interval`, and `start_date`. The `schedule_interval='@daily'` schedule says that the DAG should run daily.

The following code block defines the rest of the DAG (the second part), which contains all the tasks and the dependencies among them:

```
start = DummyOperator(task_id="start", dag=dag)
run_id = str(uuid.uuid1())
feature_eng = PapermillOperator(
    task_id="feature_engineering",
    input_nb="s3://airflow-for-ml-mar-2022/notebooks/ch6_
feature_engineering.ipynb",
    output_nb=f"s3://airflow-for-ml-mar-2022/notebooks/runs/
ch6_feature_engineering_{ run_id }.ipynb",
    dag=dag,
    trigger_rule="all_success"
)
model_prediction = PapermillOperator(
    task_id="model_prediction",
    input_nb="s3://airflow-for-ml-mar-2022/notebooks/ch6_model_
prediction.ipynb",
```

```
    output_nb=f"s3://airflow-for-ml-mar-2022/notebooks/runs/
ch6_model_prediction_{run_id}.ipynb",
    dag=dag,
    trigger_rule="all_success"
)
end = DummyOperator(task_id="end", dag=dag,
                        trigger_rule="all_success")

start >> feature_eng >> model_prediction >> end
```

As you can see in the code block, there are four steps that will execute one after the other. The `feature_engineering` and `model_prediction` steps are run using `PapermillOperator`. This takes the path to the S3 notebook as input. I have also set an output path to another S3 location so that we can check the output notebook of each run. The last line defines the dependency between the tasks. Save the preceding two code blocks (the first and second parts) as a Python file and call it `batch-model-pipeline-dag.py`. After saving the file, navigate to the S3 console to upload the file into the `dags` folder that we pointed our Airflow environment to in *Figure 6.3*. The uploaded file is processed by the Airflow scheduler. When you navigate to the Airflow UI, you should see the new DAG called **customer_segmentation_batch_model** on the screen.

The following figure displays the Airflow UI with the DAG:

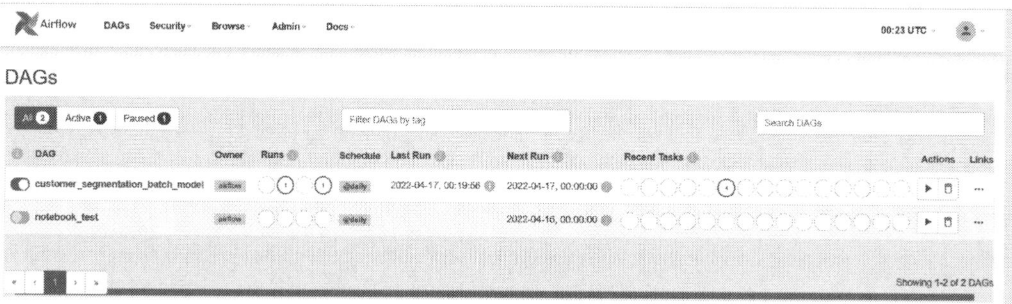

Figure 6.11 – The batch model DAG on Airflow

As we have not enabled the DAG by default option during the Airflow environment creation (which can be set in Airflow configuration variables in Amazon MWAA), when the DAG appears on the UI for the first time, it will be disabled. Click on the toggle button on the left-most column to enable it. Once enabled, the DAG will run for the first time. Click on the **customer_segmentation_batch_model** hyperlink to navigate to the details page, and feel free to look around to see the different visualization and properties of the DAG. If you navigate to the **Graph** tab, the DAG will be displayed, as shown in the following screenshot:

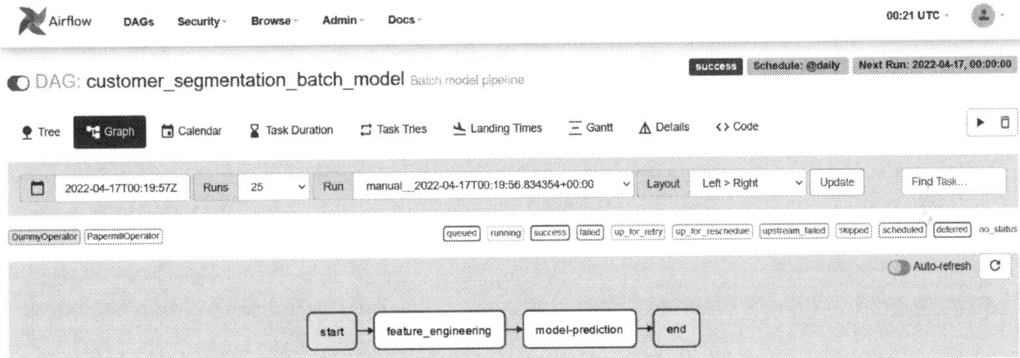

Figure 6.12 – The batch model DAG graph view

In *Figure 6.12*, you can see the graph view of the DAG. If there were any failures in the last run, they will appear in red outline. You can also view the logs of successful execution or failures for each of the tasks. As all the tasks are green, this means everything went well. You can also see the results of the last few runs in *Figure 6.11*. Airflow also provides you with the history of all the runs.

Now that the task run is complete, we can go and check the output notebook, the S3 bucket for the new set of features, or the S3 bucket for the new set of predictions. All three should be available after successful runs. Here, we will be verifying just the prediction results folder, but feel free to verify the others as well.

> **Important Note**
>
> In case of any failures, verify the logs for the failed tasks (click on the failed task in graph view to see available information). Check the permissions for Amazon MWAA, the S3 paths for input/output, and also whether all the requirements are installed in the Amazon MWAA environment.

The following screenshot shows the new prediction results in an S3 bucket:

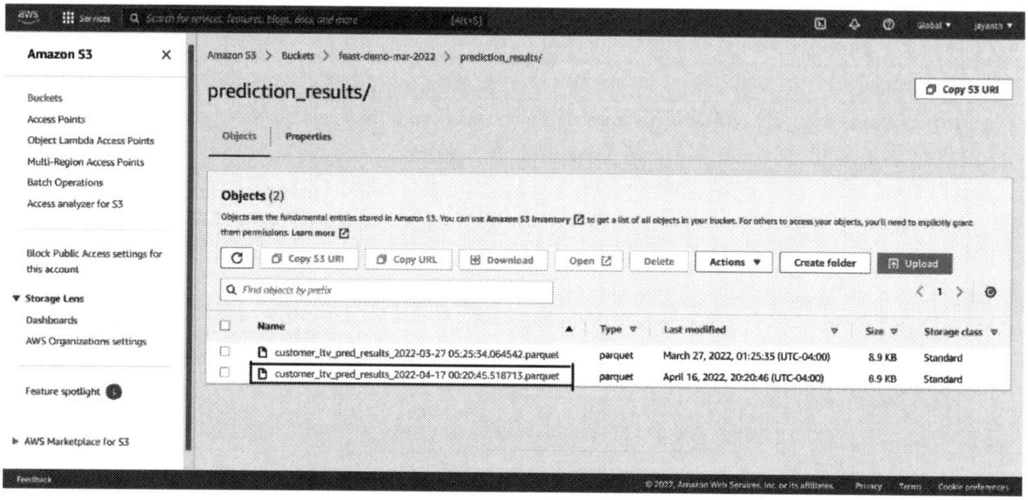

Figure 6.13 – The prediction results in an S3 bucket

In addition, you can also do all kinds of fancy things with Airflow, such as sending email notifications for failure, Slack notifications for daily runs, and integration with PagerDuty. Feel free to explore the options. Here is a list of supported providers in Airflow: `https://airflow.apache.org/docs/apache-airflow-providers/packages-ref.html`.

Now that our batch model is running in production, let's look at how to productionize the online model with Feast.

Productionizing an online model pipeline

In the previous chapter, for the online model, we built REST endpoints to serve on-demand predictions for customer segmentation. Though the online model is hosted as a REST endpoint, it needs a supporting infrastructure for the following functions:

- To serve features in real time (we have Feast for that)
- To keep features up to date (we will use the feature-engineering notebook with Airflow orchestration for this)

In this chapter, we will continue from where we left off and use the feature-engineering notebook built in *Chapter 4, Adding Feature Store to ML Models*, in combination with a notebook to synchronize offline data to an online store in Feast.

The following figure shows the operationalization of the online model pipeline:

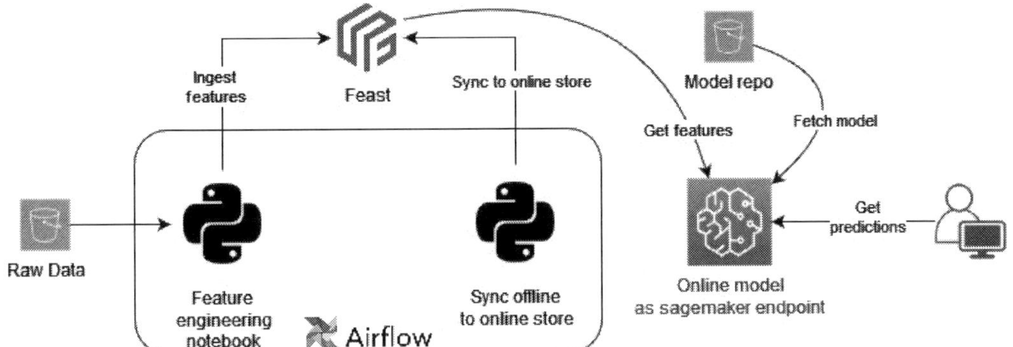

Figure 6.14 – The operationalization of the online model

As you can see in *Figure 6.14*, we will use Airflow for the orchestration of feature engineering; data freshness is still one day here, and scheduling can be done for a shorter duration. Feast can also support streaming data if there is a need. The following URL has an example you can use: `https://docs.Feast.dev/reference/data-sources/push`. The REST endpoints developed in *Chapter 5, Model Training and Inference*, will be Dockerized and deployed as a SageMaker endpoint.

> **Important Note**
>
> Once Dockerized, the Docker image can be used to deploy into any containerized environment, such as Elastic Container Service, Elastic BeanStalk, and Kubernetes. We are using SageMaker, as it takes less time to set up and also has advantages such as data capture and IAM authentication that come out of the box.

Orchestration of a feature engineering job

As we already have two notebooks (feature engineering and sync offline to online store) and we are familiar with Airflow, let's schedule the feature engineering workflow first. Again, in the notebook, I have done some minor changes. Please verify the changes before using it. You can find the notebooks (`ch6_feature_engineering.ipynb` and `ch6_sync_offline_online.ipynb`) here: `https://github.com/PacktPublishing/Feature-Store-for-Machine-Learning/tree/main/Chapter06/notebooks`. Just the way we did it for the batch model, download the notebooks and upload them to a specific S3 location. I will be uploading them to the same location as before: `s3://airflow-for-ml-mar-2022/notebooks/`.

Now that the notebooks are ready, let's write the Airflow DAG for the online model pipeline. The DAG will have the following steps in order – `start` (`dummy operator`), `feature_engineering` (`Papermill operator`), `sync_offline_to_online` (`Papermill operator`), and `end` (`dummy operator`).

The following code block contains the first part of the Airflow DAG:

```
from datetime import datetime
from airflow import DAG
from airflow.operators.dummy_operator import DummyOperator
from airflow.providers.papermill.operators.papermill import
PapermillOperator
dag = DAG('customer_segmentation_online_model',
          description='Online model pipeline',
          schedule_interval='@daily',
          start_date=datetime(2017, 3, 20), catchup=False)
```

Just like in the case of the batch model pipeline DAG, this contains the DAG parameters.

The following code block defines the rest of the DAG (the second part), which contains all the tasks and the dependencies among them:

```
start = DummyOperator(task_id="start")
run_time = datetime.now()
feature_eng = PapermillOperator(
    task_id="feature_engineering",
    input_nb="s3://airflow-for-ml-mar-2022/notebooks/ch6_
feature_engineering.ipynb",
    output_nb=f"s3://airflow-for-ml-mar-2022/notebooks/runs/
ch6_feature_engineering_{run_time}.ipynb",
    trigger_rule="all_success",
```

```
    dag=dag
)
sync_offline_to_online = PapermillOperator(
    task_id="sync_offline_to_online",
    input_nb="s3://airflow-for-ml-mar-2022/notebooks/ch6_sync_
offline_online.ipynb",
    output_nb=f"s3://airflow-for-ml-mar-2022/notebooks/runs/
ch6_sync_offline_online_{run_time}.ipynb",
    trigger_rule="all_success",
    dag=dag
)
end = DummyOperator(task_id="end", trigger_rule="all_success")
start >> feature_eng >> sync_offline_to_online >> end
```

The structure of the Airflow DAG is similar to the batch model DAG we looked at earlier; the only difference is the third task, `sync_offline_to_online`. This notebook syncs the latest features from offline data to online data. Save the preceding two code blocks (the first and second parts) as a Python file and call it `online-model-pipeline-dag.py`. After saving the file, navigate to the S3 console to upload the file into the `dags` folder that we pointed our Airflow environment to in *Figure 6.3*. As with the batch model, the uploaded file is processed by the Airflow scheduler, and when you navigate to the Airflow UI, you should see the new DAG called **customer_segmentation_online_model** on the screen.

The following screenshot displays the Airflow UI with the DAG:

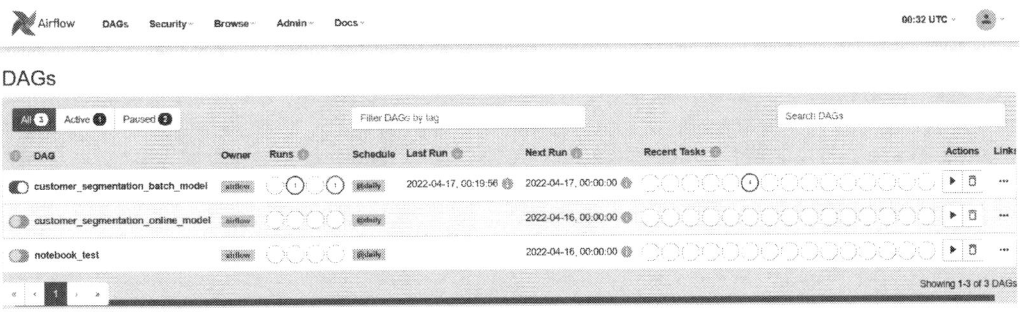

Figure 6.15 – The Airflow UI with both the online and batch models

To enable the DAG, click on the toggle button on the left-most column. Once enabled, the DAG will run for the first time. Click on the **customer_segmentation_online_model** hyperlink to navigate to the details page, and feel free to look around to see the different visualization and properties of the DAG. If you navigate to the **Graph** tab, the DAG will be displayed, as shown in the following screenshot:

Figure 6.16 – The online model pipeline graph view

As you can see in *Figure 6.16*, on successful runs, the graph will be green. As discussed during the batch model pipeline execution, you can verify the output notebook, DynamoDB tables, or S3 bucket to make sure that everything is working fine and can also check logs in case of failures.

Now that the first part of the online model pipeline is ready, let's Dockerize the REST endpoints we developed in the previous chapter and deploy them as a SageMaker endpoint.

Deploying the model as a SageMaker endpoint

To deploy the model to SageMaker, we need to first dockerize the REST API we built in *Chapter 5, Model Training and Inference*. Before we do that, let's create an **Elastic Container Registry** (**ECR**), where we can save the Docker image of the model and use it in SageMaker endpoint configurations.

An ECR for the Docker image

To create the ECR resource, navigate to the ECR console from the search bar or use the following URL: `https://us-east-1.console.aws.amazon.com/ecr/repositories?region=us-east-1`. The following page will be displayed:

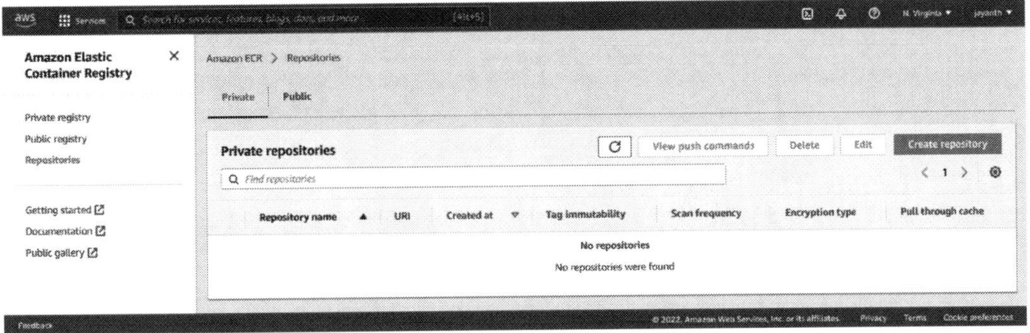

Figure 6.17 – The ECR home page

On the page displayed in *Figure 6.17*, you can choose either the **Private** or **Public** repository tab. Then, click on the **Create repository** button:

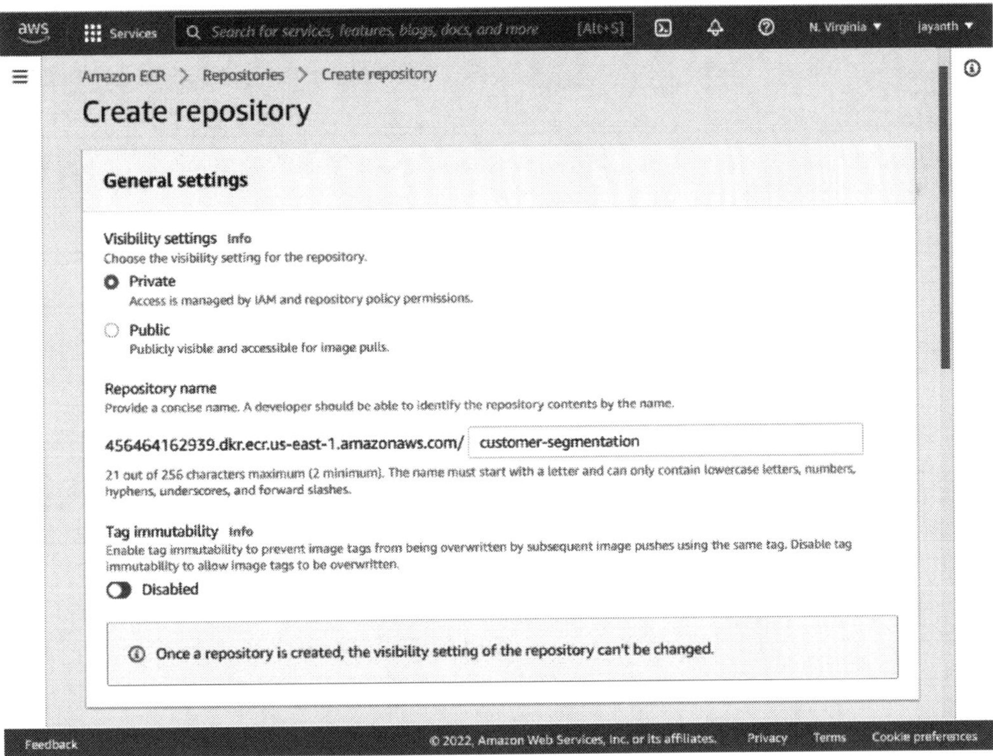

Figure 6.18 – ECR – Create repository

I have selected **Private** here; depending on whether you choose **Private** or **Public**, the options will change, but either way, it's straightforward. Fill in the required fields, scroll all the way down, and click on **Create repository**. Once the repository is created, go into the repository details page, and you should see a page similar to the one shown in *Figure 6.19*.

> **Important Note**
>
> Private repositories are secured with IAM, whereas public repositories can be accessed by anybody on the internet. Public repositories are mainly used for sharing/open sourcing your work with others outside an organization:

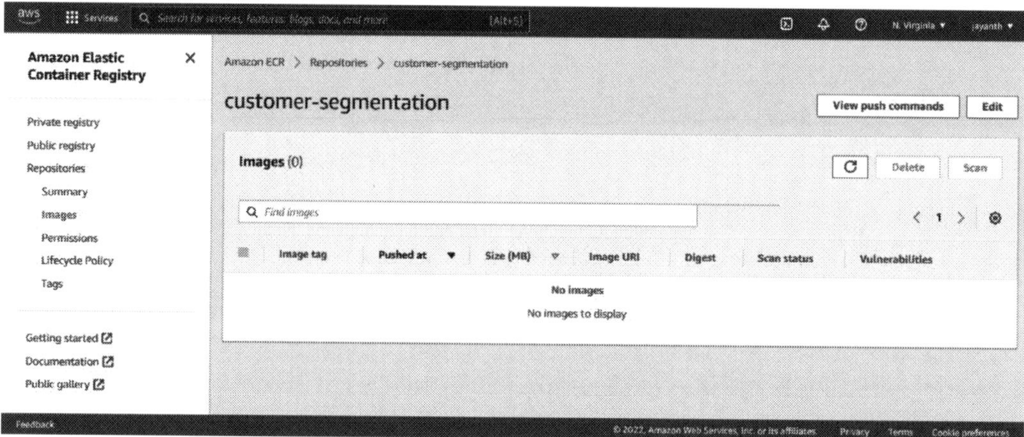

Figure 6.19 – ECR repository details

On the preceding page, click on **View push commands**, and you should see a popup, similar to the one shown in *Figure 6.20*:

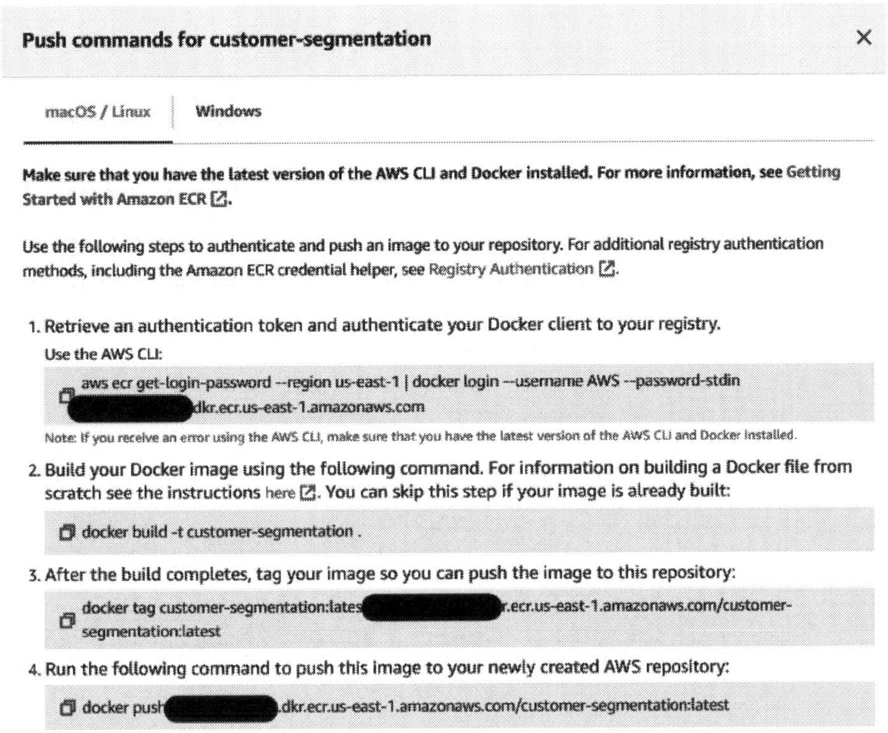

Push commands for customer-segmentation ×

macOS / Linux | Windows

Make sure that you have the latest version of the AWS CLI and Docker installed. For more information, see Getting Started with Amazon ECR.

Use the following steps to authenticate and push an image to your repository. For additional registry authentication methods, including the Amazon ECR credential helper, see Registry Authentication.

1. Retrieve an authentication token and authenticate your Docker client to your registry.
   Use the AWS CLI:
   ```
   aws ecr get-login-password --region us-east-1 | docker login --username AWS --password-stdin
   [redacted]dkr.ecr.us-east-1.amazonaws.com
   ```
   Note: If you receive an error using the AWS CLI, make sure that you have the latest version of the AWS CLI and Docker installed.
2. Build your Docker image using the following command. For information on building a Docker file from scratch see the instructions here. You can skip this step if your image is already built:
   ```
   docker build -t customer-segmentation .
   ```
3. After the build completes, tag your image so you can push the image to this repository:
   ```
   docker tag customer-segmentation:lates[redacted].ecr.us-east-1.amazonaws.com/customer-segmentation:latest
   ```
4. Run the following command to push this image to your newly created AWS repository:
   ```
   docker push[redacted].dkr.ecr.us-east-1.amazonaws.com/customer-segmentation:latest
   ```

Figure 6.20 – ECR push commands

Depending on the operating system you are using for building the Docker image, save the necessary commands. We will use these commands to build the Docker image.

Building the Docker image

As mentioned earlier, we will be using the REST endpoints built in the previous chapter in this section. If you recall correctly, we had added two REST endpoints, `ping` and `invocations`. These endpoints are not random, though the same can be hosted in any container environment. To host a Docker image in the SageMaker endpoints, the requirement is that it should have the `ping` (which is the `GET` method) and `invocations` (which is the `POST` method) routes. I have added a couple of files to the same folder structure, which will be useful for building the Docker image. The REST code and folder structure are available at the following URL: `https://github.com/PacktPublishing/Feature-Store-for-Machine-Learning/tree/main/online-model-rest-api`.

> **Important Note**
>
> The additional files are `Dockerfile`, `requirements.txt`, and `serve`.

Consecutively, clone the REST code to the local system, copy the feature repository into the `root` directory of the project, export the credentials, and then run the commands in *Figure 6.20*.

> **Important Note**
>
> You can use the same user credential that was created in *Chapter 4*, *Adding Feature Store to ML Models*. However, we had missed adding ECR permissions to the user. Please navigate to the IAM console and add **AmazonEC2ContainerRegistryFullAccess** to the user. Otherwise, you will get an access error.

The following are the example commands:

```
cd online-model-rest-api/
export AWS_ACCESS_KEY_ID=<AWS_KEY>
export AWS_SECRET_ACCESS_KEY=<AWS_SECRET>
export AWS_DEFAULT_REGION=us-east-1
aws ecr get-login-password --region us-east-1 | docker login
--username AWS --password-stdin <account_number>.dkr.ecr.
us-east-1.amazonaws.com
docker build -t customer-segmentation .
docker tag customer-segmentation:latest <account_number>.dkr.
ecr.us-east-1.amazonaws.com/customer-segmentation:latest
docker push <account_number>.dkr.ecr.us-east-1.amazonaws.com/
customer-segmentation:latest
```

The commands logs in to ECR using the credentials set in the environment, builds the Docker image, and tags and pushes the Docker image to the registry. Once the image is pushed, if you navigate back to the screen in *Figure 6.19*, you should see the new image, as shown in the following screenshot:

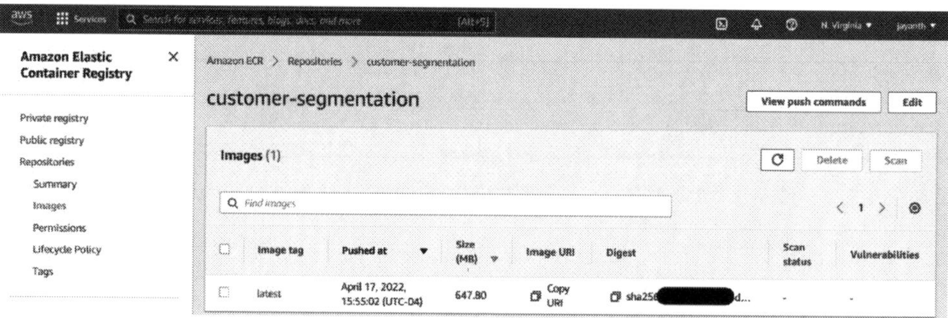

Figure 6.21 – ECR with the pushed image

Now that the image is ready, copy the image **Uniform Resource Identifier (URI)** by clicking on the icon next to **Copy URI**, as shown in *Figure 6.21*. Let's deploy the Docker image as a SageMaker endpoint next.

Creating a SageMaker endpoint

Amazon SageMaker aims at providing managed infrastructure for ML. In this section, we will only be using the SageMaker inference components. SageMaker endpoints are used for deploying a model as REST endpoints for real-time prediction. It supports Docker image models and also supports a few flavors out of the box. We will be using the Docker image that we pushed into the ECR in the previous section. SageMaker endpoints are built using three building blocks – models, endpoint configs, and endpoints. Let's use these building blocks and create an endpoint next.

A SageMaker model

The model is used to define the model parameters such as the name, the location of the model, and the IAM role. To define a model, navigate to the SageMaker console using the search bar and look for `Models` in the **Inference** section. Alternatively, visit `https://us-east-1.console.aws.amazon.com/sagemaker/home?region=us-east-1#/models`. The following screen will be displayed:

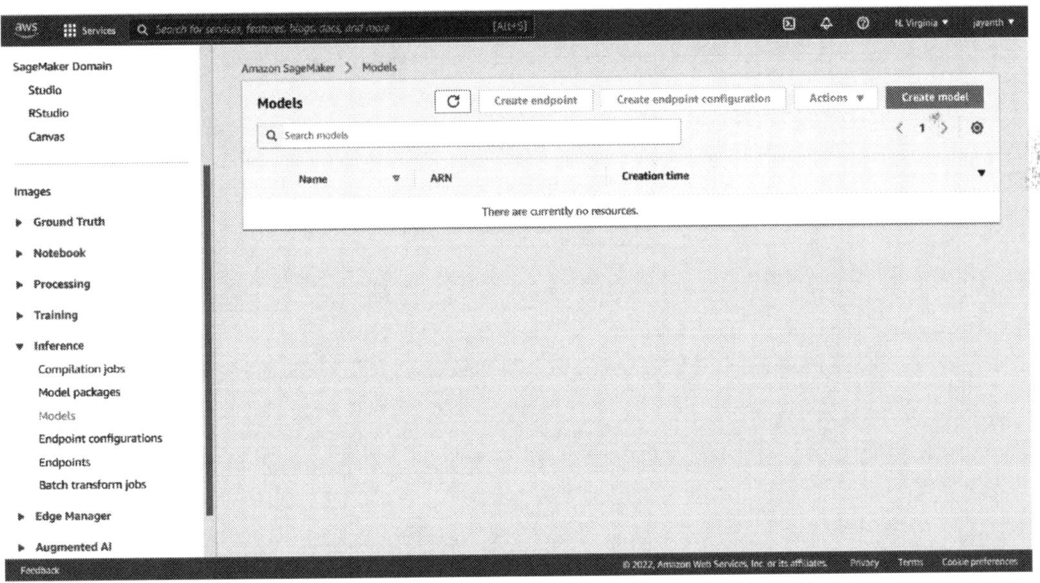

Figure 6.22 – The SageMaker Models console

On the displayed page, click on **Create model** to navigate to the next screen. The following page will be displayed:

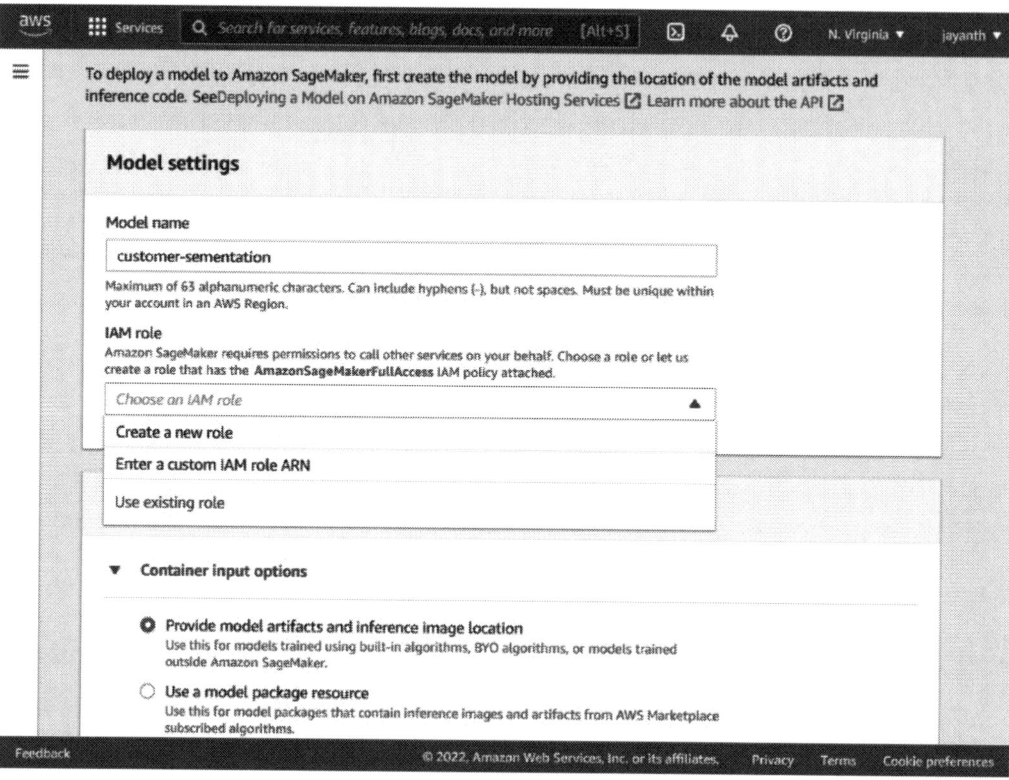

Figure 6.23 – SageMaker – Create model

As shown in *Figure 6.23*, input a model name, and for the IAM role, select **Create a new role** from the dropdown. A new popup appears, as displayed in the following screenshot:

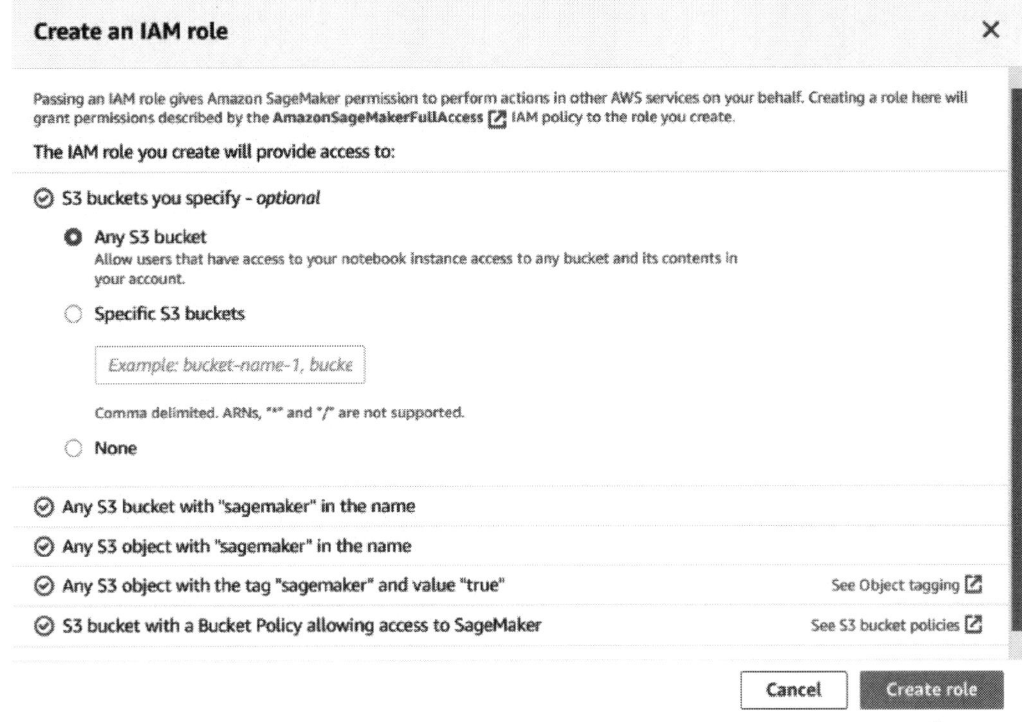

Figure 6.24 – The SageMaker model – Create an IAM role

In the popup, leave everything as default for the purpose of this exercise and click on **Create role**. AWS will create an IAM role, and on the same screen, you should see a message in the dialog with a link to the IAM role. The following figure shows the displayed message:

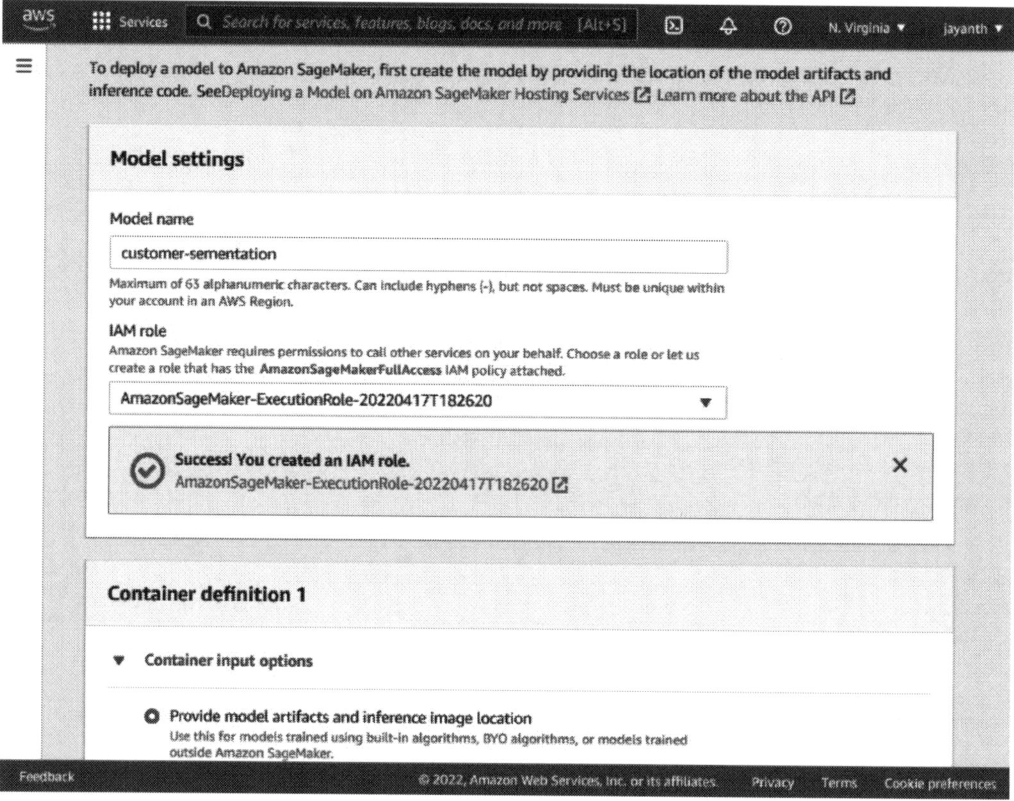

Figure 6.25 – The SageMaker model – the new execution role is created

Now, if you recall correctly, we are using DynamoDB as the online store; as we are reading data on demand from DynamoDB tables, the IAM role needs access to them. Therefore, navigate to the IAM role we just created using the link displayed on the page in a new tab, add **AmazonDynamoDBFullAccess**, and come back to this tab. Scroll down to the **Container definition 1** section, where you should see the following parameters:

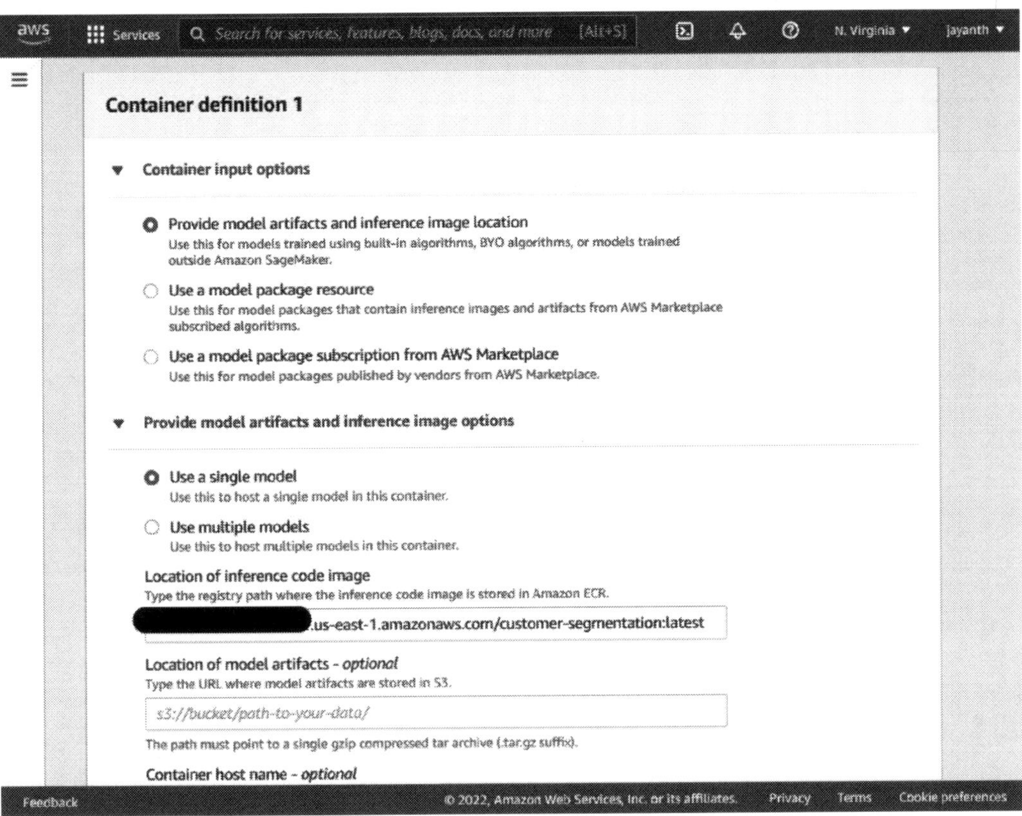

Figure 6.26 – The SageMaker model – the Container definition 1 section

For the **Location of inference code image** parameter, paste the image URI that we copied from the screen, as displayed in *Figure 6.21*. Leave the others as their defaults and scroll again to the **Network** section:

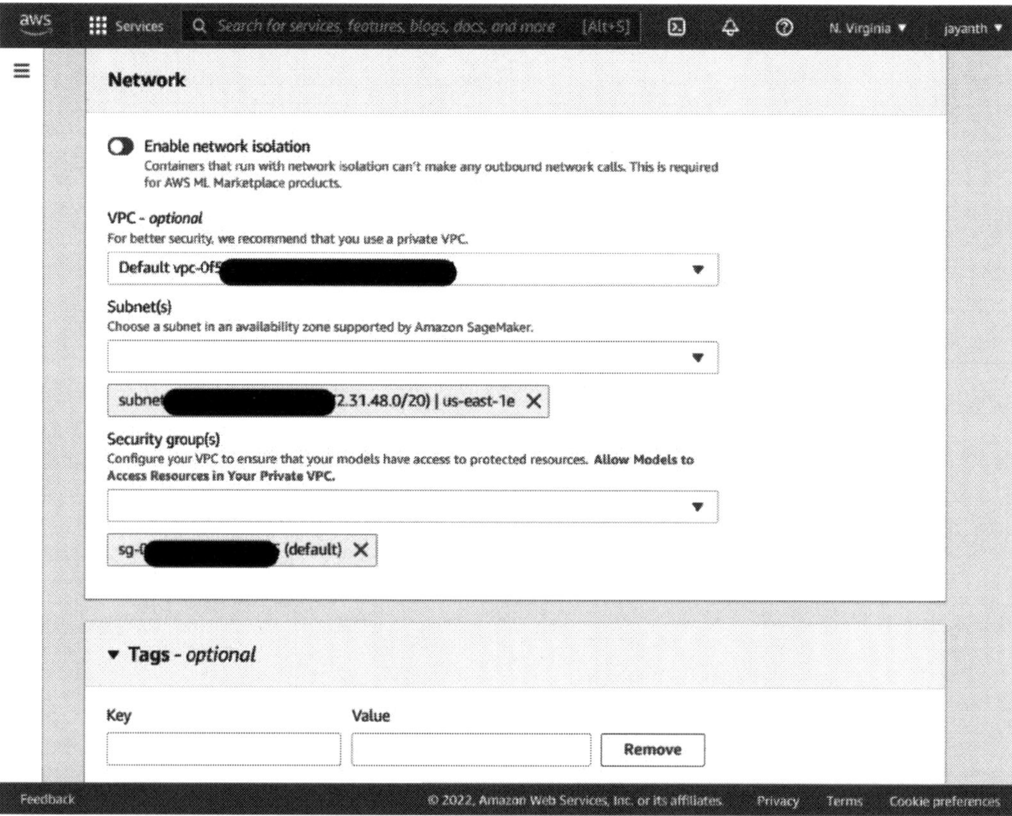

Figure 6.27 – The Sagemaker Model – the Network section

Here, select the **VPC** to **Default vpc**, select one or two subnets from the list, and choose the default security group. Scroll down to the bottom and click on **Create model**.

> **Important Note**
>
> It is never a good idea to select the default security group for production deployment, as inbound rules are not restrictive.

Now that the model is ready, let's create the endpoint configuration next.

Endpoint configuration

To set up the endpoint configuration, navigate to the SageMaker console using the search bar and look for `Endpoint Configurations` in the **Inference** section. Alternatively, visit `https://us-east-1.console.aws.amazon.com/sagemaker/home?region=us-east-1#/endpointConfig`. The following page will be displayed:

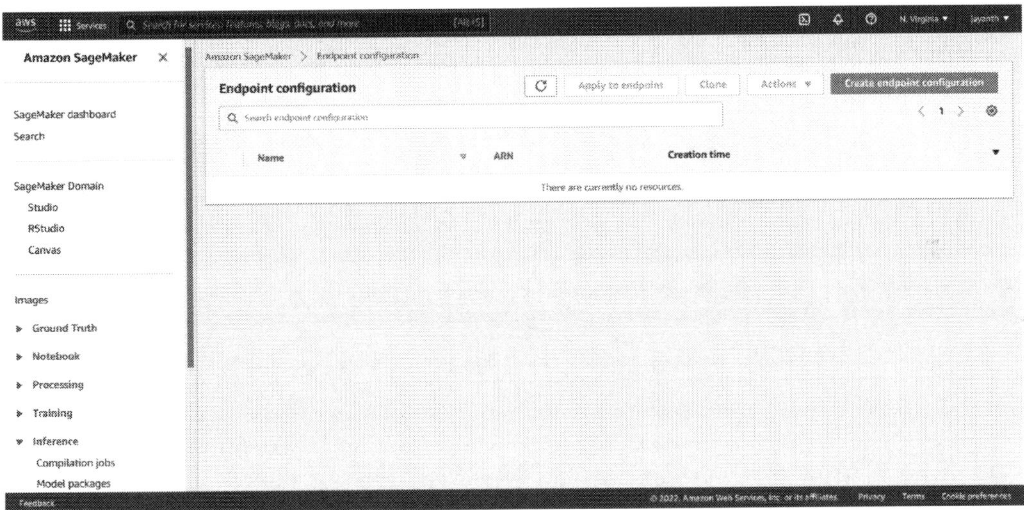

Figure 6.28 – The Sagemaker Endpoint configuration console

On the displayed web page, click on **Create endpoint configuration**. You will be navigated to the following page:

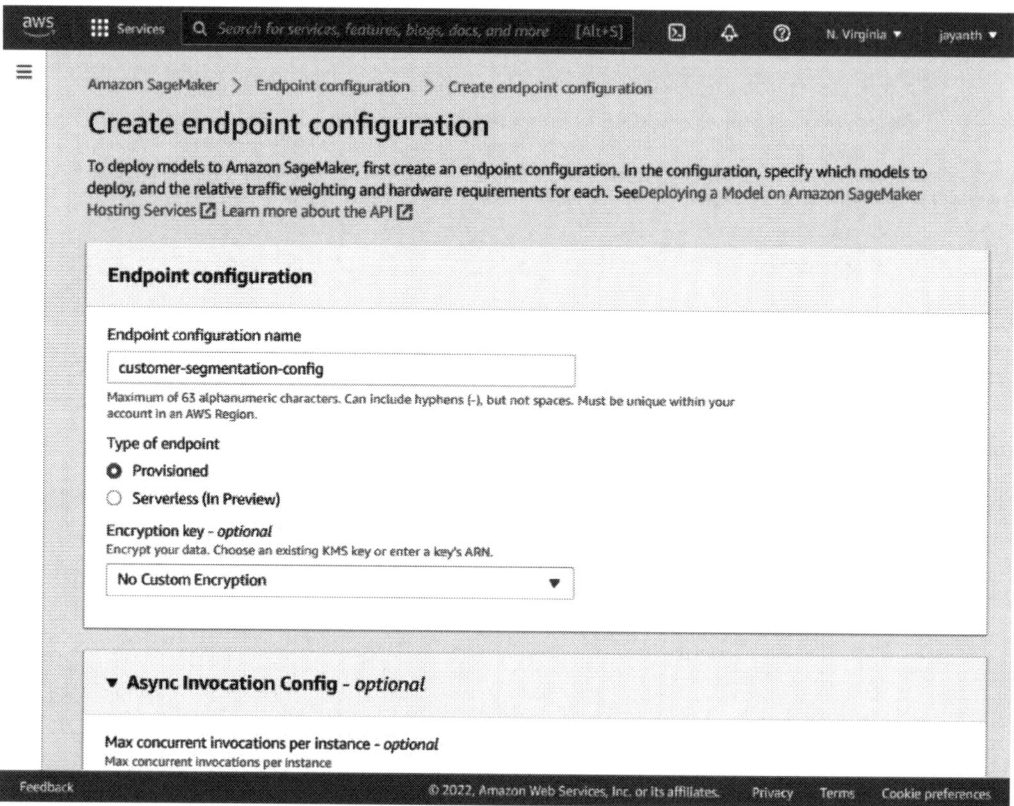

Figure 6.29 – SageMaker – Create endpoint configuration

On this screen, fill in the **Endpoint configuration name** field; I have given the name `customer-segmentation-config`. Scroll down to the **Data capture** section. This is used to define what percent of real-time inference data needs to be captured, where (the S3 location), and how it needs to be stored (JSON or CSV). You can choose to enable this or leave it disabled. I have left it disabled for this exercise. If you enable it, it will ask you for additional information. The section following **Data capture** is **Production variants**. This is used for setting up multiple model variants, and A/B testing of the models. For now, since we only have one variant, let's add that here. To add a variant, click on the **Add model** link in the section; the following popup will appear:

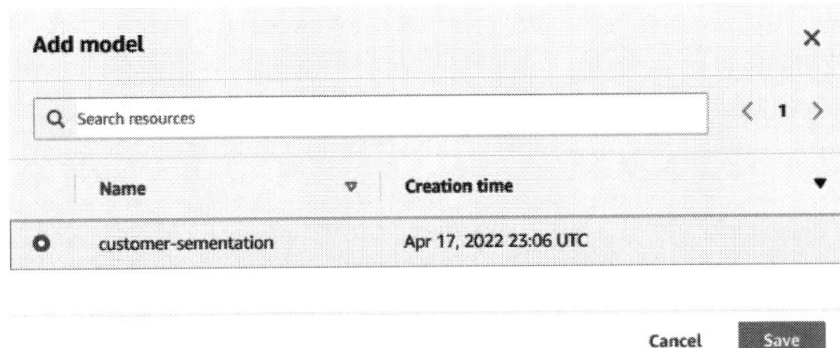

Figure 6.30 – SageMaker – adding a model to the endpoint config

In the popup, select the model that we created earlier, scroll all the way down, and click on **Create endpoint configuration**.

SageMaker endpoint creation

The last step is to use the endpoint configuration to create an endpoint. To create a SageMaker endpoint, navigate to the SageMaker console using the search bar and look for `Endpoints` in the **Inference** section. Alternatively, visit `https://us-east-1.console.aws.amazon.com/sagemaker/home?region=us-east-1#/endpoints`. The following page will be displayed:

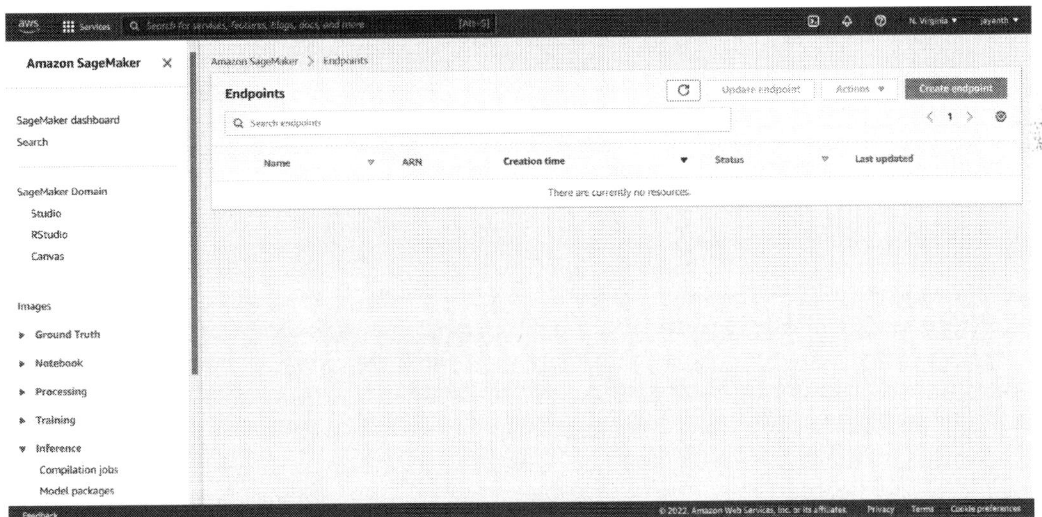

Figure 6.31 – The SageMaker Endpoints console

On the page shown in *Figure 6.31*, click on **Create endpoint** to navigate to the following page:

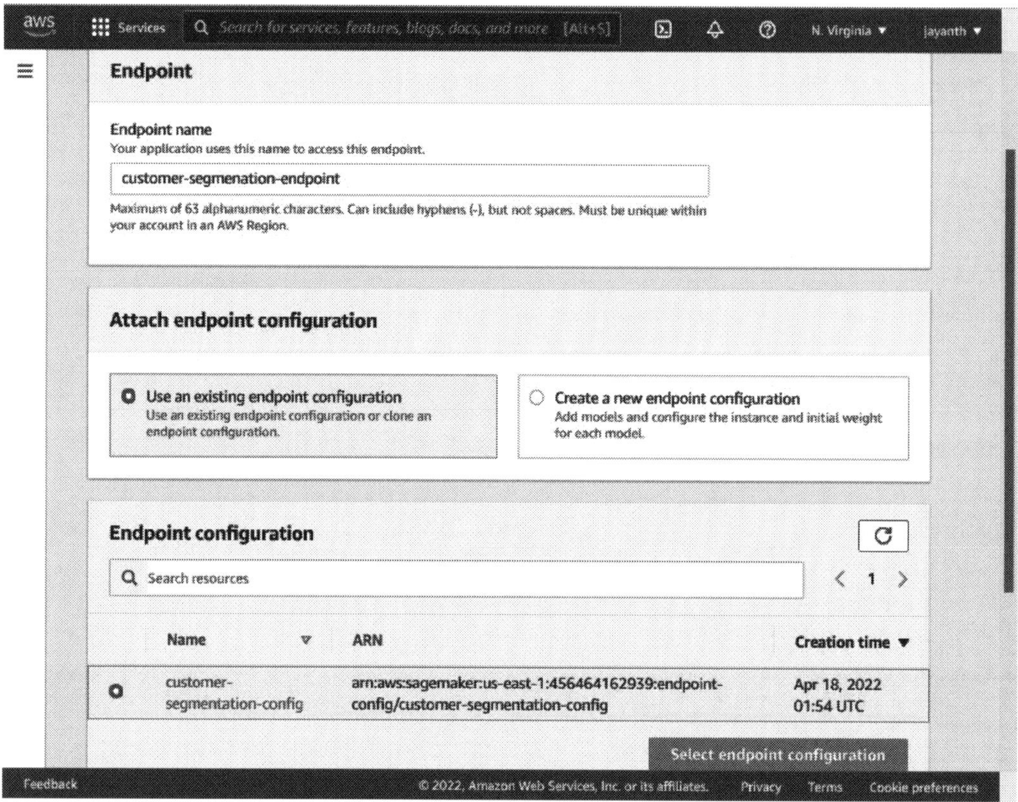

Figure 6.31 – SageMaker – creating an endpoint

On the web page displayed in *Figure 6.31*, provide an endpoint name. I have given the name `customer-segmentation-endpoint`. Scroll down to the **Endpoint configuration** section, select the endpoint configuration we created earlier, and click on the **Select endpoint configuration** button. Once it is selected, click on **Create endpoint**. It will take a few minutes to create an endpoint. When the endpoint status changes to **Available**, your model is live for serving real-time traffic.

Testing the SageMaker endpoint

The next thing we need to know is how to consume the model. There are different ways – you can use the SageMaker library, Amazon SDK client (Python, TypeScript, or any other available), or a SageMaker endpoint URL. All these methods default to AWS IAM authentication. If you have special requirements and want to expose the model without authentication or with custom authentication, it can be achieved using the API gateway and Lambda authorizer. For the purpose of this exercise, we will be using the `boto3` client to invoke the API. Irrespective of how we invoke the endpoint, the results should be the same.

The following code block invokes the endpoint using the `boto3` client:

```
import json
import boto3
import os
os.environ["AWS_ACCESS_KEY_ID"] = "<aws_key>"
os.environ["AWS_SECRET_ACCESS_KEY"] = "<aws_secret>"
os.environ["AWS_DEFAULT_REGION"] = "us-east-1"
payload = json.dumps({"customer_list":["12747.0", "12841.0"]})
runtime = boto3.client("runtime.sagemaker")
response = runtime.invoke_endpoint(
    EndpointName= "customer-segmentation-endpoint",
    ContentType="application/json", Body=payload
)
response = response["Body"].read()
result = json.loads(response.decode("utf-8"))
print(results)
```

In the preceding code block, we are invoking the endpoint that we created to run predictions for two customers with the `12747.0` and `12841.0` IDs. The endpoint will respond within milliseconds with the predictions for the given customer IDs. Now, the endpoint can be shared with the model consumers.

Now that the model is in production, let's look at a few aspects that come after a model moves to production.

Beyond model production

In this section, we will discuss the postproduction aspects of ML and how we benefit from the adoption of a feature store.

Feature drift monitoring and model retraining

Once the model is in production, the next question that will come up frequently is how the model is performing in production. There may be different metrics used to measure the performance of a model – for instance, for a recommendation model, performance may be measured by a conversion rate, which is how often the recommended product was purchased. Similarly, predicting the next action of a customer may be measured by error rate, and so on. There is no universal way of doing it. But if a model's performance is bad, it needs to be retrained or replaced with a new one.

One other aspect that defines when a model should be retrained is when the feature starts to drift away from the values with which it was trained. For example, let's say the mean frequency value of the customer during the initial model training was 10, but now, the mean frequency value is 25. Similarly, the lowest monetary value was initially $100.00 and now it is $500.00. This is called **data drift**.

Data drift monitoring measures the change in the statistical distribution of the data; in the case of feature monitoring, it is comparing the change in the statistical distribution of a feature from *t1* time to *t2* time. The article at the following URL discusses different metrics for data drift monitoring: `https://towardsdatascience.com/automating-data-drift-thresholding-in-machine-learning-systems-524e6259f59f`.

With a feature store, it is easy to retrieve a training dataset from two different points in time, namely the dataset used for model training and the latest feature values for all the features used in model training. Now, all we need to do is run data drift monitoring on schedule to generate a drift report. The standardization that Feast brought to the table is, since the data is stored and retrieved using standard APIs, a generic feature drift monitoring can be run on schedule for all the datasets in the feature store. The feature drift report can be used as one of the indicators for model retraining. If feature drift is affecting the model's performance, it can be retrained with the latest dataset, and deployed and AB-tested with the current production model.

Model reproducibility and prediction issues

If you recall from *Chapter 1, An Overview of the Machine Learning Life Cycle*, model reproducibility is one of the common problems of ML. We need a way to consistently reproduce the model (or training data used for model). Without a feature store, if the underlying raw data that is used to generate features changes, it is not possible to reproduce the same training dataset. However, with a feature store, as we discussed earlier, the features are versioned with a timestamp (one of the columns in the features DataFrame is an event timestamp). Hence, we can query the historical data to generate the same feature set used for model training. If the algorithm used for training the model is not stochastic, the model can also be reproduced. Let's try this out.

Since we have already done something similar to this in the *Model training with a feature store* section of *Chapter 5, Model Training and Inference*, we will reuse the same code to run this experiment. Copy and run all the code till you create the entity DataFrame and then replace the `event_timestamp` column with an older timestamp (the timestamp of when the model was trained), as shown here. In this case, the model was trained at `2022-03-26 16:24:21`, as shown in *Figure 5.1* of *Chapter 5, Model Training and Inference*:

```
## replace timestamp to older time stamp.
entity_df["event_timestamp"] = pd.to_datetime("2022-03-26
16:24:21")
```

Once you are done replacing the timestamp, continue running the code from the *Dee's model training experiments* section of *Chapter 5, Model Training and Inference*. You should be able to generate the exact same dataset that was used in Dee's model training (in this case, the dataset in *Figure 5.2* of *Chapter 5, Model Training and Inference*). Hence, if the model uses a nonrandom algorithm, then the model can also be reproduced using the feature set.

One other advantage of a feature store is the debugging prediction issue. Let's consider a scenario where you have a website-facing model that is classifying a transaction as fraudulent or not. During the peak hour, it flagged a few transactions as fraudulent, but the transactions were legitimate. The customer called in and complained to the customer service department, and now it's the data scientist Subbu's turn to figure out what went wrong. If there was no feature store in the project, to reproduce the issue, Subbu would have to go into the raw data, try to generate the features, and see whether the behavior still remains the same. If not, Subbu would have to go into the application log, process it, look for user behavior before the event, try to reproduce it from the user interaction perspective, and also capture the features for all these trials, hoping that the issue can be reproduced at least once.

On the other hand, with the feature store used in the project, Subbu will figure out the approximate time when the event happened, what the entities and features used in the model are, and what the version of the model that was running in production was at the time of the event. With this information, Subbu will connect to the feature store and fetch all the features used in the model for all the entities for the approximate time range when the issue happened. Let's say that the event occurred between 12:00pm to 12:15pm today, features were streaming, and the freshness interval was around 30 seconds. This means that, on average, for a given entity, there is a chance that features will change in the next 30 seconds from any given time.

To reproduce the issue, Subbu will form an entity DataFrame with the same entity ID repeated 30 times in one column and, for the event time column, a timestamp from 12:00pm to 12:15pm with 30-second intervals. With this entity DataFrame, Subbu will query the historical store using the Feast API and run the prediction for the generated features. If the issue is reproduced, Subbu has the feature set that caused the issue. If not, using the entity DataFrame, the interval will be reduced to less than 30 seconds, maybe to 10 seconds, to figure out if features changed at a faster pace than 30 seconds. Subbu can continue doing this till she finds the feature set that reproduces the issue.

A headstart for the next model

Now that the model has productionized, the data scientist Subbu picks up the next problem statement. Let's assume that the next ML model has to predict the **Next Purchase Day** (**NPD**) of a customer. The use case here could be that based on the NPD, we want to run a campaign for a customer. If a customers' purchase day is farther in the future, we want to offer a special deal so that we can encourage purchasing sooner. Now, before going to a raw dataset, Subbu can look for available features based on how the search and discoverability aspect is integrated into the feature store. Since Feast moved from service-oriented to SDK/CLI-oriented, there is a need for catalog tools, a GitHub repository of all the feature repositories, a data mesh portal, and so on. However, in the case of feature stores such as SageMaker or Databricks, users can connect to feature store endpoints (with SageMaker runtime using a boto3 or Databricks workspace) and browse through the available feature definitions using the API or from the UI. I have not used the Tecton feature store before, but Tecton also offers a UI for its feature store that can be used to browse through the available features. As you can see, this is one of the drawbacks of the different versions of Feast between 0.9.X and 0.20.X (0.20 is the version at the time of writing).

Let's assume, for now, that Subbu has a way to locate all the feature repositories. Now, she can connect and browse through them to figure out what the projects and feature definitions are that could be useful in the NPD model. So far, we have just one feature repository that has the customer RFM features that we have been using so far, and these features can be useful in the model. To use these features, all Subbu has to do is get read access to the AWS resource, and the latest RFM features will be available every day for experimentation and can also be used if the model moves to production.

To see how beneficial the feature store would be during the development of the subsequent model, we should try building the NPD. I will go through the initial few steps to get you started on the model. As we followed a blog during the development of the first model, we will be following another part in the same blog series, which can be found at `https://towardsdatascience.com/predicting-next-purchase-day-15fae5548027`. Please read through the blog, as it discusses the approach and why the author thinks specific features will be useful. Here, we will be skipping ahead to the feature engineering section.

We will be using the feature set that the blog author uses, which includes the following:

- RFM features and clusters
- The number of days between the last three purchases
- The mean and standard deviation of the differences between the purchases

The first feature set already exists in the feature store; we don't need to do anything extra for it. But for the other two, we need to do feature engineering from the raw data. The notebook at `https://github.com/PacktPublishing/Feature-Store-for-Machine-Learning/blob/main/Chapter06/notebooks/ch6_next_purchase_day_feature_engineering.ipynb` has the required feature engineering to generate the features in the preceding second and third bullet points. I will leave the ingestion of these features into a feature store and using the features (RFM) from the previous model in combination with these to train a new model as an exercise. As you develop and productionize this model, you will see the benefit of the feature store and how it can accelerate model building.

Next, let's discuss how to change a feature definition when the model is in production.

Changes to feature definition after production

So far, we have discussed feature ingestion, query, and changes to a feature set during the development phases. However, we haven't talked about changes to feature definitions when the model is in production. Often, it is argued that changing feature definition once the model moves to production is difficult. The reason for this is that there is a chance that multiple models are using feature definitions and any changes to them will have a cascading effect on the models. This is one of the reasons why some feature stores don't yet support updates on feature definitions. We need a way to handle the change effectively here.

This is still a gray area; there is no right or wrong way of doing it. We can adopt any mechanism that we use in other software engineering processes. A simple one could be the versioning of the feature views, similar to the way we do our REST APIs or Python libraries. Whenever a change is needed for a production feature set, assuming that it is being used by others, a new version of the feature view (let's call it `customer-segemantion-v2`) will be created and used. However, the previous version will still need to be managed until all the models migrate. If, for any reason, there are models that need the older version and cannot be migrated to the newer version of the feature table/views, it may have to be managed or handed over to the team that needs it. There needs to be some discussion on ownership of the features and feature engineering jobs.

This is where the concept of data as a product is very meaningful. The missing piece here is a framework for producers and consumers to define contracts and notify changes. The data producers need a way of publishing their data products; here, the data product is feature views. The consumers of the product can subscribe to the data product and use it. During the feature set changes, the producers can define a new version of the data product and depreciate the older version so that consumers will be notified of what the changes are. This is just my opinion on a solution, but I'm sure there are better minds out there who may already be implementing another solution.

With that, let's summarize what we have learned in this chapter and move on to the next one.

Summary

In this chapter, we aimed at using everything we built in the previous chapters and productionizing the ML models for batch and online use cases. To do that, we created an Amazon MWAA environment and used it for the orchestration of the batch model pipeline. For the online model, we used Airflow for the orchestration of the feature engineering pipeline and the SageMaker inference components to deploy a Docker online model as a SageMaker endpoint. We looked at how a feature store facilitates the postproduction aspects of ML, such as feature drift monitoring, model reproducibility, debugging prediction issues, and how to change a feature set when the model is in production. We also looked at how data scientists get a headstart on the new model with the use of a feature store. So far, we have used Feast in all our exercises; in the next chapter, we will look at a few of the feature stores that are available on the market and how they differ from Feast, alongside some examples.

Section 3 – Alternatives, Best Practices, and a Use Case

In this section, we will look at some of the alternatives to Feast, which include a few managed feature store offerings. We will also deep-dive into Amazon SageMaker Feature Store, which will help us compare Feast (a self-managed infrastructure) to a managed feature store. We will also run through ML best practices and, finally, an end-to-end ML use case with a managed feature store, which includes feature engineering, model training, and model inference, along with feature and model monitoring examples.

This section comprises the following chapters:

- *Chapter 7, Feast Alternatives and ML Best Practices*
- *Chapter 8, Use Case – Customer Churn Prediction*

7
Feast Alternatives and ML Best Practices

In the last chapter, we discussed how to use Amazon Managed Workflows with Apache Airflow for orchestration and productionizing online and batch models with **Feast**. So far in this book, we have been discussing one feature store – Feast. However, there are a bunch of feature stores available on the market today. In this chapter, we will look at a few of them and discuss how they are different from Feast and the advantages or disadvantages of using them over Feast.

In this chapter, we will try out one other feature store, specifically Amazon SageMaker. We will take the same feature set that we generated while building the customer **lifetime value (LTV)** model and ingest it into SageMaker Feature Store and also run a couple of queries. The reason for choosing AWS over other feature stores such as Tecton, Hopworks, and H2O.ai is the easy access to the trial version. However, choosing the right feature store for you depends on the tools and infrastructure that you already have and more, which we will discuss in this chapter.

The aim of this chapter is to give you the gist of what is available on the market and how it differs from self-managed feature stores such as Feast. We will also discuss the similarities and differences between these feature stores. The other aspect that I want to discuss in this chapter is the best practices in ML development. Irrespective of the tools/software we use for ML development, there are a few things that can be universally adopted by all of us to improve ML engineering.

In this chapter, we will discuss the following topics:

- The available feature stores on the market
- Feature management with SageMaker Feature Store
- ML best practices

Technical requirements

To run through the examples and get a better understanding of this chapter, the topics covered in previous chapters will be useful but not required. To follow the code examples in the chapter, you need familiarity with a notebook environment, which could be a local setup such as Jupyter or an online notebook environment such as Google Colab, Kaggle, or SageMaker. You will also need an AWS account with full access to SageMaker and the AWS Glue console. You can create a new account and use all the services for free during the trial period. You can find the code examples of the book using the following GitHub link:

`https://github.com/PacktPublishing/Feature-Store-for-Machine-Learning/tree/main/Chapter07`

The available feature stores on the market

In this section, we will briefly discuss some of the available feature stores on the market and how they compare with Feast, as well as some commonalities and differences between these feature stores.

The Tecton Feature Store

Tecton is an enterprise feature store, built by the creators of Uber's machine learning platform Michelangelo (`https://eng.uber.com/michelangelo-machine-learning-platform/`). Tecton is also one of the major contributors to Feast. Hence, when you look at Tecton's documentation (`https://docs.tecton.ai/index.html`), you will see a lot of similarities in the APIs and terminology. However, there are a lot of functionalities in Tecton that don't exist in Feast. Also, Tecton is a managed feature store, which means that you don't need to build and manage the infrastructure; it will be managed for you.

As with most feature stores, Tecton uses online and offline stores for low latency and historical storage respectively. However, there are fewer options for online and offline stores compared to Feast, and it is currently supported only on AWS. If you prefer Azure or GCP, you don't have any other option but to wait for now. I believe multiple cloud providers and data stores will be eventually supported. Tecton uses a **Software as a Service** (**SaaS**) deployment model and separates deployment into data and control planes. You can find their deployment model at the following link: `https://docs.tecton.ai/setting-up-tecton/07a-deployment_saas.html`. The best part is that data never leaves the customer's AWS account, and only the metadata required for the control panel to work is accessed by the Tecton-owned AWS account; also, the UI will be hosted in their account. However, if you want to expose online data through a REST/gRPC API endpoint, the service will be hosted in Tecton's AWS account. The online feature request and response will be routed through their account.

Once Tecton is deployed into your AWS account, you can interact with it using the Python SDK. The CLI commands are similar to Feast commands; however, there are options such as being able to manage versions of your feature definitions and downgrading to a previous version of the definitions. As well as the common workflows that you can do with a feature store such as ingesting, querying at low latency, and performing point-in-time joins, with Tecton, you can define transformation as part of the feature store. This is one of my favorite features of Tecton. Here is the link to the feature views and transformation page in the feature store: `https://docs.tecton.ai/overviews/framework/feature_views/feature_views.html`. What this means is that you can define a raw data source configuration for a data warehouse (Snowflake), database, Kinesis, or Kafka, and define a PySpark, Spark SQL, or pandas transformation to generate features. Tecton orchestrates these jobs on a defined schedule and generates features, and ingests them into online and offline stores. This can help in tracking data lineage.

The following is an example code snippet on how to define feature views and transformation:

```
# Feature View type
@batch_feature_view(
    # Pipeline attributes
    inputs=...
    mode=...
    # Entities
    entities=...
    # Materialization and serving configuration
    online=...
    offline=...
    batch_schedule=...
    feature_start_time=...
    ttl=...
    backfill_config=...
    # Metadata
    owner=...
    description=...
    tags=...
)
# Feature View name
def my_feature_view(input_data):
    intermediate_data = my_transformation(input_data)
    output_data = my_transformation_two(intermediate_data)
    return output_data
```

You may recognize some of the parameters that you see in the preceding code block. Here, the annotation says it's a batch transformation on which you can define parameters such as which entities to use, what the schedule is, and whether it should ingest data into online and offline stores. In the method definition, input data will be injected based on whatever is assigned to the `input` parameter in the annotation definition (you can assume it to be a DataFrame from a raw data source). On the DataFrame, you add your transformation and return the output DataFrame, which will be features. These features will be ingested into the online and offline stores on the defined schedule. Once you define the preceding transformation, you will have to run `tecton apply`, which is similar to the `feast apply` command, to register this transformation. The other functionalities are similar to what other feature stores offer; hence, I will skip over them and let you explore their documentation.

What is worth keeping in mind though is that the Tecton deployments are single-tenant at the time of writing, which means that if there are teams that cannot share data, you might need multiple deployments. There is a set of roles that needs to be created that will allow Tecton to install and create required resources using cross-account roles, which involves a one-time initial setup from you.

Databricks Feature Store

Databricks Feature Store is another option that is available out there for users. It makes sense if you are already using Databricks as your notebook environment and for data processing jobs. It comes with the Databricks workspaces, so you can't have just the feature store. However, you can get a workspace and not use anything else except the feature store. It can be hosted on AWS, GCP, or Azure. So, if you are on any of the major cloud providers, this could be an option.

The concepts are similar to other feature stores, such as feature tables, timestamp versioning on the rows, the ability to do point-in-time joins, and online and offline stores. It uses a delta lake for its offline store and uses one of the key-value stores, available on a cloud based on which cloud provider you are on. The best part about Databricks Feature Store is that it integrates well with all the other aspects and components of Databricks, such as Spark DataFrame ingestion, retrieval, out-of-the-box integration with the MLflow model repository, access control, and tracking the lineage of notebooks that are used to generate a particular feature table. It also has a nice UI where you can browse and search for features. The next best part is there is no setup required if you already have the Databricks workspace. Here is a link to the notebook, which features examples of feature creation, ingestion, retrieval, training, and model scoring: `https://docs.databricks.com/_static/notebooks/machine-learning/feature-store-taxi-example.html`.

However, there are a few things to keep in mind. Databricks Feature Store doesn't have a concept of projects; hence, feature tables are the highest level of abstraction, and access control is at the feature table level. Additionally, Databricks' online model hosting is still in public preview (although no doubt it will eventually become a standard offering). This means that if you use Databricks Feature Store for an online model that is hosted outside of Databricks, it might have to connect to the online store using the direct client. For example, if you use DynamoDB as an online store (Databricks offers multiple choices, depending on the cloud provider) and host the model in Amazon **Elastic Container Service (ECS)**, you may have to implement the logic query for DynamoDB directly using the `boto3` client for features during prediction. Also, sharing features across the workspace might need additional configuration for either access tokens or using a central workspace for the feature store. Here is the link to the Databricks Feature Store documentation for more details: `https://docs.databricks.com/applications/machine-learning/feature-store/index.html`.

Google's Vertex AI Feature Store

Google's Vertex AI is a **Platform as a Service** (**PaaS**) offering from Google for ML and AI. Vertex AI aims at offering an end-to-end ML platform that provides a set of tools for ML development, training, orchestration, model deployment, monitoring, and more. The tool that we are most interested in is Vertex AI Feature Store. If you are already using GCP for your services, it should be an automatic pick.

The concepts and terminology are very similar to that of Feast. The highest level of abstraction in Vertex AI is called a *featurestore*, similar to a *project* in Feast, and a *featurestore* can have *entities*, and *features* should belong to *entities*. It supports online and batch serving, just like all the other feature stores. However, unlike Feast and Tecton, there are no options available for online and historical stores. Since it is a managed infrastructure, users don't need to worry about installation and choosing online and offline stores – probably just the pricing. Here is a link to its prices: `https://cloud.google.com/vertex-ai/pricing#featurestore`. It uses **IAM** (short for **Identity and Access Management**) for authentication and authorization, and you also get a UI to search and browse features.

The best part of Vertex AI is its integration with other components of GCP and the Vertex AI service itself for feature generation, pipeline management, and data lineage tracking. One of my favorite features is drift monitoring. You can set up a feature monitoring configuration on the feature tables, which can generate data distribution reports for you without requiring any additional work.

Again, there are a few things to keep in mind. For online serving, you need to do capacity sizing and set up the number of nodes required to handle your traffic. The autoscaling option for online serving is still in public preview (although it's just a matter of time before it becomes a standard offering), but capacity planning should be a major problem to solve. A few load test simulations should help you figure that out easily. Also, there are quotas and limits on the number of online serving nodes you can have for a feature store, the length of data retention, and the number of features per entity. Some of these can be increased on request whereas others can't. Here is a link to the list of quotas and limits on a feature store: `https://cloud.google.com/vertex-ai/docs/quotas#featurestore`.

The Hopsworks Feature Store

Hopsworks is another open source feature store under the AGPL-V3 license that can be run on-premises, on AWS or Azure. It also has an enterprise version of the feature store that supports GCP as well as any Kubernetes environment. Similar to other ML platform services, it also offers multiple components, such as model management and compute environment management.

The concepts are similar to that of other feature stores; however, the terminology is different. It doesn't have a concept of entities, and *featuregroups* in *Hopsworks* are analogous to *featureviews* in *Feast*. Just like other feature stores, Hopsworks supports online and offline serving. It uses Apache Hive with Apache Hudi as an offline store and MySQL Cluster as an online store. Again, there are no options for online or offline stores. However, there are different storage connectors developed by Hopsworks that can be used to create on-demand external feature groups, such as *RedShiftSource*, which we defined in *Feast* in *Chapter 4*, *Adding Feature Store to ML Models*. But there is a limitation on external feature groups, meaning there is no time travel, online serving, and so on.

There are a lot of features in the Hopsworks Feature Store that are fancy and very interesting. Some of the best ones are as follows:

- **Project-level multi-tenancy**: Each project has an owner and can share resources with other members in the team and across teams.
- **Feature group versioning**: Hopsworks supports feature group versioning, which is not currently supported by any other feature stores on the market.

- **Statistics on feature groups**: It provides a few out-of-the-box statistics on feature groups, such as feature co-relation computation, a frequency histogram on features, and uniqueness. The following is an example feature group:

```
store_fg_meta = fs.create_feature_group(
    name="store_fg",
    version=1,
    primary_key=["store"],
    description="Store related features",
    statistics_config={"enabled": True,
                       "histograms": True,
                       "correlations": True})
```

- **Feature validation**: This is another fancy feature that is available out of the box. This is a set of predefined validation rules that exist on feature groups such as the minimum and maximum values of a feature, a uniqueness count of features, the entropy of a feature, and the maximum length of features. It has enough rule types that you won't have a use case where you need to customize a validation rule. The following are a couple of example rules:

```
#the minimum value of the feature needs to be between 0
and 10
rules=[Rule(name="HAS_MIN", level="WARNING",
            min=0, max=10)]

#Exactly 10% of all instances of the feature need to be
contained in the legal_values list
rules=[Rule(name="IS_CONTAINED_IN", level="ERROR",
            legal_values=["a", "b"], min=0.1,
            max=0.1)]
```

- **Transformation functions**: Similar to Tecton transformations for feature views, in Hopsworks, you can define or use built-in transformation on a training dataset (Hopsworks has a concept of training data where you can pick features from different feature groups and create a training dataset definition on top of them– a concept similar to database views).

There are some things to keep in mind though. If you choose the open source version, you may not have several features, and infrastructure will have to be self-managed. Conversely, for the enterprise version, you will have to collaborate with a Hopsworks engineer and create a few resources and roles required for the installation of Hopsworks on the cloud provider. Here is a link to all the documentation: `https://docs.hopsworks.ai/feature-store-api/2.5.8/`. I recommend having a look at the features even if you don't use them; this might give an idea of some of the features you might want to build or have in your feature store.

SageMaker Feature Store

SageMaker is an end-to-end ML platform offered by AWS. Just like Vertex AI, it has a notebook environment, AutoML, processing jobs and model management, a feature store, and so on. If you are an AWS-focused company, this must be a natural pick over the others.

The concepts are close to that of other feature stores, although some of the terms are different. For example, SageMaker Feature Store also doesn't have the concept of entities, and *featureviews* in Feast are analogous to *featuregroups* in SageMaker. It has all the basic features, such as online and offline stores and serving. However, you don't have options to pick from. It uses S3 as an offline store and one of the key-value stores as an online store (AWS doesn't say what is used for an online store in its documentation). AWS uses IAM for authentication and authorization. To access feature store currently, you need full access to SageMaker and the AWS Glue console. If you compare SageMaker to Feast, both use/support S3 as an offline store, a key-value store as an online store, and a Glue catalog for managing the schema. Apart from SageMaker being a managed feature store, another difference is that Feast uses Redshift for querying offline data, whereas SageMaker uses Amazon Athena (serverless) for querying. You can add this functionality to Feast if you are a fan of serverless technologies.

One of my favorite things about SageMaker Feature Store is that there is no infrastructure management. Apart from creating an IAM role to access the feature store, you don't need to manage anything. All the resources for any given load are managed by AWS. All you need to worry about is just developing and ingesting features. SageMaker Feature Store also supports ingestion using Spark on EMR or Glue jobs (serverless). Along with the features, it also adds metadata, such as `write_time` and `api_invocation_time`, that can be used in queries. The best part is that you can query offline data using Amazon Athena SQL queries.

There are a few things to keep in mind though. The current implementation doesn't yet have granular access management. Right now, you need full access to SageMaker to use Feature Store, although I believe that it's only a matter of time before AWS starts offering granular access. Point-in-time joins are not available out of the box; however, these can be achieved using SQL queries or Spark.

So far, we have looked at a few of the available options on the market; you can find other feature stores that are available at this link: `https://www.featurestore.org/`. However, picking the right feature store for your project or team can be tricky. The following are a few things to keep in mind while picking a feature store:

- Your primary cloud provider makes a huge difference. If you are GCP-focused, it doesn't make sense to use SageMaker Feature Store and vice versa. If you are multi-cloud, then you will have more options.
- The data processing framework is also another key factor that decides what feature store to use. For example, if you use SageMaker as your ML platform, trying out SageMaker Feature Store before others makes more sense.
- Integration with other components in your ecosystem is also key – for instance, answering questions such as how well it integrates with your processing platform, the orchestration framework, the model management service, data validation frameworks, and your ML development process can really help in picking the right feature store.
- The required functionalities and your team structure make a big difference. If you are a small team who wants to just concentrate on ML, then a managed offering of a feature store makes sense, whereas if you have a platform team to manage the infrastructure, you may look into open source offerings and also evaluate the build versus buy options. If you have a platform team, they might look for additional features such as multi-tenancy, granular access control, and SaaS/PaaS.

In conclusion, a lot of factors influence the choice of a feature store other than the functionalities it offers, as it must integrate well with a broader ecosystem.

Next, let's look at how a managed feature store works.

Feature management with SageMaker Feature Store

In this section, we will look into what action we might have to take if we were to use a managed feature store instead of Feast in *Chapter 4, Adding Feature Store to ML Models.*

> **Important Note**
>
> All managed feature stores have a similar workflow; some may be API-based and some work through a CLI. But irrespective of this, the amount of work involved in using the feature store would be similar to what we will discuss in this section. The only reason I am going through SageMaker is familiarity and ease of access to it, using the free trial as a featured product in AWS.

Resources to use SageMaker

In *Chapter 4, Adding Feature Store to ML Models*, before we started using the feature store, we created a bunch of resources on AWS, such as an S3 bucket, a Redshift cluster, an IAM role, and a Glue catalog table. Conversely, for a managed feature store such as SageMaker, all you need to have is an IAM role that has full access to SageMaker and you are all set. Let's try that out now.

We need some IAM user credentials and an IAM role that SageMaker Feature Store can assume. Creating an IAM user is similar to what we have done before. Follow the same steps and create an IAM user, and assign **AmazonS3FullAccess** and **AmazonSageMakerFullAccess** permissions. IAM role creation is the same as we have done before; however, we need to allow the SageMaker service to assume the role.

> **Important Note**
>
> As mentioned many times before, it is never a good idea to assign full access; permissions should always be restrictive based on resources.

Let's create an IAM role:

1. Log in to your AWS account and navigate to the IAM role page, using the search bar; alternatively, visit the following URL: `https://us-east-1.console.aws.amazon.com/iamv2/home#/roles`. The following page will be displayed:

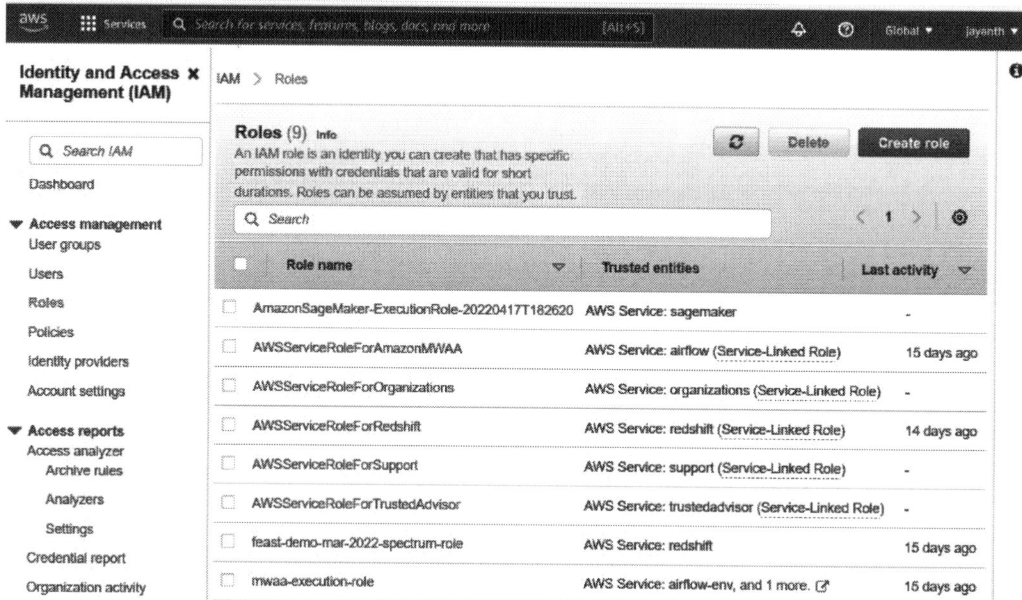

Figure 7.1 – The IAM role home page

2. On the displayed web page, click on **Create role** to navigate to the following screen:

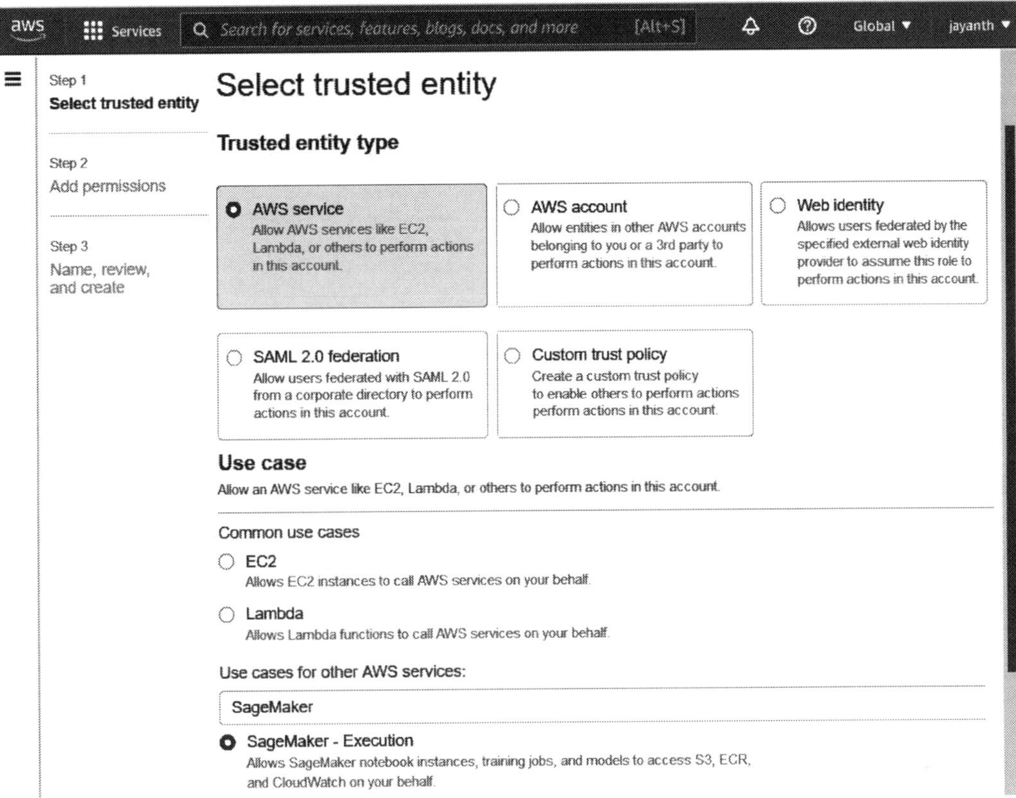

Figure 7.2 – The IAM role creation page

3. On the screen displayed in *Figure 7.2*, in the **Use cases for other AWS services** dropdown, select **SageMaker** and then click the **SageMaker - Execution** radio button. Scroll down and click on **Next**, leaving everything as default on the **Add Permissions** page, and then click on **Next**. The following page will be displayed:

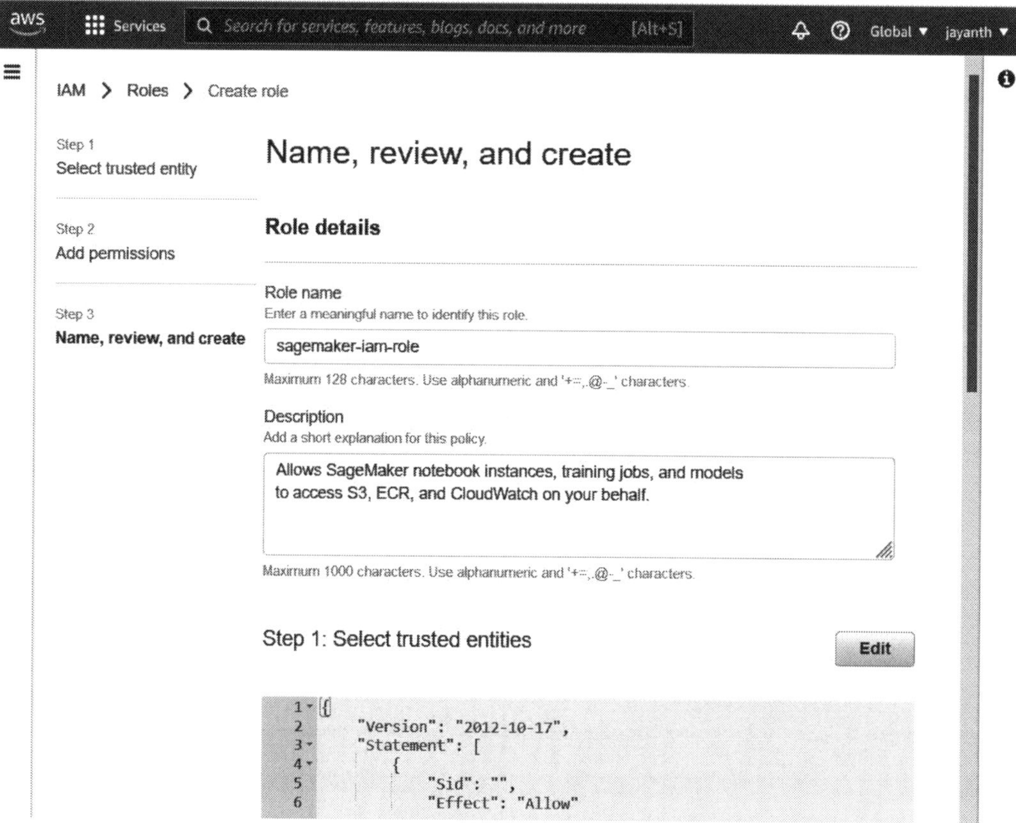

Figure 7.3 – The Name, review and create page

4. On the displayed web page, fill in the **Role name** field. We'll set the role name as `sagemaker-iam-role`. Scroll all the way down and click on **Create role**. Once the role is created, navigate to the IAM role details page and add the **AmazonS3FullAccess** permission, similar to how we did before. Also, copy the role **ARN** (short for **Amazon Resource Name**), which will be of the following format: `arn:aws:iam::<account_number>:role/sagemaker-iam-role`.

That's all we need to access SageMaker Feature Store. Let's create the feature definitions next.

Generating features

To define the feature group, since we are trying to compare how it differs from Feast, we will take the same feature set. You can download the previously ingested features from an S3 bucket or download it from the GitHub link: `https://github.com/PacktPublishing/Feature-Store-for-Machine-Learning/blob/main/Chapter07/rfm_features.parquet`. After downloading the Parquet file, copy it to a location that can be accessed from the notebook. The next step is to create a new notebook, which I am calling `ch7-sagemaker-feature-store.ipynb`:

1. Let's install the required libraries first:

```
!pip install sagemaker pandas
```

2. After installing the libraries, let's generate the features. Here, we will be just reading the copied file from the location and making minor modifications to the dataset:

```
import pandas as pd
import time
df = pd.read_parquet(path="/content/rfm_features.
parquet")
df = df.drop(columns=["created_timestamp"])
df["event_timestamp"] = float(round(time.time()))
df["customerid"] = df['customerid'].astype(float)
df.head()
```

The preceding code block reads the file and drops the `created_timestamp` column, as it is not required by SageMaker. We are also updating the `event_timestamp` column to the latest time and changing the type to `float` instead of `datetime`. The reason for this is that SageMaker only supports the `int`, `float`, and `string` features at the time of writing, and `datetime` files can either be a `float` or `string` object in the `datetime` ISO format.

The code block produces the following output:

	customerid	recency	frequency	monetaryvalue	r	f	m	rfmscore	revenue6m	ltvcluster	segmenthighvalue	segmentlowValue	segmentmidvalue	event_timestamp
0	12747.0	7	35	1082.09	3	2	3	8	1666.11	1	1	0	0	1.651455e+09
1	12748.0	1	582	4336.73	3	3	3	9	18679.01	2	1	0	0	1.651455e+09
2	12749.0	8	54	782.10	3	3	3	9	2323.04	1	1	0	0	1.651455e+09
4	12823.0	63	1	459.00	0	0	2	2	765.00	1	0	1	0	1.651455e+09
7	12836.0	28	62	814.71	1	3	3	7	951.46	1	1	0	0	1.651455e+09

Figure 7.4 – Recency, Frequency, and Monetary value (RFM) features

Now that we have RFM features, the next step is to define the feature group. If you recall correctly from *Chapter 4, Adding Feature Store to ML Models*, after generating the features, we created the feature definitions and applied them to the feature store.

Defining the feature group

To define the feature group, since it's a one-time activity, it should be done in a separate notebook rather than by feature engineering. For this exercise, let's continue in the same notebook and define the feature group:

1. The following code block defines a few imports and creates the SageMaker session:

```
import sagemaker
import sys
import boto3
from sagemaker.session import Session
from sagemaker import get_execution_role
import os
os.environ["AWS_ACCESS_KEY_ID"] = "<aws_key_id>"
os.environ["AWS_SECRET_ACCESS_KEY"] ="<aws_secret_id>"
os.environ["AWS_DEFAULT_REGION"] = "us-east-1"
prefix = 'sagemaker-featurestore-introduction'
role = "arn:aws:iam::<account_number>:role/sagemaker-iam-role"
sagemaker_session = sagemaker.Session()
region = sagemaker_session.boto_region_name
s3_bucket_name = "feast-demo-mar-2022"
```

In the code block, replace `<aws_key_id>` and `<aws_secret_id>` with the key and secret of the IAM user created earlier. Also, assign `role` with your IAM role ARN.

2. The following code block creates the feature group object and loads the feature definitions from the input DataFrame:

```
from sagemaker.feature_store.feature_group import \
  FeatureGroup
customers_feature_group = FeatureGroup(
    name="customer-rfm-features",
    sagemaker_session=sagemaker_session
)
customers_feature_group.load_feature_definitions(df)
```

The preceding code block produces the following output:

```
[FeatureDefinition(feature_name='customerid', feature_type=<FeatureTypeEnum.FRACTIONAL: 'Fractional'>),
 FeatureDefinition(feature_name='recency', feature_type=<FeatureTypeEnum.INTEGRAL: 'Integral'>),
 FeatureDefinition(feature_name='frequency', feature_type=<FeatureTypeEnum.INTEGRAL: 'Integral'>),
 FeatureDefinition(feature_name='monetaryvalue', feature_type=<FeatureTypeEnum.FRACTIONAL: 'Fractional'>),
 FeatureDefinition(feature_name='r', feature_type=<FeatureTypeEnum.INTEGRAL: 'Integral'>),
 FeatureDefinition(feature_name='f', feature_type=<FeatureTypeEnum.INTEGRAL: 'Integral'>),
 FeatureDefinition(feature_name='m', feature_type=<FeatureTypeEnum.INTEGRAL: 'Integral'>),
 FeatureDefinition(feature_name='rfmscore', feature_type=<FeatureTypeEnum.INTEGRAL: 'Integral'>),
 FeatureDefinition(feature_name='revenue6m', feature_type=<FeatureTypeEnum.FRACTIONAL: 'Fractional'>),
 FeatureDefinition(feature_name='ltvcluster', feature_type=<FeatureTypeEnum.INTEGRAL: 'Integral'>),
 FeatureDefinition(feature_name='segmenthighvalue', feature_type=<FeatureTypeEnum.INTEGRAL: 'Integral'>),
 FeatureDefinition(feature_name='segmentlowvalue', feature_type=<FeatureTypeEnum.INTEGRAL: 'Integral'>),
 FeatureDefinition(feature_name='segmentmidvalue', feature_type=<FeatureTypeEnum.INTEGRAL: 'Integral'>),
 FeatureDefinition(feature_name='event_timestamp', feature_type=<FeatureTypeEnum.FRACTIONAL: 'Fractional'>)]
```

Figure 7.5 – The load feature definitions call

As you can see in *Figure 7.5*, the `load_feature_definitions` call reads the input DataFrame and loads the feature definition automatically.

3. The next step is to create the feature group. The following code block creates the feature group in SageMaker:

```
customers_feature_group.create(
    s3_uri=f"s3://{s3_bucket_name}/{prefix}",
    record_identifier_name="customerid",
    event_time_feature_name="event_timestamp",
    role_arn=role,
    enable_online_store=True
)
```

The preceding code block invokes the create API by passing the following parameters:

- `s3_uri`: The location where the feature data will be stored
- `record_identifier_name`: The name of the `id` column (the same as the entity column in Feast)
- `event_time_feature_name`: The timestamp column that will be used for time travel
- `role_arn`: The role that SageMaker Feature Store can assume
- `enable_online_store`: Whether to enable online serving or not for this feature group

The code block produces the following output on the successful creation of the feature group:

```
{'FeatureGroupArn': 'arn:aws:sagemaker:us-east-[redacted]feature-group/customer-rfm-features',
 'ResponseMetadata': {'HTTPHeaders': {'content-length': '98',
   'content-type': 'application/x-amz-json-1.1',
   'date': 'Mon, 02 May 2022 01:30:15[redacted]
   'x-amzn-requestid': '4fb00252-deb[redacted]'},
  'HTTPStatusCode': 200,
  'RequestId': '4fb00252-de[redacted]',
  'RetryAttempts': 0}}
```

Figure 7.6 – Feature group creation

That's all – our feature group is ready to use. Let's ingest the features next.

Feature ingestion

Feature ingestion in SageMaker Feature Store is simple. It is a simple API call, as shown in the following code block:

```
ingestion_manager = customers_feature_group.ingest(df))
ingestion_manager.wait()
ingestion_manager.failed_rows
```

The preceding code block will ingest the features and print the failed row numbers if there are any.

One thing to keep in mind here is that, like Feast, you don't need to do anything extra to materialize the latest features from an offline to an online store. If the online store is enabled, the data will be ingested to both online and offline stores, and the latest data will be available in the online store for querying right away.

Let's query the online store next.

Getting records from an online store

Like Feast, querying from an online store is simple. All you need is the record ID and the feature group name. The following code block gets the record from the online store:

```
customer_id = 12747.0
sg_runtime_client = sagemaker_session.boto_session.client(
    'sagemaker-featurestore-runtime',
    region_name=region)
record = sg_runtime_client.get_record(
    FeatureGroupName="customer-rfm-features",
    RecordIdentifierValueAsString=str(customer_id))
print(record)
```

The preceding code block gets all the features for the customer with the `12747.0` ID from the online store. The query should return the results within milliseconds. The output will be similar to the following code block:

```
{'ResponseMetadata': {'RequestId': '55342bbc-c69b-49ca-
bbd8-xxxx', 'HTTPStatusCode': 200, 'HTTPHeaders': {'x-amzn-
requestid': '55342bbc-c69b-49ca-bbd8-xxx, 'content-type':
'application/json', 'content-length': '729', 'date': 'Mon, 02
May 2022 01:36:27 GMT'}, 'RetryAttempts': 0},
'Record': [{'FeatureName': 'customerid', 'ValueAsString':
'12747.0'}, {'FeatureName': 'recency', 'ValueAsString':
'7'}, {'FeatureName': 'frequency', 'ValueAsString':
'35'}, {'FeatureName': 'monetaryvalue', 'ValueAsString':
'1082.09'}, {'FeatureName': 'r', 'ValueAsString': '3'},
{'FeatureName': 'f', 'ValueAsString': '2'}, {'FeatureName':
'm', 'ValueAsString': '3'}, {'FeatureName': 'rfmscore',
'ValueAsString': '8'}, {'FeatureName': 'revenue6m',
'ValueAsString': '1666.1100000000001'}, {'FeatureName':
'ltvcluster', 'ValueAsString': '1'}, {'FeatureName':
'segmenthighvalue', 'ValueAsString': '1'}, {'FeatureName':
'segmentlowValue', 'ValueAsString': '0'}, {'FeatureName':
'segmentmidvalue', 'ValueAsString': '0'}, {'FeatureName':
'event_timestamp', 'ValueAsString': '1651455004.0'}]}
```

As you can see, the output contains all the features and corresponding values.

Now that we have looked at querying an online store, let's check out how to generate the training dataset and query historical data next.

Querying historical data with Amazon Athena

As mentioned previously, SageMaker Feature Store offers the ability to run SQL queries on a historical store using Amazon Athena.

The following code block generates the latest snapshot of all customers and their features:

```
get_latest_snapshot_query = customers_feature_group.athena_
query()
query = f"""SELECT *
FROM
    (SELECT *,
         row_number()
        OVER (PARTITION BY customerid
    ORDER BY  event_timestamp desc, Api_Invocation_Time DESC,
write_time DESC) AS row_num
    FROM "{get_latest_snapshot_query.table_name}")
WHERE row_num = 1 and
NOT is_deleted;"""
get_latest_snapshot_query.run(query_string=query, output_
location=f"s3://{s3_bucket_name}/output")
get_latest_snapshot_query.get_query_execution()
```

The code block uses a nested SQL query, where the inner query gets all customers and their features, in descending order, from the `event_time`, `Api_Invocation_Time`, and `write_time` columns. The outer query selects the first occurrence of every customer from the results of the inner query. On successful execution of the query, the code block outputs the location of the query results along with additional details.

The results can be loaded as a DataFrame, as shown in the following code block:

```
latest_df = get_latest_snapshot_query.as_dataframe()
latest_df.head()
```

The preceding code block output the following:

customerid	recency	frequency	monetaryvalue	r	f	m	rfmscore	revenue6m	ltvcluster	segmenthighvalue	segmentlowvalue	segmentmidvalue	event_timestamp	write_time
12747.0	7	35	1082.09	3	2	3	8	1666.11	1	1	0	0	1.651455e+09	2022-05-02 01:36:31.398
12823.0	63	1	459.00	0	0	2	2	765.00	1	0	1	0	1.651455e+09	2022-05-02 01:36:31.406
12836.0	28	62	814.71	1	3	3	7	951.46	1	1	0	0	1.651455e+09	2022-05-02 01:36:31.391
12748.0	1	582	4336.73	3	3	3	9	18679.01	2	1	0	0	1.651455e+09	2022-05-02 01:36:31.400
12749.0	8	54	782.10	3	3	3	9	2323.04	1	1	0	0	1.651455e+09	2022-05-02 01:36:31.397

Figure 7.7 – Athena query results

Feel free to try out other Athena queries on Feature Store. Here is the documentation of the Amazon Athena query: `https://docs.aws.amazon.com/athena/latest/ug/what-is.html`.

Cleaning up a SageMaker feature group

Let's clean up the SageMaker resources to save costs before we move forward. The cleanup is pretty easy; it is just another API call to delete the feature group. The following code block performs that:

```
customers_feature_group.delete()
```

That's all. After successful execution, it deletes the feature group but leaves behind the data in S3 and the Glue catalog, which can still be queried with Amazon Athena (using the `boto3` client) if required. Just to make sure everything is cleaned up, run the following code block in the same notebook. It should return an empty list of feature groups:

```
sagemaker_client = sagemaker_session.boto_session.client(
    "sagemaker", region_name=region
)
sagemaker_client.list_feature_groups()
```

Now that we have looked at the SageMaker feature group, let's look into ML best practices next.

ML best practices

So far in the book, we have discussed feature stores, how to use them for ML development and production, and what the available options are when choosing a feature store. Though a feature store is one of the major components/aspects of ML, there are other aspects of ML that we haven't concentrated on much in this book. In this section, let's briefly talk through some of the other aspects and best practices in ML.

Data validation at source

Irrespective of the technologies, algorithms, and infrastructure we use for building an ML model, if there are errors and anomalies in data, model performance will be severely impacted. Data should be treated as a first-class citizen of any ML system. Hence, it is very important to detect errors and anomalies in the data before it enters the ML pipeline.

To run validation on raw data sources, we need a component to create and orchestrate the validation rules against the data. Users of the data should be able to write any custom rules in SQL queries, Python scripts, or Spark SQL. Any failures in the rule should be notified to the data consumers who, in turn, should be able to make a decision on whether to stop the pipeline execution, retrain the model, or take no action.

Some of the common rules include descriptive analytics of the dataset on schedule, which can provide insights into data drift. More advanced statistics such as **Kullback–Leibler (KL)** divergence and the **Population Stability Index (PSI)** are good to have. Having simple data validation rules such as data freshness, unique values, string field length, patterns, and value range thresholds can be very beneficial. Schema validation is another important aspect of data validation. Any changes in the validation can affect all the consumers and pipelines. The better data validation we have at source, the healthier and more performant our models and pipeline will be.

Breaking down ML pipeline and orchestration

One bad practice is to develop everything in a single notebook, from data validation and feature engineering to model prediction. This is not a scalable or reusable approach. Most of the time is spent cleaning up unwanted code and productionizing the model. Hence, it is always a good idea to break down the ML pipeline into multiple smaller steps, such as data validation, cleaning, transformation, feature engineering, model training, and model prediction. The smaller the transformation steps, the more readable, reusable, and easy it will be to debug code for errors. This is one of the reasons that Feature Views and transformation in Tecton, and storage connectors and transformation functions in Hopsworks are great features. Similar features are also offered by many **Extract, Transform and Load (ETL)** frameworks.

Apart from breaking down the ML pipeline, orchestration is another important part of ML platforms. Every cloud provider has one, and there are many open source offerings as well. Developing pipeline steps that can be orchestrated without much work is key. Nowadays, there are a lot of tools for orchestration, and as long as the steps are small and meaningful, it should be easy to orchestrate with any of the existing frameworks.

Tracking data lineage and versioning

If you recall *Chapter 6, Model to Production and Beyond*, we discussed debugging prediction issues. In that example, we discussed generating the same feature set that produced the anomaly in prediction; however, many times it won't be enough to figure out what went wrong in the system and whether it was caused by code or the dataset. Hence, along with that, being able to track the data lineage of that feature set all the way to the data source can be very helpful in debugging the issue.

For every run of the pipeline, saving the input and output of every step with the timestamp version is the key here. With this, we can track the anomaly in prediction all the way back to its source, which is data. For example, instead of just having the features that generated a bad recommendation for a customer on a website, it would be better to also have the ability to trace the features all the way back to their interactions at the time of the event and the different transformation that was generated in the ML pipeline when this event occurred.

The following is some of the pipeline information that can help in better lineage tracking:

- Versions of all the libraries used in the steps
- Versions of code that was run in the pipeline, including the pipeline version itself
- Input arguments and artifacts produced by every step of the pipeline, such as the raw data, the dataset, and models

Next, let's look at the feature repository.

The feature repository

Having a feature repository can be very beneficial for ML development. Though there are a few gray areas in respect of updates to feature table schema, the benefits of a feature store, such as reusability, browsable features, the readiness of online serving, time travel, and point-in-time joins, are very useful in model development. As we observed in the previous chapter, the features developed during the development of the customer lifetime value model were useful in the Next Purchase Day model. Similarly, as the feature repository grows in size, more and more features become available for use, and there is less duplication of work for data scientists and engineers to do, thereby accelerating the development of the model.

The following screenshot depicts the cost of developing an ML model versus the number of curated features in the feature store:

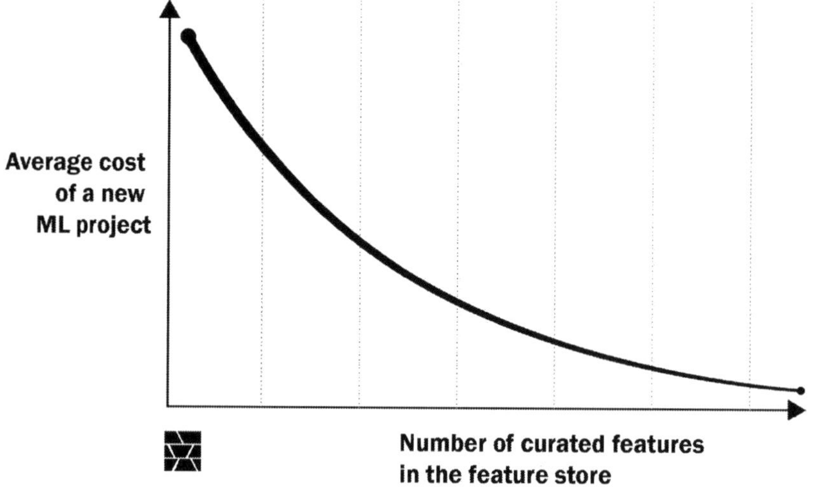

Figure 7.8 – The average cost of the model versus the number of curated features in the feature store

As shown in *Figure 7.8*, the cost of developing and productionizing the model goes down as the feature repository grows. Going by the reuse and add new if not available, all the features available in the feature repository are either production-ready or serving production models. We will be just adding delta features for each new model. This means that the only additional cost on the infrastructure would be to run these additional feature engineering transformations and new feature tables, and the rest is assumed to auto-scale for the production load if we are using a managed feature store. Hence, the cost involved in the development and production of the new model should decrease over time and flatten once the feature repository is saturated.

Experiment tracking, model versioning, and the model repository

Experiment tracking and the model repository are other important aspects of ML development. When developing a model, we run different experiments – it could be different algorithms, different implementations such as TensorFlow versus PyTorch, hyperparameter tuning, a different set of features for the model, a different training dataset, and also different transformations on the training dataset. Keeping track of these experiments is not easy, as some of these experiments can go on for days or weeks. Hence, using experiment-tracking software that comes out of the box with many of the notebook environments is very important.

Every run should log the following:

- The version of model training notebooks or scripts.
- Some parameters about the dataset that can be used to reproduce the same training and evaluation dataset. If you are using a feature store, then it could be the timestamps and entities used; if not, you can also save the training dataset to a file and log the location of the dataset.
- All the parameters that are used in the training algorithm.
- The performance metrics of each run.
- Any visualization of the results can also be very useful.

The logged metrics for each run can be used for comparing the performance metrics of the models for different runs. These metrics will be critical in making a decision on which run of the model is better performing and should be moved to new stages, such as stage deployment, and AB testing. In addition, each run also helps you browse through the history of the experiments if you or anybody else on the team ever need to look back and reproduce some specific run.

Similarly, a model repository can help in keeping track of all the different versions of the model. The model registry/repository stores the information required to load and run the model – for instance, an MLflow model repository stores information such as the conda environment, the model's `pickle` file, and any other additional *dependencies* of the model. If you have a central repository of the model, it can be useful for consumers to browse and search, and also for the life cycle management of models, such as moving models to different stages – development, staging, production, and archived. Model repositories can also be used for scanning any vulnerabilities in code and any packages used in the model. Hence, the model repository plays a key role in ML development.

Feature and model monitoring

As we discussed in the previous chapter, feature monitoring is another important aspect. An important counterpart of the feature repository is monitoring for changes and anomalies. The feature monitoring rules will be similar to that of data monitoring. Some of the useful rules of features are feature freshness, minimum and maximum rules, monitoring for outliers, descriptive statistics of the latest features, and metrics such as KL divergence and PSI. The Hopsworks monitoring rules should be a good starting point for the list of rules that you may have on features. Here is a link to the documentation: `https://docs.hopsworks.ai/feature-store-api/2.5.8/generated/feature_validation/`.

Model monitoring is another important aspect. After moving a model to production, it tends to decay in performance over time. This happens as user behaviors change; hence the data profiles. It is important to keep track of how the model is performing in production. These performance reports should be generated on schedule, if not in real time, and appropriate actions must be taken, such as model retraining with the new data or starting a new iteration altogether.

Miscellaneous

A few other things to keep in mind during ML development include keeping track of runtime environments, library upgrades, and depreciations. It is better to proactively act on these. For instance, if you use tools that are strictly tied to a specific environment, such as a Python or Spark version, once a specific runtime is deprecated and removed from production support, the jobs might start failing and the production system may be hampered. Another example could be that Databricks has runtimes that are tied to specific Python and Spark versions. If you are running jobs on a deprecated version, once it goes out of support, the jobs might start failing if there are breaking changes in the new version. Hence, it is better to upgrade proactively.

With that, let's summarize what we have learned in this chapter before looking at an end-to-end use case in the next chapter.

Summary

In this chapter, we took a look at some of the available feature stores on the market. We discussed five of them, namely Tecton, Databricks, Vertex AI, Hopsworks, and SageMaker Feature Store. We also did a deep dive into SageMaker Feature Store to get a feel of using a managed feature store instead of Feast and how it differs when it comes to resource creation, feature ingestion, and querying. In the last section, we briefly discussed a set of best practices for ML development.

In the next chapter, we'll go through an end-to-end use case on a managed ML platform.

8
Use Case – Customer Churn Prediction

In the last chapter, we discussed the alternatives to the **Feast** feature store available on the market. We looked at a few feature store offerings from cloud providers that are part of **Machine Learning** (**ML**) platform offerings, namely, SageMaker, Vertex AI, and Databricks. We also looked at a couple of other vendors that offer managed feature stores that can be used with your cloud provider, namely, Tecton and Hopsworks, of which Hopsworks is also open source. To get a feel for a managed feature store, we tried out an exercise on the SageMaker Feature Store and also briefly discussed ML best practices.

In this chapter, we will discuss an end-to-end use case of customer churn using a telecom dataset. We will walk through data cleaning, feature engineering, feature ingestion, model training, deployment, and monitoring. For this exercise, we will use a managed feature store – Amazon SageMaker. The reason for choosing SageMaker over other alternatives that we discussed in the last chapter is simply the easy accessibility to the trial version of the software.

The aim of this chapter is to go through a customer churn prediction ML use case, step by step, using a managed feature store. This should give you an idea of how it differs from self-managed feature stores and also basic feature monitoring and model monitoring aspects the feature store helps with.

In this chapter, we will discuss the following topics in order:

- Infrastructure setup
- Introduction to the problem and the dataset
- Data processing and feature engineering
- Feature group definitions and ingestion
- Model training
- Model prediction
- Feature monitoring
- Model monitoring

Technical requirements

To run through the examples and to get a better understanding of this chapter, an understanding of the topics covered in previous chapters will be useful but is not required. To follow the code examples in this chapter, you need familiarity with a notebook environment, which could be a local setup such as the Jupyter Notebook or an online notebook environment such as Google Colab, Kaggle, or SageMaker. You will also need an AWS account with full access to SageMaker and the Glue console. You can create a new account and use all the services for free during the trial period. You can find the code examples of the book at the following GitHub link:

`https://github.com/PacktPublishing/Feature-Store-for-Machine-Learning/tree/main/Chapter08`

Infrastructure setup

For the exercises in this chapter, we will need an S3 bucket to store data, an IAM role, and an IAM user that has access to both the SageMaker Feature Store and the S3 bucket. Since we have already gone through creating all these resources, I will skip through this. Please refer to *Chapter 4*, *Adding Feature Store to ML Models*, for S3 bucket creation, and *Chapter 7*, *Feast Alternatives and ML Best Practices*, for IAM role and IAM user creation. That is all we need, in terms of initial setup for this chapter.

> **Important Note**
>
> I am trying to use as few resources of AWS SageMaker as possible since it will incur costs if your free trial has come to an end. You can use SageMaker Studio for a better experience with notebooks and also the UI of the feature store.

Introduction to the problem and the dataset

In this exercise, we will use the telecom customer churn dataset, which is available on Kaggle at the URL `https://www.kaggle.com/datasets/blastchar/telco-customer-churn`. The aim of the exercise is to use this dataset, prepare the data for model training, and train an XGBoost model to predict customer churn. The dataset has 21 columns and the column names are self-explanatory. The following is a preview of the dataset:

	customerID	gender	SeniorCitizen	Partner	Dependents	tenure	PhoneService	MultipleLines	InternetService	OnlineSecurity	OnlineBackup
0	7590-VHVEG	Female	0	Yes	No	1	No	No phone service	DSL	No	Yes
1	5575-GNVDE	Male	0	No	No	34	Yes	No	DSL	Yes	No
2	3668-QPYBK	Male	0	No	No	2	Yes	No	DSL	Yes	Yes
3	7795-CFOCW	Male	0	No	No	45	No	No phone service	DSL	Yes	No
4	9237-HQITU	Female	0	No	No	2	Yes	No	Fiber optic	No	No

	DeviceProtection	TechSupport	StreamingTV	StreamingMovies	Contract	PaperlessBilling	PaymentMethod	MonthlyCharges	TotalCharges	Churn
0	No	No	No	No	Month-to-month	Yes	Electronic check	29.85	29.85	No
1	Yes	No	No	No	One year	No	Mailed check	56.95	1889.5	No
2	No	No	No	No	Month-to-month	Yes	Mailed check	53.85	108.15	Yes
3	Yes	Yes	No	No	One year	No	Bank transfer (automatic)	42.30	1840.75	No
4	No	No	No	No	Month-to-month	Yes	Electronic check	70.70	151.65	Yes

Figure 8.1 – Telecom dataset

Figure 8.1 shows the labeled telecom customer churn dataset. The `customerID` column is the ID of the customers. All other columns except `Churn` represent the set of attributes, and the `Churn` column is the target column.

Let's get our hands dirty and perform feature engineering next.

Data processing and feature engineering

In this section, let's use the telecom customer churn dataset and generate the features that can be used for training the model. Let's create a notebook, call it `feature-engineering.ipynb`, and install the required dependencies:

```
!pip install pandas sklearn python-slugify s3fs sagemaker
```

Once the installation of the libraries is complete, read the data. For this exercise, I have downloaded the data from Kaggle and saved it in a location where it is accessible from the notebook.

The following command reads the data from S3:

```
import os
import numpy as np
import pandas as pd
from slugify import slugify
from sklearn.preprocessing import LabelEncoder
from sklearn.preprocessing import StandardScaler
""" If you are executing the notebook outside AWS(Local jupyter
lab, google collab or kaggle etc.), please uncomment the
following 3 lines of code and set the AWS credentials """
#os.environ["AWS_ACCESS_KEY_ID"] = "<aws_key>"
#os.environ["AWS_SECRET_ACCESS_KEY"] = "<aws_secret>"
#os.environ["AWS_DEFAULT_REGION"] = "us-east-1"

telcom = pd.read_csv("s3://<bucket_name_path>/telco-customer-
churn.csv")
```

> **Important Note**
>
> If you are executing the notebook outside AWS, then set the user credentials using the environment variables.

If you preview that dataset, there are a few columns that need to be reformatted, converted into a categorical column, or have empty values removed. Let's perform those transformations one after the other.

The `TotalCharges` column contains a few empty strings. Let's remove the rows that contain empty or null values for `TotalCharges`:

```
# Replace empty strings with nan
churn_data['TotalCharges'] = churn_data["TotalCharges"].
replace(" ",np.nan)
# remove null values
churn_data = churn_data[churn_data["TotalCharges"].notnull()]
churn_data = churn_data.reset_index()[churn_data.columns]
churn_data["TotalCharges"] = churn_data["TotalCharges"].
astype(float)
```

The preceding code block replaces all the empty strings with `np.nan` and drops all the rows that contain null in the `TotalCharges` column.

Next, let's look at the tenure column. This one has integer values that represent the tenure of the customer in months. Along with the value, we can also group the customers into three groups: short (0-24 months), mid (24-48 months), and long (greater than 48 months).

The following code adds the customer tenure_group column with the defined groups:

```
# Create tenure_group columns using the tenure
def tenure_label(churn_data) :
    if churn_data["tenure"] <= 24 :
        return "0-24"
    elif (churn_data["tenure"] > 24) & (churn_data["tenure"] <=
48) :
        return "24-48"
    elif churn_data["tenure"] > 48:
        return "48-end"
churn_data["tenure_group"] = churn_data.apply(
    lambda churn_data: tenure_label(churn_data), axis = 1)
```

The preceding code block creates the categorical column tenure_group, which will have three values, 0-24, 24-48, and 48-end, depending on the length of the customer tenure.

A few columns in the dataset are dependent on others. For example, OnlineSecurity depends on whether the customer has InternetService or not. Hence, some of these columns, namely, OnlineSecurity, OnlineBackup, DeviceProtection, TechSupport, StreamingTV, and StreamingMovies have No internet service as the value instead of No. Let's replace No internet service with No in those columns.

The following code block performs the replacement:

```
# Replace 'No internet service' to No for the following columns
replace_cols = ['OnlineSecurity', 'OnlineBackup',
                'DeviceProtection', 'TechSupport',
                'StreamingTV', 'StreamingMovies']
for i in replace_cols :
    churn_data[i] = churn_data[i].replace({'No internet
service' : 'No'})
```

We have done a set of data cleaning operations so far. Let's preview the dataset once before we proceed and do further transformations.

The following code samples the `churn_data` DataFrame:

```
churn_data.sample(5)
```

The following code outputs a sample preview as shown in the following screenshot:

	customerID	gender	SeniorCitizen	Partner	Dependents	tenure	PhoneService	MultipleLines	InternetService	OnlineSecurity	OnlineBackup	DeviceProtection
4850	3950-VPYJB	Male	0	Yes	Yes	57	Yes	No	DSL	Yes	Yes	No
2622	4213-HKBJO	Female	0	No	No	33	Yes	Yes	No	No	No	No
4773	9814-AOUDH	Male	0	No	No	53	Yes	No	No	No	No	No
490	6778-YSNIH	Female	0	No	No	2	Yes	No	DSL	No	Yes	No
1085	4546-FOKWR	Female	0	No	No	16	Yes	Yes	Fiber optic	No	No	No

	TechSupport	StreamingTV	StreamingMovies	Contract	PaperlessBilling	PaymentMethod	MonthlyCharges	TotalCharges	Churn	tenure_group
4850	Yes	No	No	One year	No	Mailed check	59.60	3509.40	No	48-end
2622	No	No	No	Two year	No	Credit card (automatic)	25.70	826.10	No	24-48
4773	No	No	No	Two year	No	Credit card (automatic)	19.50	1050.50	No	48-end
490	No	Yes	No	Month-to-month	Yes	Electronic check	59.00	114.15	No	0-24
1085	No	No	No	Month-to-month	Yes	Credit card (automatic)	74.75	1129.35	No	0-24

Figure 8.2 – Churn dataset

As you can see in *Figure 8.2*, the dataset is clean and only has categorical or numerical columns. The next step is to covert these categorical values into numerical encoding. Let's look at the dataset and see which ones are categorical and which ones are numerical.

The following code calculates the unique values in every column:

```
churn_data.nunique()
```

The preceding code displays the following output:

```
customerID          7032
gender                 2
SeniorCitizen          2
Partner                2
Dependents             2
tenure                72
PhoneService           2
MultipleLines          3
InternetService        3
OnlineSecurity         2
OnlineBackup           2
DeviceProtection       2
TechSupport            2
StreamingTV            2
StreamingMovies        2
Contract               3
PaperlessBilling       2
PaymentMethod          4
MonthlyCharges      1584
TotalCharges        6530
Churn                  2
tenure_group           3
dtype: int64
```

Figure 8.3 – Unique value count of every column

As you can see in *Figure 8.3*, except `MonthlyCharges`, `tenure`, and `TotalCharges`, all other columns are categorical.

In the dataset, there are binary columns and multi-value category columns. Let's find out which ones are binary and which ones are multi-value columns. The following code block checks if the column is binary from the list of columns:

```
# filter all the col if unique values in the column is 2
bin_cols = churn_data.nunique()[churn_data.nunique() ==
2].keys().tolist()
```

Now that we have the list of binary columns, let's transform them into 0s and 1s using the label encoder.

The following code uses the label encoder to perform the transformation on the binary columns:

```
le = LabelEncoder()
for i in bin_cols :
    churn_data[i] = le.fit_transform(churn_data[i])
```

The next step is to transform the multi-value categorical columns into 0s and 1s. To do that, let's filter out the multi-value column names first.

The following code block selects the multi-value columns:

```
all_categorical_cols = churn_data.nunique()[churn_data.
nunique() <=4].keys().tolist()
multi_value_cols = [col for col in all_categorical_cols if col
not in bin_cols]
```

The preceding code block filters out all the categorical columns first and filters out the binary columns so that we are left with only the multi-value columns.

The following code block transforms the multi-value columns into binary encodings:

```
churn_data = pd.get_dummies(data = churn_data, columns=multi_
value_cols)
```

The last part is transforming the numerical values. Since numerical columns can have different ranges, scaling the columns to a standard range can be beneficial for ML algorithms. It also helps algorithms converge faster. Hence, let's scale the number columns to a standard range.

The following code block uses `StandardScaler` to scale all the numerical columns to a standard range:

```
numerical_cols = ['tenure','MonthlyCharges','TotalCharges']
std = StandardScaler()
churn_data[numerical_cols] = std.fit_transform(churn_
data[numerical_cols])
```

The preceding code block scales the numerical columns: `tenure`, `MonthlyCharges`, and `TotalCharges`. Now that our feature engineering is complete, let's preview the final feature set and ingest it into the SageMaker Feature Store.

The following code block shows the feature set preview:

```
churn_data.columns = [slugify(col, lowercase=True,
separator='_') for col in churn_data.columns]
churn_data.head()
```

The preceding code block formats the column names as lowercase and replaces all the separators in the string, such as spaces and hyphens, with an underscore. The final features are shown in the following screenshot:

	customerid	gender	seniorcitizen	partner	dependents	tenure	phoneservice	onlinesecurity	onlinebackup	deviceprotection	techsupport	streamingtv
0	7590-VHVEG	0	0	1	0	-1.280248	0	0	1	0	0	0
1	5575-GNVDE	1	0	0	0	0.064303	1	1	0	1	0	0
2	3668-QPYBK	1	0	0	0	-1.239504	1	1	1	0	0	0
3	7795-CFOCW	1	0	0	0	0.512486	0	1	0	1	1	0
4	9237-HQITU	0	0	0	0	-1.239504	1	0	0	0	0	0

	streamingmovies	paperlessbilling	monthlycharges	totalcharges	churn	multiplelines_no	multiplelines_no_phone_service	multiplelines_yes	internetservice_dsl
0	0	1	-1.161694	-0.994194	0	0	1	0	1
1	0	0	-0.260878	-0.173740	0	1	0	0	1
2	0	1	-0.363923	-0.959649	1	1	0	0	1
3	0	0	-0.747850	-0.195248	0	0	1	0	1
4	0	1	0.196178	-0.940457	1	1	0	0	0

	internetservice_fiber_optic	internetservice_no	contract_month_to_month	contract_one_year	contract_two_year	paymentmethod_bank_transfer_automatic
0	0	0	1	0	0	0
1	0	0	0	1	0	0
2	0	0	1	0	0	0
3	0	0	0	1	0	1
4	1	0	1	0	0	0

	paymentmethod_credit_card_automatic	paymentmethod_electronic_check	paymentmethod_mailed_check	tenure_group_0_24	tenure_group_24_48	tenure_group_48_end
0	0	1	0	1	0	0
1	0	0	1	0	1	0
2	0	0	1	1	0	0
3	0	0	0	0	1	0
4	0	1	0	1	0	0

Figure 8.4 – Feature set

The final feature set has 33 columns as shown in *Figure 8.4*. If you recall in *Chapter 4, Adding Feature Store to ML Models*, while creating feature definitions, we identified entities and grouped features based on their entities or logical groups. Though these features can be grouped into multiple groups, we will be creating a single feature group and ingesting all the features into it.

In the next section, let's create the feature definitions and ingest the data.

Feature group definitions and feature ingestion

Now that we have the feature set ready for ingestion, let's create the feature definitions and ingest the features into a feature store. For this exercise, as mentioned before, we will be using the SageMaker Feature Store. If you recall from the previous chapters, we always kept feature definitions in a separate notebook, as it is a one-time activity. In this exercise, we are going to try a different method, which is using a conditional statement to create a feature group if it doesn't exist. You can use either of the approaches.

Let's continue in the same notebook and initialize the boto3 session and check whether our feature group exists already or not:

```
import boto3
FEATURE_GROUP_NAME = "telcom-customer-features"
feature_group_exist = False
client = boto3.client('sagemaker')
response = client.list_feature_groups(
    NameContains=FEATURE_GROUP_NAME)
if FEATURE_GROUP_NAME in response["FeatureGroupSummaries"]:
  feature_group_exist = True
```

The preceding code block queries SageMaker to check whether the feature group with the name `telcom-customer-features` exists or not and sets a Boolean based on that. We will use this Boolean to either create the feature group or to skip creation and just ingest the data into the feature store.

The following code block initializes the objects required for interacting with the SageMaker Feature Store:

```
import sagemaker
from sagemaker.session import Session
import time
from sagemaker.feature_store.feature_definition import
FeatureDefinition, FeatureTypeEnum
role = "arn:aws:iam::<account_number>:role/sagemaker-iam-role"
sagemaker_session = sagemaker.Session()
```

```
region = sagemaker_session.boto_region_name
s3_bucket_name = "feast-demo-mar-2022"
```

> **Important Note**
> Use the IAM role created in the earlier section, in the preceding code block. The IAM role should have **AmazonSageMakerFullAccess** and **AmazonS3FullAccess**.

The next step is to initialize the `FeatureGroup` object. The following code initializes the feature group object:

```
from sagemaker.feature_store.feature_group import FeatureGroup
customers_feature_group = FeatureGroup(
    name=FEATURE_GROUP_NAME,
    sagemaker_session=sagemaker_session
)
```

Now we will use the Boolean that was set earlier to conditionally create the feature group if the feature group doesn't exist. The following code block loads the feature definitions and calls `create` if the feature group doesn't exist:

```
churn_data["event_timestamp"] = float(round(time.time()))
if not feature_group_exist:
  customers_feature_group.load_feature_definitions(
      churn_data[[col
                  for col in churn_data.columns
                  if col not in ["customerid"]]])
  customer_id_def = FeatureDefinition(
      feature_name='customerid',
      feature_type=FeatureTypeEnum.STRING)
  customers_feature_group.feature_definitions = [customer_id_
def] + customers_feature_group.feature_definitions
  customers_feature_group.create(
    s3_uri=f"s3://{s3_bucket_name}/{FEATURE_GROUP_NAME}",
    record_identifier_name="customerid",
```

```
    event_time_feature_name="event_timestamp",
    role_arn=role,
    enable_online_store=False
    )
```

> **Important Note**
>
> In the `load_feature_definitions` call, if you notice, I'm loading all the feature definition columns except the `customerid` column and manually adding the `customerid` column to the feature definitions list in the following line. The reason for this is the `sagemaker` library fails to figure out the `string` data type as the pandas `dtype` for `string` is `object`.

The `create` feature group call is straightforward. I am disabling the online store by passing `enable_online_store` as `False`, since we will be trying out the batch pipeline and I will leave the online model as an exercise. Once the preceding code block executes, based on the conditional statement, for the first time, it will create the feature group and for the subsequent runs, it will skip the feature group creation.

The final step is to ingest the DataFrame. The following code block performs the ingestion and prints any failures:

```
ingestion_results = customers_feature_group.ingest(
    churn_data, max_workers=1)
ingestion_results.failed_rows
```

> **Important Note**
>
> If you only have the batch use case, SageMaker has a Spark library that can be used to ingest to the offline store directly, which is also cost-effective.

That completes the feature engineering and ingestion. In the next section, let's look at model training.

Model training

As before, for the model training, the feature store is the source. Hence, let's create our model training notebook and install and initialize the required objects for querying the feature store. Here is the link to the notebook:

`https://github.com/PacktPublishing/Feature-Store-for-Machine-Learning/blob/main/Chapter08/Ch8_model_training.ipynb`

The following code block installs the required libraries for model training:

```
!pip install sagemaker==2.88.0 s3fs joblib scikit-learn==1.0.2
xgboost
```

After installing the required libraries, initialize the SageMaker session and the required objects:

```
import sagemaker
from sagemaker.session import Session
from sagemaker.feature_store.feature_group import FeatureGroup
#import os
#os.environ["AWS_ACCESS_KEY_ID"] = "<aws_key_id>"
#os.environ["AWS_SECRET_ACCESS_KEY"] = "<aws_secret>"
#os.environ["AWS_DEFAULT_REGION"] = "us-east-1"
role = "arn:aws:iam::<account_number>:role/sagemaker-iam-role"
FEATURE_GROUP_NAME = "telcom-customer-features"
sagemaker_session = sagemaker.Session()
region = sagemaker_session.boto_region_name
s3_bucket_name = "feast-demo-mar-2022"
customers_feature_group = FeatureGroup(
    name=FEATURE_GROUP_NAME,
    sagemaker_session=sagemaker_session
)
```

The preceding code block initializes the SageMaker session and initializes the feature group object. The `name` of the feature group should be the same as the `name` of the feature group that we created in our feature engineering notebook.

> **Important Note**
>
> Assign the IAM role that was created earlier to the `role` variable. Also, if you are running the notebook outside AWS, you need to uncomment and set up AWS credentials in the preceding code block.

The next part is to query the historical store to generate the training data. Unlike Feast, we don't need an entity DataFrame here. Instead, we use SQL queries to fetch the historical data. It has the same time travel capabilities as Feast has. For this exercise, let's fetch the latest features for all customers, using a similar query to one that we used in the last chapter, during the SageMaker overview:

```
get_latest_snapshot_query = customers_feature_group.athena_
query()
query = f"""SELECT *
FROM
    (SELECT *,
        row_number()
        OVER (PARTITION BY customerid
    ORDER BY  event_timestamp desc, Api_Invocation_Time DESC,
write_time DESC) AS row_num
    FROM "{get_latest_snapshot_query.table_name}")
WHERE row_num = 1 and
NOT is_deleted;"""
get_latest_snapshot_query.run(
    query_string=query,
    output_location=f"s3://{s3_bucket_name}/output")
get_latest_snapshot_query.wait()
```

If you recall correctly, we used a similar nested query in the last chapter. The preceding code block fetches all the customers and their latest features. The output of the query will be written to a specific S3 location as mentioned in the `run` API call.

Once the query runs successfully, the dataset can be fetched using the following code block:

```
churn_data = get_latest_snapshot_query.as_dataframe()
churn_data = churn_data.drop(columns=["event_timestamp",
"write_time", "api_invocation_time", "is_deleted", "row_num"])
```

> **Important Note**
>
> Please note that, we will perform the same steps for model prediction and feature monitoring as we have in this section (*Model training*) from the beginning till the preceding code block.

The preceding code block fetches the dataset and drops the unwanted columns. The fetched dataset is similar to the data shown in *Figure 8.4* with additional columns: `write_time`, `api_invocation_time`, `is_deleted`, and `row_num`. The first three are additional metadata columns added by SageMaker during ingestion and `row_num` is the column that we created in the query for fetching the latest features for every customer.

Now that we have the dataset, let's split it for training and testing. The following code block drops the columns unwanted for training from the dataset and splits the data for training and testing:

```
from sklearn.model_selection import train_test_split
from sklearn.linear_model import LogisticRegression
from sklearn.metrics import confusion_matrix,accuracy_
score,classification_report
from sklearn.metrics import roc_auc_score,roc_curve
from sklearn.metrics import precision_score,recall_score
Id_col = ["customerid"]
target_col = ["churn"]

# Split into a train and test set
train, test = train_test_split(churn_data,
                               test_size = .25,
                               random_state = 111)
cols    = [i for i in churn_data.columns if i not in Id_col +
target_col]
training_x = train[cols]
training_y = train[target_col]
testing_x  = test[cols]
testing_y  = test[target_col]
```

The preceding code block leaves out the ID column and performs a 75/25 split for training and testing.

The rest of it is straightforward, which is basically training an XGBoost model, parameter tuning, and comparing the performance. The following is an example code block for training, sample analysis, and logging the model:

```
import joblib
import boto3
model = XGBClassifier(max_depth=7,
```

```
                      objective='binary:logistic')
model.fit(training_x, training_y)
predictions = model.predict(testing_x)
probabilities = model.predict_proba(testing_x)
print("\n Classification report : \n",
      classification_report(testing_y, predictions))
print("Accuracy   Score : ",
      accuracy_score(testing_y, predictions))
# confusion matrix
conf_matrix = confusion_matrix(testing_y, predictions)
model_roc_auc = roc_auc_score(testing_y, predictions)
print("Area under curve : ", model_roc_auc, "\n")
joblib.dump(model, '/content/customer-churn-v0.0')
s3_client = boto3.client('s3')
response = s3_client.upload_file('/content/customer-
churn-v0.0', s3_bucket_name, "model-repo/customer-churn-v0.0")
```

The preceding code block also logs the model to a specific location in S3. This is a crude way of doing it. It is always better to use an experiment training tool for logging the performance and the model.

Now that the model training is complete, let's look at model scoring.

Model prediction

As mentioned in the last note in the previous section, as this is a batch model, the steps are similar for model scoring for fetching the data from the offline store. However, depending on which customers need to be scored (maybe all), you might filter out the dataset. Once you filter out the dataset, the rest of the steps are again straightforward, which is to load the model, run predictions, and store the results.

The following is a sample code block for loading the model, running predictions, and also storing the results back in S3 for consumption:

```
import boto3
from datetime import date
s3 = boto3.client('s3')
s3.download_file(s3_bucket_name, f"model-repo/customer-
churn-v0.0", "customer-churn-v0.0")
features = churn_data.drop(['customerid', 'churn'], axis=1)
```

```
loaded_model = joblib.load('/content/customer-churn-v0.0')
prediction = loaded_model.predict(features)
prediction.tolist()
file_name = f"customer_churn_prediction_{date.today()}.parquet"
churn_data["predicted_churn"] = prediction.tolist()
s3_url = f's3://{s3_bucket_name}/prediction_results/{file_
name}'
churn_data.to_parquet(s3_url)
```

The preceding code block downloads the model from S3, loads the model, scores it against the data fetched from the historical store, and also stores the result in the S3 bucket for consumption.

> **Note**
>
> The library versions of XGBoost, Joblib, and scikit-learn should be the same as what was used while saving the model, otherwise loading of the model might fail.

To productionize this ML pipeline, we can use orchestration similar to what we did in *Chapter 6, Model to Production and Beyond*. I will leave that as an exercise since it's duplicate content. Let's look at an example of feature monitoring next.

Feature monitoring

We have discussed how important feature monitoring is in an ML system a few times in the book. We have also talked about how a feature store standardizes feature monitoring. In this section, let's look at an example of feature monitoring that can be useful for any model. As feature monitoring is calculating a set of statistics on feature data and notifying the data scientist or data engineer of changes, it needs the latest features used by the model.

In this section, let's calculate the summary stats on the feature data and also feature correlation, which can be run on a schedule and sent to people of interest regularly so that they can take action based on it. As mentioned in the last note of the *Model training* section, the steps to fetch the features are the same as what was done in that section. Once you have all the features, the next step is to calculate the required stats.

> **Important Note**
>
> Please note you may have to install additional libraries. Here is the URL for the notebook: `https://github.com/PacktPublishing/Feature-Store-for-Machine-Learning/blob/main/Chapter08/Ch8_feature_monitoring.ipynb`.

The following code block calculates the summary stats on the feature data and also plots the correlation metrics:

```
import numpy as np
import warnings
warnings.filterwarnings("ignore")
import plotly.offline as py
import plotly.graph_objs as go
churn_data.describe(include='all').T
```

The preceding line of code produces a descriptive statistic of the dataset, which includes min, max, count, standard deviation, and more.

Apart from the descriptive statistics, the correlation matrix of the features is another thing that could be useful for all the ML models. The following code block calculates the correlation matrix of the features and plots a heatmap:

```
corr = churn_data.corr()
cols = corr.columns.tolist()
trace = go.Heatmap(z=np.array(corr),
                   x=cols,
                   y=cols,
                   colorscale="Viridis",
                   colorbar=dict(
                       title="Pearson Coefficient",
                       titleside="right"
                       ),
                   )
layout = go.Layout(dict(title="Correlation Matrix",
                        height=720,
                        width=800,
                        margin=dict(r=0, l=210,
                                    t=25, b=210,
```

```
                                              ),
                                 )
                            )
fig = go.Figure(data=[trace], layout=layout)
py.iplot(fig)
```

The preceding code block outputs the following heatmap:

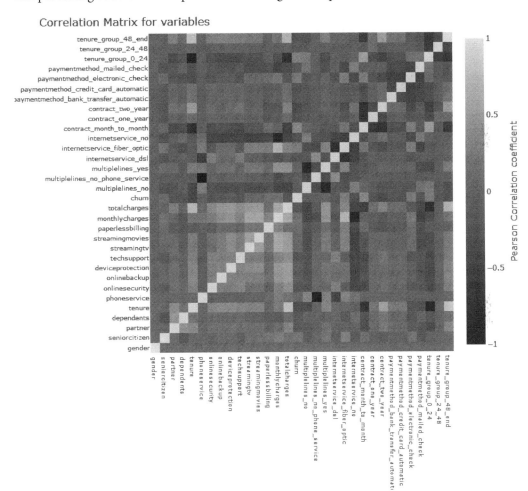

Figure 8.5 – Feature correlation

You can add more statistics, in comparison to the previous run, alerts through emails, Slack notifications, and more. This could be in another notebook/Python script, which can be scheduled at the same or at a lesser frequency than the feature engineering notebook and have automated reports sent to you. Here is the link to the complete notebook: `https://github.com/PacktPublishing/Feature-Store-for-Machine-Learning/blob/main/Chapter08/Ch8_feature_monitoring.ipynb`.

> **Important Note**
>
> This is just an example of feature monitoring. There are more sophisticated statistics and metrics that can be used to determine the health of the features.

Let's look at model monitoring next.

Model monitoring

Another important aspect of ML is model monitoring. There are different aspects of model monitoring: one could be system monitoring in the case of online models, where you monitor the latency, CPU, memory utilization, requests per minute of the model, and more. The other aspect is performance monitoring of the model. Again, there are many different ways of measuring performance. In this example, we will look at a simple classification report and the accuracy of the model.

To generate the classification report and calculate the accuracy of the live model, you need the prediction data and also the ground truth of the live data. For this example, let's say that the churn model is run once a week to generate the churn prediction and the ground truth will be available every 4 weeks from the day the model is run. That means if the model predicts customer x's churn as `True`, and within the next 4 weeks, if we lose the customer for any reason, the model predicted correctly; otherwise, the prediction was wrong. Hence, for every run of the model prediction, we need to wait for 4 weeks to have the ground truth.

For the simplicity of this exercise, let's also assume that the ground truth is filled back into the feature store every week. That means the feature store always has the latest ground truth. Now, our job is to fetch the prediction results that correspond to the latest features in the feature store (the prediction that was run 4 weeks ago) and calculate the required metrics. Let's do that next.

As mentioned before, the steps to fetch the latest feature from the feature store are the same as what we did in the last three sections. Once you have fetched the data from the feature store, the following code fetches the corresponding prediction results and merges the dataset:

```
from datetime import date, timedelta
import pandas as pd
pred_date = date.today()-timedelta(weeks=4)
file_name = f"customer_churn_prediction_{pred_date}.parquet"
prediction_data = pd.read_parquet(f"s3://{s3_bucket_name}/
prediction_results/{file_name}")

prediction_y = prediction_data[["customerid",
                                 "predicted_churn"]]
acutal_y = churn_data[["customerid", "churn"]]

merged_data = prediction_y.merge(acutal_y, on="customerid")
merged_data.head()
```

The preceding code block should produce an output similar to the following snapshot.

	customerid	predicted_churn	churn
0	7590-VHVEG	0	0
1	5575-GNVDE	0	0
2	3668-QPYBK	0	1
3	7795-CFOCW	0	0
4	9237-HQITU	1	1

Figure 8.6 – Merged data for model monitoring

> **Important Note**
>
> As we have assumed the prediction and ground truth to be 4 weeks apart, the previous code block tries to fetch the data that is 4 weeks from today. For the exercise, you can replace the `file_name` variable with the prediction output Parquet file.

Once you have the DataFrame in *Figure 8.6*, the following code block uses the `predicted_churn` and `churn` columns to produce the classification report and accuracy:

```
testing_y = merged_data["churn"]
predictions = merged_data["predicted_churn"]
print("\n Classification report : \n",
      classification_report(testing_y, predictions))
print("Accuracy   Score : ",
      accuracy_score(testing_y, predictions))
# confusion matrix
conf_matrix = confusion_matrix(testing_y, predictions)
# roc_auc_score
model_roc_auc = roc_auc_score(testing_y, predictions)
print("Area under curve : ", model_roc_auc, "\n")
```

The previous code block produces output similar to the following.

```
Classification report :
              precision    recall  f1-score   support

           0       0.82      0.90      0.86      1268
           1       0.65      0.48      0.56       490

    accuracy                           0.78      1758
   macro avg       0.74      0.69      0.71      1758
weighted avg       0.77      0.78      0.77      1758

Accuracy   Score :  0.7849829351535836
Area under curve :  0.6925465138736883
```

Figure 8.7 – Classification report

As mentioned before, this is sample monitoring. This can be scheduled at the same interval as the feature engineering notebook, though it would fail for the first four iterations due to the unavailability of the prediction data. Also make sure you adjust the prediction filename appropriately for your needs. Here is the URL for the complete notebook: `https://github.com/PacktPublishing/Feature-Store-for-Machine-Learning/blob/main/Chapter08/Ch8_model_monitoring.ipynb`.

With that, let's summarize what we have learned in this chapter.

Summary

In this chapter, we set out with the aim of trying out a use case, namely telecom customer churn prediction using a dataset available from Kaggle. For this use case, we used a managed SageMaker Feature Store, which was introduced in the last chapter. In the exercise, we went through the different stages of ML, such as data processing, feature engineering, model training, and model prediction. We also looked at a feature monitoring and model monitoring example. The aim of this chapter was not model building but to showcase how to use a managed feature store for model building and the opportunities it opens for monitoring. To learn more about feature stores, the apply conference (`https://www.applyconf.com/`) and feature store forum (`https://www.featurestore.org/`) are good resources. To stay updated with new developments in ML and how other firms are solving similar problems, there are a few interesting podcasts, such as TWIML AI (`https://twimlai.com/`) and Data Skeptic (`https://dataskeptic.com/`). These resources should help you find more resources based on your area of interest in ML. With that, let's end this chapter and the book. I hope I was effective in conveying the importance of feature stores in the ML process and it was a good use of your time, and mine. Thank you!

Index

D

E

F

G

H

I

K

L

M

N

O

P

R

S

T

U

`Packt.com`

Subscribe to our online digital library for full access to over 7,000 books and videos, as well as industry leading tools to help you plan your personal development and advance your career. For more information, please visit our website.

Why subscribe?

- Spend less time learning and more time coding with practical eBooks and Videos from over 4,000 industry professionals
- Improve your learning with Skill Plans built especially for you
- Get a free eBook or video every month
- Fully searchable for easy access to vital information
- Copy and paste, print, and bookmark content

Did you know that Packt offers eBook versions of every book published, with PDF and ePub files available? You can upgrade to the eBook version at `packt.com` and as a print book customer, you are entitled to a discount on the eBook copy. Get in touch with us at `customercare@packtpub.com` for more details.

At `www.packt.com`, you can also read a collection of free technical articles, sign up for a range of free newsletters, and receive exclusive discounts and offers on Packt books and eBooks.

Other Books You May Enjoy

If you enjoyed this book, you may be interested in these other books by Packt:

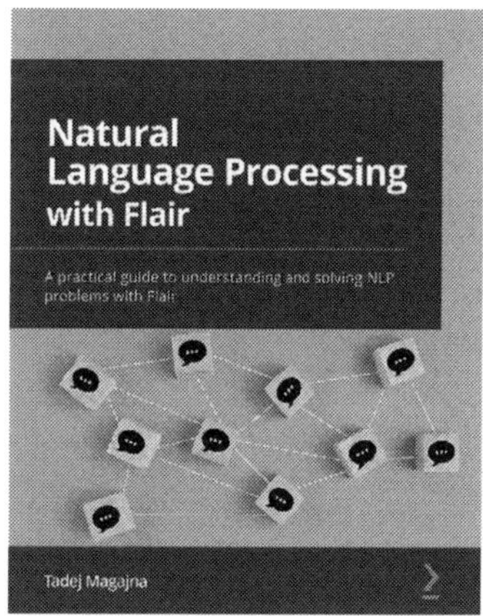

Natural Language Processing with Flair

Tadej Magajna

ISBN: 9781801072311

- Gain an understanding of core NLP terminology and concepts
- Get to grips with the capabilities of the Flair NLP framework
- Find out how to use Flair's state-of-the-art pre-built models
- Build custom sequence labeling models, embeddings, and classifiers
- Learn about a novel text classification technique called TARS
- Discover how to build applications with Flair and how to deploy them to production

Machine Learning on Kubernetes

Faisal Masood, Ross Brigoli

ISBN: 9781803241807

- Understand the different stages of a machine learning project
- Use open source software to build a machine learning platform on Kubernetes
- Implement a complete ML project using the machine learning platform presented in this book
- Improve on your organization's collaborative journey toward machine learning
- Discover how to use the platform as a data engineer, ML engineer, or data scientist
- Find out how to apply machine learning to solve real business problems

Packt is searching for authors like you

If you're interested in becoming an author for Packt, please visit `authors.packtpub.com` and apply today. We have worked with thousands of developers and tech professionals, just like you, to help them share their insight with the global tech community. You can make a general application, apply for a specific hot topic that we are recruiting an author for, or submit your own idea.

Share Your Thoughts

Now you've finished F*eature Store for Machine Learning*, we'd love to hear your thoughts! Scan the QR code below to go straight to the Amazon review page for this book and share your feedback or leave a review on the site that you purchased it from.

`https://packt.link/r/1-803-23006-1`

Your review is important to us and the tech community and will help us make sure we're delivering excellent quality content.

Made in the USA
Middletown, DE
08 July 2022

68483894R00157